Lawrenceville Press

A Guide to Structured Programming in BASIC

Third Edition

For the IBM® PC and compatibles

Bruce Presley
William Freitas

First Edition published 1982
Second Edition published 1985
Copyright © 1992
by

ISBN 0-931717-58-2 Softcover
0-931717-89-2 Hardcover

Printed in the United States of America

All orders including educational, Canadian, foreign, FPO and APO addresses may be placed by contacting:

Lawrenceville Press, Inc.
P.O. Box 704
Pennington, NJ 08534-0704
1-609-737-1148
1-609-737-8564 FAX

16 15 14 13 12 11 10 9 8 7 6 5 4 3 2

Preface

We believe this to be the clearest, most comprehensible BASIC text available. Great effort has been made to avoid the confusing language and hard-to-follow examples that so often frustrate and discourage the beginning student. Because this text is software-specific we are able to present the exact commands the student will use, thus avoiding the confusion caused by a generic text which attempts to satisfy all users.

It is our belief that learning to program offers the student an invaluable opportunity to develop problem-solving skills. The process of defining a problem, breaking it down into a series of smaller problems and finally writing a computer program to solve it is an exercise in learning to think logically. In addition, the student is made aware of the capabilities and limitations of the computer and soon realizes that the programmer — the human element — is more important than the machine.

A Guide to Structured Programming in BASIC is written for a one or two-term course. No previous programming experience is required or assumed. It is the goal of this text to provide the best possible introduction for students learning BASIC, whether they will continue on to more advanced computer science courses or end their computer education with this introductory course.

Topic Organization

Chapter One discusses the history of computers and gives an introduction to how computers work. An emphasis is placed on defining terms which students will need to know. Careers in computing are presented and the educational requirements needed to pursue them. Ethical problems created by computers are also discussed.

Chapter Two introduces problem solving and algorithm design. Students are taught to start BASIC and write simple programs using the PRINT statement.

Variables and FOR...NEXT loops are introduced in Chapter Three allowing students to begin learning structured programming techniques. This chapter ends, as do most subsequent chapters, with a problem which is solved by first developing a detailed algorithm.

Chapter Four introduces the conditional statement IF...THEN, the WHILE...WEND loop, and counters and accumulators. The concept of formatted output with PRINT USING is presented.

Evaluating mathematical expressions using order of operations and random numbers are introduced in Chapter Five. An algorithm for rounding floating point numbers to a desired number of decimal places is developed in a step-by-step process.

Chapter Six emphasizes problem-solving techniques when presenting the use of subroutines as a method of breaking a problem down into well defined tasks. Methods of debugging are also presented.

Nested loops, arrays and subscripted variables are presented in Chapter Seven. Both single subscripted and double subscripted arrays are used to solve a variety of problems, some of which make use of the subroutines presented in the previous chapter.

Chapter Eight introduces the binary number system and the ASCII code. The functions needed for string manipulation are explained and demonstrated.

A detailed explanation of the three graphics modes are presented in Chapter Nine. Students are taught how to draw a variety of diagrams and how to add sound to them.

Chapter Ten presents mathematical functions, including trigonometric functions. User-defined functions are employed to solve a variety of problems.

Chapters 11 and 12 explain how sequential and random-access files are used to store data on disk. Problems are solved which employ most of the programming techniques previously introduced in earlier chapters.

A brief introduction to searching and sorting algorithms is presented in Chapter 13. Both the bubble sort and binary search are explained and demonstrated.

Design and Features

Classroom Tested

This text has been written based upon the authors' more than twenty-five years of experience in teaching programming. All of the material in this text has been tested and developed in their classrooms.

Problem Solving

From the very beginning, students are taught to solve problems using proper structured programming techniques.

Software Specific

All programs and solutions have been produced using BASIC running on an IBM PC or compatible.

Demonstration Programs and Runs	Many demonstration programs are included, complete with sample runs, so that students are shown both proper programming techniques and the actual output produced by their programs.
Format	Each BASIC statement is given a clear definition, shown in a single program line and then demonstrated in a complete, working program. Statements are also highlighted in the Table of Contents, making this text easy to use as a reference guide.
End of Chapter Problems	Most chapters end by stating a problem, developing an appropriate algorithm, naming the necessary variables, and then finally writing the code. These are an especially important feature of this text because it is by studying these solutions that the student reinforces proper problem-solving strategies.
Review Problems	Numerous review problems are presented throughout each chapter which provide immediate reinforcement to newly learned concepts. Solutions to the problems are given in the Teacher's Resource Package described below.
Chapter Summaries	At the end of each chapter a summary is given of the chapter's contents including definitions for the BASIC statements that have been introduced. These summaries offer the student a quick review of the important concepts presented.
Vocabulary	A review of newly introduced terms and BASIC statements is provided at the end of each chapter.
Exercises	Each chapter includes a large set of exercises of varying difficulty, making them appropriate for students with a wide range of abilities. Many of the exercises contain a demonstration run to help make clear what output is expected from the student's program. Included are advanced exercises which require carefully thought-out algorithms. Answers to the exercises are included in the Teacher's Resource Package.
Illustrations	Considerable care has been taken to make the illustrations in this text meaningful so that they serve to increase the student's understanding of topics being discussed.

Teacher's Resource Package and Diskette

An extensive Teacher's Resource Package and Diskette is available to accompany this text. It contains the following features:

- **Lessons** - Each chapter of the text is broken down into a series of lessons which include a set of objectives and student assignments.

- **Discussion Topics** - Additional material is presented which supplements the text and can be used in leading classroom discussions.

- **Transparency Masters** - Where programs or diagrams are used as part of the classroom discussion, transparency masters are provided.

- **Worksheets** - Each lesson contains a set of problems which can be assigned to be done in or out of class. These problems do not usually require use of the computer.

- **Tests** - Examinations are provided for all chapters plus a mid-term and final examination along with detailed answer keys and grading scales.

- **Answers** - Answers are given for all review, exercise and advanced exercise questions.

- **Diskette** - A diskette is included which contains programs that are to be modified by students, the longer programs from the text, the end of chapter programs, and answers to all exercises which may be run as demonstrations.

For the convenience of the instructor, this material is contained in a 3-ring binder so that pages may be removed for duplication and the instructor's own notes may be inserted. Note: The Resource Package and Diskette are available only when ordered by an educational institution.

Acknowledgements

We wish to acknowledge our debt to the following people whose talents contributed to the development of this text.

Beth Brown reviewed the text for technical accuracy and prepared many of the exercise answers. We are indebted to her keen eye for detail and her expertise in programming.

Elizabeth Dole designed the text's format and Greg Schwinn the cover. The text was typeset directly from disk at Marketing Design Concepts by José, Rachel and Bill. We wish to thank Heffernan Press, especially Bill Daley who supervised the printing of the text.

The success of this and our other texts is due to the efforts of Heidi Crane, Vice President of Marketing at Lawrenceville Press. She has developed the promotional material which has been so well received by schools around the world. Michael Porter, director of distribution, is responsible for the efficient manner in which educational orders are filled.

We would like to thank the St. Andrew's School for allowing us the flexible schedules to produce this text. A very special note of appreciation is due our friend, colleague, and chairperson of the Computer Science department, Ruth Wagy.

Finally, we wish to thank our students, for whom and with whom this text was written. Their candid evaluation of each lesson has been the driving force behind the creation of *A Guide to Structured Programming in BASIC.*

Bruce Presley
William Freitas

Preface to the Third Edition

In the years since the publication of the first edition of *A Guide to Programming the IBM Personal Computers* many changes have taken place in the field of computer science education. Teachers have become more aware of the issues involved in teaching students to be effective programmers, and new teaching techniques have been introduced and accepted. In addition, there has been significant improvement in the computers and hardware available to educators.

This text is a major revision of the two earlier editions with major emphasis placed on structured programming techniques. For example, there is not a single GOTO statement anywhere in the text. Students are taught programming techniques that will be completely compatible with those they will encounter when studying more advanced structured languages such as Pascal or C. In addition most of the exercises have been rewritten for clarity, and 25% new exercises have been added.

More emphasis has been placed on the real-world use of computers. Students are given an introduction to computer history, ethics and careers in computing in Chapter 1. Useful commands such as SAVE and LOAD have been moved from the Appendices to Chapter 2. New material covering the importance of making backups and the use of subdirectories has been added. Interesting and useful commands such as PLAY are introduced. In all, we are certain that you will find this to be the most clear and comprehensible text for introducing structured BASIC programming.

Table of Contents

Chapter 1

An Introduction to Computing

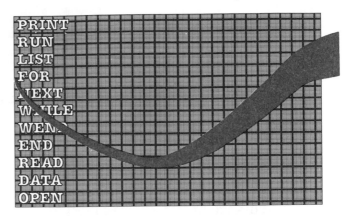

Objectives

Chapter One

After completing this chapter you will be able to:

1. Define what a computer is.

2. Discuss the history of computers.

3. Understand how a computer operates.

4. Identify the components of a modern computer system.

5. Define telecommunications and describe its uses.

6. Describe different careers in computing and their educational requirements.

7. Understand the ethical responsibilities of computer use and programming.

8. Describe several objectives for the future of computing.

*T*his text is about computers and how they can be programmed. We will employ a popular computer language named BASIC to teach you how to write your own computer programs. When discussing computers, it is convenient to divide the subject into two broad categories — hardware and software. Hardware refers to the computer itself and its peripheral devices — disk drives, printers, etc. whereas software refers to the programs or instructions which are entered into the computer to make it perform specific tasks. Since it is the purpose of this text to teach you how to program a computer, it is a guide to producing software.

1.1 Computers and Programs

A computer is an electronic machine that accepts information (called "data"), processes it according to specific instructions, and provides the results as new information. It can store and move large quantities of data at very high speed and even though it cannot think, it can make simple decisions and comparisons. For example, a computer can decide which of two numbers is larger or which of two names comes first alphabetically and then act upon that decision. Although the computer can help to solve a wide variety of problems, it is merely a machine and cannot solve problems on its own. It must be provided with instructions in the form of a "program."

A program is a list of instructions written in a special language that the computer understands. It tells the computer which operations to perform and in what sequence to perform them. In this text we will learn the BASIC programming language.

1.2 Why Learn to Program?

The primary reason for learning to program are the skills you will acquire in developing problem-solving techniques. Learning how to define a problem, break it down into manageable parts and then design a series of operations to reach a solution are invaluable skills that may be applied to all fields of work and study.

Secondly, and of equal importance, is that you will be able to use the computer efficiently for your own purposes. While there are many programs available commercially, they may not be written for an individual's specific needs. By learning to write your own programs, you can develop software designed to meet your requirements.

Thirdly, it is recognized that computers have become a major factor in our lives, affecting virtually every profession and business. By possessing even a limited knowledge of programming you will be aware of the capabilities and limitations of computers, which will enable you to deal with them both knowledgeably and confidently.

Finally, programming is fun. The intellectual challenge of controlling the operations of a computer is not only rewarding but an invaluable skill.

1.3 Early Calculating Machines

Many of the advances made by science and technology are dependent upon the ability to perform complex mathematical calculations and to process large amounts of data. It is therefore not surprising that for thousands of years mathematicians, scientists and business people have searched for "computing" machines that could perform calculations and analyze data quickly and accurately.

As civilizations began to develop, they created both written languages and number systems. These number systems were not originally meant to be used in mathematical calculations, but rather were designed to record measurements. Roman numerals are a good example of this type of system. Calculations in ancient times were carried out with a device known as an abacus which is still in use in many parts of the world, especially in the Orient. The abacus works by sliding beads back and forth on a frame with the beads on the top of the frame representing fives and on the bottom, ones.

Toward the end of the middle ages, Roman numerals were replaced by a new number system borrowed from the Arabs, therefore called Arabic numerals. This system uses ten digits and is the system we use today. Because the Arabic system made calculations with pencil and paper easier, the abacus and other such counting devices became less common.

One of the earliest mechanical devices for calculating was the Pascaline, invented by the French philosopher and mathematician Blaise Pascal in 1642. Being a gifted thinker, Pascal thought that the task of adding numbers should be able to be done by a mechanism that would resemble the way a clock keeps time. The Pascaline he invented was a complicated set of gears which could only be used to perform addition and not at all for multiplication or division. Unfortunately, Pascal never got the device to work properly.

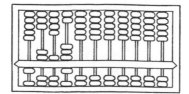 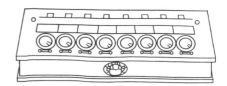

An abacus and the Pascaline, two early calculating devices

Later in the 17th century, Gottfried Wilhelm von Leibniz, a famous mathematician who is credited with being one of the developers of calculus, invented a device that was designed to add and subtract, as well as multiply, divide and extract square roots. Though both Pascal's and Leibniz's machines held great promise, they did not work well because the craftsmen of their time were unable to make machined parts that were accurate enough to carry out the inventor's design. Because of mechanically unreliable parts, the devices tended to jam and malfunction.

In 1810 Joseph Jacquard, a French weaver, made a revolutionary discovery. He realized that the weaving instructions for his looms could be stored on cards with holes punched in them. As the cards moved through the loom in sequence, needles passed through the holes and picked up threads of the correct color or texture. By rearranging the cards, a weaver could change the pattern being woven without stopping the machine to change threads. The idea that information could be stored by punching holes on a card was to be of great use in the later development of the computer.

Jacquard's loom used punched cards to store instructions

1.4 Babbage's Difference and Analytical Engines

In 1822 Charles Babbage began work on the Difference Engine. The original purpose of this machine was to produce tables of numbers that would be used by naval navigators. At the time navigation tables were often highly inaccurate due to calculation errors. In fact, several ships were known to have been lost at sea because of these errors. Again because of the mechanical problems that plagued Pascal and Leibniz, the Difference Engine never worked properly.

Undaunted, Babbage later planned and began work on a considerably more advanced machine, called the Analytical Engine. This machine was to perform a variety of calculations by following a set of instructions, or "program", entered into it using punched cards similar to the ones used by Joseph Jacquard. During processing, the Analytical Engine was to store information in a memory unit that would allow it to make decisions and then carry out instructions based on those decisions. For example, in comparing two numbers it could be programmed to determine which was larger and then follow different sets of instructions. The Analytical Engine was no more successful than its predecessors, but its design was to serve as a model for the modern computer.

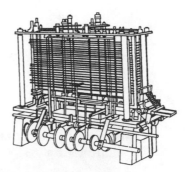

The Analytical engine attempted to be the first computer

Babbage's chief collaborator on the Analytical Engine was Lady Ada Augusta, Countess of Lovelace, the daughter of Lord Byron. Interested in mathematics, Lady Lovelace was a sponsor of the Engine and one of the first people to realize its power and significance. She also tested the device and wrote of its achievements in order to gain support for it. Because of her involvement she is often called the first programmer.

Babbage had hoped that the Analytical Engine would be able to play chess, thinking out and making brilliant moves. Lady Lovelace, however, said that the Engine could never "originate anything", meaning that she did not believe that a machine, no matter how powerful, could think. To this day her statement about computing machines remains true.

1.5 *The First Electric Calculating Machines*

By the end of the 19th century, U.S. Census officials were concerned about the time it took to tabulate the count of the increasing number of Americans. The Census of 1880, for example, took nine years to compile, making the figures highly inaccurate by the time they were published.

To solve the problem, Herman Hollerith invented a calculating machine that used electricity rather than mechanical gears. Holes representing information to be tabulated were punched in cards similar to those used in Jacquard's loom, with the location of each hole representing a specific piece of information (male, female, age, etc.). The cards were then inserted into the machine and metal pins used to open and close electrical circuits.

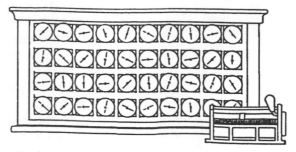

Hollerith's calculating machine used punched cards to store input data

Hollerith's machine was immensely successful and based on its success Hollerith and some friends formed a company that eventually became known as International Business Machines (IBM).

The first computer-like machine is generally thought to be the Mark I, which was built by a team from IBM and Harvard University. The Mark I used mechanical telephone relay switches to store information and accepted data on punched cards, processed it and then output the new data. Because it could not make decisions about the data it processed, the Mark I was not, however, a real computer but was instead a highly sophisticated calculator. It was, nevertheless, impressive, measuring over 51 feet in length and weighing 5 tons! It also had over 750,000 parts, many of them moving mechanical parts which made the Mark I not only huge but unreliable.

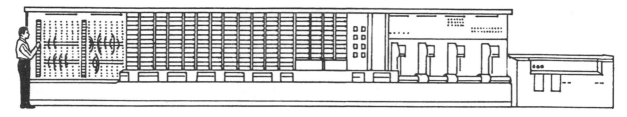

The Mark 1 was a sophisticated electronic calculating machine

1.6 ENIAC, the First Electronic Computer

In 1943 work began on the Electronic Numerical Integration and Calculator, or ENIAC. It was originally a secret military project which was to be used to calculate the trajectory of artillery shells. In one of its first demonstrations it was given a problem that would have taken a team of mathematicians three days to solve. It solved the problem in twenty seconds.

ENIAC was different from the Mark I in several important ways. First, it occupied 1500 square feet, which is the same area taken up by the average two bedroom house and it weighed 30 tons. Second, it used 17,000 vacuum tubes instead of relay switches. Most importantly, because it was able to make decisions, it was the first true computer.

The ENIAC weighed 30 tons and used 17,000 vacuum tubes

ENIAC had two major shortcomings. First, it was difficult to change its instructions to allow the computer to solve different problems. It had originally been designed only to compute artillery trajectory tables, but when it needed to work on another problem it could take up to three days of wire pulling, replugging and switch flipping to change instructions. Second, because the tubes it contained were constantly burning out, the ENIAC was unreliable.

Today, much of the credit for ENIAC's success is given to John Atanasoff. Atanasoff, a physics professor at Iowa State, developed a similar computer with graduate student Clifford Berry during 1939-1942. Because of World War II, little was known about his invention until the 1950's.

1.7 The Stored Program Computer

In the late 1940's, John von Neumann considered the idea of storing computer instructions and data in memory, which was accessed by a central processing unit, or CPU. The CPU would control all the functions of the computer electronically so that it would not be necessary to flip switches or pull wires to change the instructions. Now it would be possible to solve many different problems by simply typing in new instructions at a keyboard. Together with other computer scientists, von Neumann designed and built the EDVAC (Electronic Discrete Variable Automatic Computer) and the EDSAC (Electronic Discrete Storage Automatic Computer).

With the development of the concept of stored instructions or "programs", the modern computer age was ready to begin. Since then the development of new computers has progressed rapidly, but von Neumann's concept has remained, for the most part, unchanged. The next computer to employ von Neumann's concepts was the UNIVersal Automatic Computer, called UNIVAC, developed in 1951.

Computers at this time continued to use many vacuum tubes which made them large and expensive. UNIVAC weighed 35 tons. These computers were so expensive to purchase and run that only the largest corporations and the U.S. government could afford them. Their ability to perform up to 1000 calculations per second, however, made them popular.

It was the invention of the transistor that made smaller and less expensive computers possible, with increased calculating speeds of up to 10,000 calculations per second. Although the size of the computers shrank, they were still large and expensive. In 1963, IBM, using ideas it had learned while working on projects for the military, introduced the first medium-sized computer named the model 650. It was still expensive, but it was capable of handling the flood of paperwork produced by many government agencies and businesses.

The vacuum tube was replaced by the smaller, more reliable transistor

These new computers also saw a change in the way data was stored. Punched cards were replaced by magnetic tape and high speed reel-to-reel tape machines. Using magnetic tape gave computers the ability to read (access) and write (store) data quickly and reliably.

Another important advance occurring at this time was the development of programming languages. Previously, computers had to be programmed by setting different switches to their On or Off positions. The first programming languages were very similar, being strings of 1's and 0's representing the status of the switches (1 for On and 0 for Off). These were called "low-level" languages. Languages such as FORTRAN (FORmula TRANslator), which was the first popular "high-level" language, allowed programmers to use English-like instructions such as READ and WRITE. With them, it was possible to type instructions directly into the computer or on punched cards, eliminating the time consuming task of re-wiring.

Perhaps the most widely used high-level programming language today is COBOL (COmmon Business Oriented Language) developed by the Department of Defense in 1959 to provide a common language for use on all computers. The designer of COBOL was Grace Murray Hopper, a Commodore in the Navy at the time. Commodore Hopper was the first person to apply the term "debug" to the computer. While working on the Mark II computer in 1945, a moth flew into the circuitry, causing an electrical short which halted the computer. While removing the dead moth, she said that the program would be running again after the computer had been "debugged." Today, the process of removing errors from programs is still called debugging.

A number of new high-level languages have been developed since that time including BASIC (Beginner's All-purpose Symbolic Instruction Code), which was originally developed by John Kemeny and Tom Kurtz at Dartmouth College. This text will teach you how to program in BASIC. Other popular computer languages include Ada, C, and Pascal.

1.8 Integrated Circuits and the Microprocessor

The next major technological advancement was the replacement of transistors by tiny integrated circuits or "chips." Chips are blocks of silicon with logic circuits etched into their surface. They are smaller and cheaper than transistors and can contain thousands of circuits on a single chip. Integrated circuits also give computers tremendous speed allowing them to process information at a rate of 1,000,000 calculations per second.

One of the most important benefits of using integrated circuits is to decrease the cost and size of computers. The IBM System 360 was one of the first computers to use integrated circuits and was so popular with businesses that IBM had difficulty keeping up with the demand. Computers had come down in size and price to such a point that smaller organizations such as universities and hospitals could now afford them.

The most important advance to occur in the early 70's was the invention of the microprocessor, an entire CPU on a single chip. In 1970, Marcian Hoff, an engineer at Intel Corporation, designed the first of these chips. As a result, in 1975 the ALTAIR microcomputer was born. In 1977, working originally out of a garage, Stephen Wozniak and Steven Jobs designed and built the first Apple computer. Microcomputers were now inexpensive and therefore available to many people. Because of these advances almost anyone could own a machine that had more computing power and was faster and more reliable than either the ENIAC or UNIVAC. As a comparison, if the cost of sports cars had dropped as quickly as that of computers, a new Porsche would now cost about one dollar.

1.9 Mainframe, Mini and Microcomputers

There are three general size categories by which computers are classified. The choice of which size computer to use depends on what tasks are planned for it and how much data it must store.

Mainframe computers are large computer systems costing many hundreds of thousands, if not millions, of dollars. Because they are so large, mainframes can carry out many different tasks at the same time. They are used by large corporations, banks, government agencies and universities.

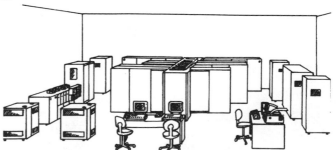

A mainframe computer is often tended by several "systems operators"

Minicomputers are smaller than mainframes, usually taking up the space of one or two bookcases. They are also less expensive, costing from about ten thousand to one hundred thousand dollars. Minicomputers are used by smaller businesses, schools and research institutions. Like mainframes, minicomputers can perform more than one task at a time. Although minicomputers store large amounts of data, they cannot store as much as a mainframe or process it as fast.

Most people using mainframe and minicomputers communicate with them by using "terminals." A terminal consists of a keyboard where commands and data are entered and monitors which display the output produced by the computer. The terminal is connected by wires to the computer, which may be located on a different floor or in a building a few blocks away. Some mainframe computers have over a hundred terminals attached and working at the same time.

Microcomputers are small and usually inexpensive. Often called "personal computers" or PC's, they can cost as little as one hundred dollars and fit on a desk top. Unlike mainframes and minicomputers, most microcomputers can only carry out one task at a time. During the past few years the processing speed and ability of microcomputers to store large quantities of data has increased at such a rapid rate that some of them now rival both mini and mainframe computers. Through the use of local area networks (LANs), where a number of microcomputers are linked together to a common data storage device, the differences between mainframe, mini and microcomputers are blurring.

1.10 How Computers Work

All computers process information, or "data." This data may be in the form of numbers, letters, words, pictures or symbols. In order to process data, a computer must carry out four specific activities:

1. Input data.
2. Store data while it is being processed.
3. Process data according to specific instructions.
4. Output the results in the form of new data.

As an example of computer processing, it is possible to input a list containing the names and addresses of one hundred thousand people and then ask the computer to search through this data and print only the names and addresses of those people who live in Florida. Another example would be to ask the computer to add all integers from 1 to 1000 and print their sum (i.e., $1 + 2 + 3... + 1000 = ?$). In each of these examples, data must be input so that it may be processed by the computer. In the first case, the input is a list of names and addresses, while in the second, a list of numbers.

Computers contain four major components. Each component performs one of the four tasks we have described:

1. **Input Device**: a device from which the computer can accept data. Keyboards and disk drives are both examples of input devices.

2. **Memory**: an area inside the computer where data and instructions can be stored electronically.

3. **Central Processing Unit (CPU)**: processes data and controls the flow of data between the computer's other units. It is here that the computer executes instruction and makes decisions.

4. **Output Device**: a device that displays or stores processed data. Monitors and printers are the most common visual output devices while disk drives are the most common storage devices.

The following diagram illustrates the direction in which data flows between the separate units:

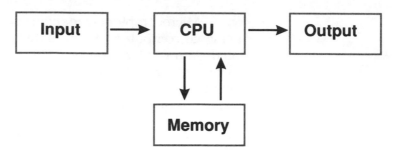

Data is input, stored in memory, processed and then output under the control of the CPU

Notice that all information first flows through the CPU. Because one of the jobs of the CPU is to control the order in which tasks are completed, it is often referred to as the "brain" of the computer. This comparison with the human brain, however, has an important flaw. The CPU only executes tasks according to the instructions it has been given; it cannot think for itself.

Most computers have two types of memory chips, ROM and RAM. Read Only Memory or ROM contains the most basic operating instructions for the computer. It is made a permanent part of the system and cannot be changed. The instructions in ROM enable the computer to complete simple jobs such as placing a character on the screen or checking the keyboard to see if a key has been pressed.

Random Access Memory or RAM is temporary memory where data and instructions can be stored. Data stored here can be changed or erased. When the computer is first turned on this part of memory is empty and when turned off, any data it stores is lost. Because RAM storage is temporary, computers use disks as auxiliary memory storage. Before turning the computer off, the data stored in RAM can be saved on a disk so that it can be used again at a later time.

1.11 Central Processing Unit

The Central Processing Unit (CPU) directs all the activities of the computer. It can only follow instructions that it receives either from ROM or from a program stored in RAM. In following these instructions, the CPU guides the processing of information throughout the computer.

The Arithmetic Logic Unit, or ALU, is the part of the CPU where the "intelligence" of the computer is located. It can perform only two operations. It can add numbers and compare numbers. Then the question is: How does the computer subtract, multiply or divide numbers? The answer is by first turning problems like multiplication and division into addition problems. This would seem to be a very inefficient way of doing things, but it works because the ALU is so fast. For example, to solve the problem 5×2, the computer adds 5 two's, $2 + 2 + 2 + 2 + 2$ to calculate the answer, 10. The time it takes the ALU to carry out a single addition of this type is measured in nanoseconds (billionths of a second). The other job of the ALU is to compare numbers and then decide whether a number is greater than, less than or equal to another number. This ability is the basis of the computer's decision-making power.

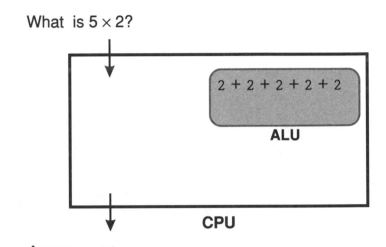

What is 5×2?

ALU

CPU

Answer: 10

The CPU directs math instructions to the ALU, where they are performed as addition operations

Memory storage, both RAM and ROM, and the CPU are made of tiny chips of silicon. These chips are so small that they must be housed in special plastic cases that have metal pins coming out of them. The pins allow the chips to be plugged into circuit boards that have their wiring printed on them.

Chips are covered by intricate circuits that have been etched into their surface and then coated with a metallic oxide that fills in the etched circuit patterns. This enables the chips to conduct electricity along the many paths of its circuits. Because there are as many as millions of circuits on a single chip, the chips are called integrated circuits.

The electrical circuits on a chip have one of two states, OFF or ON. Therefore, a system was developed that uses only two numbers, 0 and 1: 0 representing OFF and 1 representing ON. A light switch is similar to a single computer circuit. If the light is off, it represents a 0, and if on, a 1. This number system, which uses only two digits, is called the "binary" (base 2) system, and is explained in more detail in Chapter Eight.

1.12 Tele-communications

One of the most important advances made in computing has been in the field of "telecommunications." By telecommunications we mean the sending of computer data over telephone lines. To do this an additional piece of hardware called a "modem" is required to translate the binary data of the computer into waves which can then be transmitted over phone lines. To receive data a modem has the capability of translating the waves back into binary form. This process involves what is called signal <u>mo</u>dulation and <u>dem</u>odulation, hence the name modem. In addition to the modem, special telecommunications software is required so that the computer can transmit and receive data.

Modems can be "external", outside the computer, or built in

With a modem a microcomputer is capable of transmitting and receiving data between any two locations connected by phone. This includes cellular and satellite phone links. The rate at which each character of data is sent is measured in "baud", one baud representing the transmission of one character per second. Common rates are 1200, 2400 and 9600 baud which means 1200, 2400 and 9600 characters per second. However, newer modems are being created which are capable of communicating at even higher speeds.

Any type of data that a computer is capable of storing can be sent and received by modem. Using a modem it is possible to access and search very large data bases which might store financial data, news reports, travel information or a company's sales data. Because of tele-communications it is now possible for many people to work at home rather than in an office. Computer programmers often work at home producing their programs on a microcomputer while news reporters can write their stories at home on a word processor and then transmit their word processing files to a central office many miles away.

One of the most popular forms of telecommunication is the "electronic bulletin board" or "BBS." People who subscribe to a bulletin board service can call another computer and transmit messages to it which are then stored. When other subscribers of the service call the bulletin board it allows them to list all of the messages that have been "posted."

Telecommunications allows two computers to exchange information over telephone lines

Electronic mail or "E-Mail" is similar to an electronic bulletin board, but is used instead to send and receive private messages meant for one person or a small group. The person sending the message contacts the electronic mail service using a computer and modem, and then types in the name of the recipient and the message. When the recipient calls the electronic mail service he or she receives the message. Electronic mail is especially popular in universities where students and faculty can easily send messages to each other.

A growing number of universities now require all of their students to purchase microcomputers and modems. Among many other advantages, it has allowed everyone on their campuses to make use of electronic mail services.

1.13 The Future of Computing

Earlier in the chapter we traced the history of computing and discovered that, as technology improved, computers increased in speed, stored more data, decreased in size and most importantly became less expensive. This trend will, in all probability, continue. As it does, one of the advances will be the continued development of small microprocessors which will be found in an ever increasing number of appliances and devices.

Besides the development of better microprocessors, software will also improve. Software developers are attempting to make their software increasingly "user friendly", which means easier to learn and use. In learning to program you will want to make your programs user friendly so that other people can make easy use of them.

Although computers cannot think, one of the major areas of research continues to be the development of software programs that are capable of making increasingly complex decisions. The concept of using computers to make decisions which would normally be made by human beings is called "artificial intelligence." Herbert Schorr, a computer scientist at IBM, has declared that the development of artificial intelligence is the "second wave" of the information revolution. The first wave was the development of automated data processing. According to Schorr "the second wave will automate decision making."

In a recent newspaper article the Internal Revenue Service (I.R.S.) defined artificial intelligence as "the science of making machines do things that would require intelligence if done by man." As an example, there are currently computers which can play chess so well that they can beat all but the best players. Universities actually challenge each other's computers to play chess to determine which has the best chess playing program. Are these computers really intelligent? Most computer scientists would say no. They are simply programmed to make a series of decisions in response to the moves made by their opponents. It is merely their speed and ability to access huge amounts of stored data which make them appear to be intelligent.

Some specialized computers are capable of playing master level chess

Many computer scientists believe that future advances in artificial intelligence will depend upon the development of radically new technologies. To be truly useful as artificial intelligence machines, computers will have to possess some form of "common sense." Until this is accomplished we would be wise to give artificial intelligence systems only limited trust, being on guard against the errors in judgement they may make.

Another application of artificial intelligence is in "robotics." To be defined as a robot a machine must be able to be programmed and also be capable of motion. Most robots, unlike an R2D2 or C3PO in the movies, are simply moveable arms that can be directed to perform a task. Because they can be programmed, robots can make simple decisions and then act upon them.

Of the robots currently "employed", most are used in the automobile industry to spot weld and spray paint cars. As robots become capable of performing increasingly complicated tasks, they will undoubtedly be used in many more industries. There are a number of advantages to using robots. One is their ability to perform tasks too dangerous for humans. Robots have been developed which can remove and defuse bombs, work in highly radioactive environments, or under conditions of extreme noise or temperature. Their use in aiding handicapped people is also a very promising area. A major advantage of robots is that they can perform their tasks tirelessly, willing to work twenty-four hour days without rest or vacations.

1.14 Careers in Computing

As computers become more powerful they will play an ever increasing role in the world in which we live. Consequently most people, no matter what field they are employed in, will encounter computers. It is estimated that by the end of the 1990's over 90% of all office personnel will have a computer terminal or PC at their desks.

Doctors, lawyers, accountants, business people, educators, farmers and almost any profession you can think of are currently using or will soon make use of computers. It is the purpose of this text to introduce you to many of the varied tasks that a computer can perform and to help prepare you for almost any career you might consider.

After you finish this text you may well become interested in considering a career in computing. According to recent government projections the computer field will continue to hire people at an increasing rate. In this section we discuss some of the careers that you might consider and the education required to enter them.

Data Processing

The area of computing that employs the largest number of people is data processing. Data processing involves the electronic storage, manipulation and retrieval of data. Banks, businesses, educational institutions — almost any organization requires large amounts of data and therefore people capable of data processing. Careers in data processing (or DP) are usually divided into the following six categories:

1. System Analyst	4. Computer Operator
2. System Manager	5. Data-entry Operator
3. System Developer-Programmer	6. Computer Science and Research

We will consider each area separately, outlining the qualifications expected of a person entering the area.

System Analyst

Before a data processing system can be set up a system analyst must first analyze and design the system. The analyst must determine how an organization will use their computer system, what data they will store, how they will access it, and how they expect the system to grow in the future. The success or failure of the data processing system will be primarily determined by how well the analyst does his or her job.

Most system analysts are college graduates who have majored in computer science or business administration or both. A good way to start preparing yourself to be a system analyst is to take a programming course such as the one in BASIC outlined by this text and business courses such as management and accounting.

System Manager

Companies with large data processing requirements usually employ a manager who is responsible for running the Management Information Systems department (MIS). The MIS manager must organize the computer and human resources of the department in order to best achieve the organization's goals.

A college degree in business administration with a concentration in information systems is desirable to be a system manager. Since a system manager is an administrator he or she will usually possess previous management experience.

System Developer-Programmer

After the system analyst has determined what type of system should be installed, it is the job of the system developer to provide the necessary software. This is accomplished by writing three types of programs:

1) system programs — programs that operate the system's hardware. The disk operating system (DOS) booted on your microcomputer is an example of a system program.

2) applications programs — programs that solve specific problems. In a business these might be problems such as customer billing or inventory control.

3) program maintenance — many businesses need their programs expanded or changed to meet new demands or to correct errors. This is called program maintenance.

The education required to be a programmer is usually determined by the needs of the employer. Many businesses employ programmers who have taken only technical school or junior college programming courses. Large or specialized companies, which need highly sophisticated programming, usually require college graduates. A good way to start in preparing for a career as a programmer is to take the programming and computer science courses as well as the mathematics courses offered by your school.

Computer Operator

A computer operator is responsible for setting up equipment, mounting and removing tapes and disks, and monitoring the computer's operation. Often the computer operator must help the programmers and users of a computer when problems arise.

Systems operators get hands-on experience with computer hardware

Most computer operators have technical school or junior college educations. Because of the many different types of computers, the majority of their training is usually received on the job. A good way to prepare for a career as a computer operator is to take computer courses in school and assist, if possible, in the operation and maintenance of the school's computers.

Data-Entry Operator

It is the job of a data-entry operator to type data into a computer. This is usually done at a computer terminal which is very similar to the computer you will use in this class. Data-entry operators may work for banks entering cancelled checks, department stores entering inventory figures, or educational institutions entering student records. Often data is entered from various locations and then sent over phone lines to a central computer. Because of this it is sometimes possible for data-entry operators to work at home.

Usually a high school diploma is sufficient to gain a job as a data-entry operator. Often several weeks of on the job training will be offered by the employer. To begin to prepare for a position as a data-entry operator it is advisable to take courses in typing and word processing.

Computer Scientist   The study of computer science is a very broad field involving many disciplines including science, electronics and mathematics. A computer scientist often works in research at a university or computer manufacturer developing new computer applications software and hardware. It is computer scientists who first design robotics software or any of the other applications that we have mentioned.

A computer scientist usually has both undergraduate and graduate school degrees. To prepare to be a computer scientist it is advisable to take science courses, especially physics, mathematics courses including calculus, and programming and computer science courses.

1.15 The Social and Ethical Consequences of Computers

The society in which we live has been so profoundly affected by computers that historians refer to the present time as "the information age." This is due to the computer's ability to store and manipulate large amounts of information (data). Computers have become such a dominant force that if all of them were to disappear much of our society would be unable to function. Because of computers we are evolving out of an industrial into an information society much as over a hundred years ago we evolved from an agricultural into an industrial society. Such fundamental changes in society cause disruptions which must be planned for. For this reason it is crucial that we consider both the social and ethical consequences of our increasing dependence on computers.

We have already mentioned the impact of telecommunications. By allowing people to work anywhere that telephones or satellite communications are available, we are likely to become a more diversified society. Large cities with their centralized offices will no longer be as necessary. This diversification could reduce traffic congestion, air pollution and many of the other consequences of an urban society.

In our discussion of robots we mentioned their ability to work twenty-four hour days without vacations. While this is obviously a major benefit to an employer, it could have a negative impact on employees. Manufacturers are increasingly able to replace factory workers with machines, thereby increasing efficiency and saving money. This trend, however, also leads to increased unemployment of those factory workers who lack technical skills.

The argument is often used that new technologies such as robotics create jobs for the people who design, build, install and service them. While this is true, these new jobs require well educated, highly trained people. For this reason it is important to think carefully about the educational requirements needed for employment. As we become an increasingly "high-tech" society, those properly prepared for technical jobs will be the most likely to find employment.

1.16 The Right to Privacy

With computers impacting on our lives in an ever increasing number of ways, serious ethical questions arise. By ethical questions we mean asking what are the right and wrong ways to use computers. As human beings we want to insure that our rights as individuals are not encroached upon by the misuse of these machines.

Probably the most serious problem created by computers is in invading our right to privacy. Because computers can store vast amounts of data we must decide what information is proper to store, what is improper, and who should have access to the information. Every time you use a credit card, make a phone call, withdraw money from the bank, reserve a flight on an airplane, or register to take a course at school a computer records the transaction. Using these records it would be possible to learn a great deal about you — where you have been, when you were there, and what you have done.

Computers are also used to store information dealing with your credit rating, which determines your ability to borrow money. If you want to buy a car and finance it at the bank, the bank first checks your credit records on a computer to determine if you have a good credit rating. If you are able to purchase the car and then apply for automobile insurance, another computer will check to determine if you have traffic violations or have been involved in any activities which would make you a poor risk. How do you know if the information being used is accurate? Would it be fair if your neighbors could access this information without your approval? To protect both your privacy and the accuracy of data stored about you, a number of laws have been passed.

The Fair Credit Reporting Act of 1970 deals with data collected for use by credit, insurance and employment agencies. The act gives individuals the right to see information maintained about them. If a person is denied credit they are allowed access to the files used to make the credit determination. If any of the information is incorrect, the person has the right to have it changed. More laws are under consideration today that deal with restricting access to computer data bases and protecting the privacy of computer communications.

1.17 Protecting Computer Software and Data

Because computer software can be copied electronically it is easy to duplicate. Such duplication is usually illegal because the company producing the software is not paid for the copy. This has become an increasingly serious problem as the number of illegal software copies distributed by computer "pirates" has grown. Developing, testing and marketing software is an expensive process. If the software developer is then denied rightful compensation, the future development of all software is jeopardized. Software companies are increasingly vigilant in detecting and prosecuting those who illegally copy their software. Therefore, when using software it is important to use only legally acquired copies, and to not make illegal copies for others.

Another problem that is growing as computer use increases is the willful interference with or destruction of computer data. Because computers can transfer and erase data at high speeds, it makes them especially vulnerable to acts of theft or vandalism. Newspapers have carried numerous reports of home computer users gaining access to large computer data bases. Sometimes these "hackers" change or erase data stored in the system. These acts are usually illegal and can cause very serious and expensive damage. One especially harmful act is the planting of a "virus" into computer software. A virus is a series of instructions buried into a program which cause the computer to destroy data when given a certain signal.

Most people are becoming aware that the willful destruction of computer data is no different than any other vandalization of property. Since the damage is done electronically the result is often not as obvious as destroying physical property, but the consequences are much the same. It is estimated that computer crimes cost the nation as much as 30 billion dollars a year, a figure that is expected to rise.

1.18 The Ethical Responsibilities of the Programmer

As you will learn when you write your own programs, it is extremely difficult, if not impossible, for a computer programmer to guarantee that a program will always operate properly. The programs used to control complicated devices contain millions of instructions and as the programs grow longer the likelihood of errors increases. A special cause for concern is the increased use of computers to control potentially dangerous devices such as aircraft, nuclear reactors, military weapons and sensitive medical equipment. This places a strong ethical burden on the programmer to insure, as best he or she can, the reliability of computer software.

The Defense Department is currently supporting research aimed at detecting and correcting program errors. Because it spends an estimated 18 billion dollars annually developing software, much of it for use in situations which can be life threatening, the department is especially interested in having reliable programs.

As capable as computers have proven to be, we must be cautious in allowing them to replace human beings in areas where judgement is crucial. Because we are intelligent, humans can often detect that something out of the ordinary has occurred and then take actions which have not been previously anticipated. Computers, on the other hand, will only do what they have been programmed to do, even if it is to perform a dangerous act.

Chapter Summary

Computer hardware refers to the computer itself and its peripheral devices — disk drives, printers, etc., whereas software refers to the programs or instructions which are entered into the computer to make it perform specific tasks. Using this text you will learn to write computer programs in the BASIC language.

The earliest calculating machines were mechanical, requiring gears, wheels and levers, and were often unreliable. The advent of electricity brought about machines which used vacuum tubes, and were capable of performing thousands of calculations a minute. The unreliability of the vacuum tube lead to the development of the transistor and integrated circuit. Computers based on these devices were smaller, faster, more reliable and less expensive.

All computers have several parts in common: (1) an input device which allows data and commands to be entered, (2) a way of storing commands and data, (3) a Processing Unit which controls the processing, and (4) a way of returning the processed information in the form of output. In general, a computer is a machine which accepts information, processes it according to some specific instructions called a program, and then returns new information as output.

Today's microcomputer makes use of a CPU on a chip, the microprocessor which controls the actions of the computer. The CPU contains a special device called the Arithmetic Logic Unit (ALU) which performs math and comparison operations. Based on von Neumann's concept, the computer stores both data and instructions in its memory at the same time. Memory comes in two forms, RAM chips which can be erased and used over, and ROM chips, which is permanent. Keyboards and disk drives are used to input data. Monitors and printers are used to output data. Because the contents of RAM are lost when the computer's power is turned off, disks are used to store data.

One of the most important advances in the field of computing has been in telecommunications, which means the sending of computer data over phone lines. Modems are used both to transmit and receive computer data. Because of telecommunications many people may be able to work at home. A popular form of telecommunications is the electronic bulletin board which allows users to transmit and receive messages. A similar form of telecommunications is electronic mail (E-mail) where single users are able to receive messages meant only for them.

The continued development of microprocessors will affect many products including automobiles and home appliances. With their ability to make simple decisions, microprocessors can automate many of the functions performed by these devices.

Using computers to make decisions normally made by human beings is called artificial intelligence. Although computers cannot think, they can be programmed to make decisions which, for example, allow them to play chess. Artificial intelligence shows great promise for use with robotics. A robot is a machine that can be programmed and also move. Robots are currently used to perform simple manufacturing tasks, but will take on more complex jobs in the future.

Careers in computing were discussed in this chapter and the educational requirements needed to pursue them. Careers which required only a high school education as well as those requiring a college education were presented. The government estimates that the need for data processing employees will continue to grow at a rapid rate.

Historians refer to the present time as the "information age" due to the computer's ability to store and manipulate large amounts of data. As the use of computers increases they will profoundly affect society including what jobs will be available. A problem created by computers is their potential for invading our right to privacy. Laws have been passed to protect us from the misuse of data stored in computers.

Because computer software is easy to copy, illegal copies are often made, denying software manufacturers of rightful compensation. Another problem has been the willful destruction of computer files by erasing data or planting a "virus" into programs that can spread when the programs are copied.

As computers are increasingly used to made decisions in situations which can threaten human life it becomes the responsibility of programmers to do their best to insure the reliability of the software they have developed. We must continue to be cautious not to replace human beings with computers in areas where judgement is crucial.

Vocabulary

ALU - Arithmetic Logic Unit, the part of the CPU that handles math operations.

Artificial intelligence - Using computers to make decisions which would normally be made by a human being.

CPU - Central Processing Unit, the device which electronically controls the functions of the computer.

Data - Information either entered into or produced by the computer.

Electronic bulletin board (BBS) - Telecommunications service which allows subscribers using a computer and modem to transmit messages that can be received by other subscribers.

Electronic mail (E-Mail) - Telecommunications service which allows a person using a computer and modem to send a private message to another person's computer.

Hacker - Person who uses a computer and modem to enter a computer system without authorization.

Hardware - Physical devices which make up the computer and its peripherals.

Information service - A company that provides different telecommunications services, usually for a fee.

Input - Data used by the computer.

Keyboard - Device resembling a typewriter used for inputting data into a computer.

Local Area Network (LAN) - A small network consisting primarily of microcomputers, usually all in a single building.

Memory - Electronic storage used by the computer.

Microprocessor - CPU on a single chip.

Modem - Device which translates binary data into waves and waves back into binary data so that computer data can be sent over telephone lines.

Monitor - Television-like device used to display computer output.

Network - Connecting computers by wires so that data can be transmitted between them.

Output - Data produced by a computer program.

Peripheral - Secondary hardware device connected to a computer such as a printer, monitor or disk drive.

Pirate - Person who illegally copies computer software.

Program - Series of instructions written in a special language directing the computer to perform certain tasks.

PC - Personal Computer, a small computer employing a microprocessor.

RAM - Random Access Memory, memory which the computer can both read and write.

Robot - Machine which can be programmed and is also capable of motion.

ROM - Read Only Memory, memory from which the computer can read only.

Software - Computer programs.

Telecommunications - Sending of computer data over telephone lines.

Terminal - Keyboard and monitor combination used to communicate with a mainframe or minicomputer.

Virus - Program which hides within another program for the purpose of destroying or altering data.

Review

Sections 1.1-1.6

1. What is the primary difference between a computer and a calculator?

2. What is a computer program?

3. Why did early calculating devices not work well?

4. Was Pascal's Pascaline a computer? Why or why not?

5. If successful, could Babbage's Analytical Engine been considered a computer? Why or why not?

6. a) What was the first calculating machine to make use of punched cards?
   b) What were the cards used for?

7. Why did scientists and business people want computers rather than calculators?

8. a) The Mark I was considered a calculator rather than a computer. Why?
    b) Why was the Mark I unreliable?
    c) What was the most important difference between the ENIAC and Mark I?

Sections 1.7-1.9

9. John von Neumann made one of the most important contributions to the development of modern computers. What was this contribution and why was it so important?

10. What made early computers so expensive?

11. What two innovations made the IBM Model 650 superior to earlier computers?

12. High level programming languages such as FORTRAN and BASIC were developed in the 1960's. Why were they important?

13. a) What is an integrated circuit?
    b) In what ways is it superior to a transistor?

14. What invention made the microcomputer possible?

15. Compare a microcomputer with ENIAC. What advantages does the microcomputer have?

16. List three jobs which could best be performed on each of the following computers:

    a) mainframe computer
    b) minicomputer
    c) microcomputer

Sections 1.10-1.13

17. a) List three tasks for which a computer would be better than a human working without a computer. Tell why the computer is better.
    b) List three tasks for which a human would be better than a computer. Tell why the human is better.

18. a) What is computer hardware?
    b) What is software?

19. Which of the four major components of a computer would be used to perform each of the following tasks?

    a) display a column of grade averages
    b) calculate grade averages
    c) store electronically a set of grades
    d) type in a set of grades
    e) decide which of two grades was higher
    f) store a set of grades outside of the computer

20. What is the primary difference between the two types of memory contained in a computer?

21. How would the computer solve the problem 138×29?

22. Why does the computer use binary numbers?

23. Besides those listed in the text, list three occupations where people would be able to work at home rather than in an office using telecommunications.

24. What is the difference between an electronic bulletin board and electronic mail?

25. If all of the students in your school had computers and modems at home, in what ways could they be used by teachers and students?

26. What is artificial intelligence?

27. What devices owned by your family contain microprocessors and what are they used for?

28. If you could have a robot built to your own specifications, what would you have it be capable of doing?

Section 1.14-1.18   The six computer careers mentioned in this chapter include:

(1) system analyst
(2) system developer - programmer
(3) system manager
(4) computer operator
(5) data-entry operator
(6) computer scientist

29. Which of the above careers require only a:

a) high school diploma
b) college diploma
c) college and graduate school degrees

30. For each of the following students list the careers above that he or she should consider:

a) a student who likes mathematics.
b) a student who wants to be involved in the management of a business.
c) a student who wants to work in the development of rocket guidance systems.
d) a student who likes to think through problems in a methodical, logical way.

31. What is meant by the term "high-tech" society?

32. a) How do you believe society will benefit from the information age?
b) What might be the negative aspects of the information age?

33. How can a computer be used to invade your privacy?

34. What can you do if you are turned down for credit at a bank and believe

that the data used to deny credit is inaccurate?

35. What ethical responsibilities does a programmer have when writing a program that will be used to design a bridge? Can the programmer absolutely guarantee that the program will operate properly? Why?

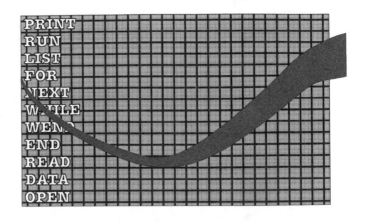

An Introduction to BASIC

PRINT

END

RUN

LIST

NEW

Home, CLS

REM

SAVE, LOAD, FILES

SYSTEM, BASIC

Objectives

Chapter Two

After completing this chapter you will be able to:

1. Determine the steps required to solve a problem on the computer.

2. Start the computer and load the disk operating system (DOS) and BASIC.

3. Use immediate mode to execute statements.

4. Enter and RUN programs containing PRINT, END and REM statements.

5. Locate and correct errors in a program.

6. Use the LIST, NEW and CLS commands.

7. Save programs on disk using the SAVE command, and access saved programs using LOAD.

8. List the names of files stored on disk using the FILES command.

9. Use the SYSTEM command to exit BASIC and return to DOS.

*I*n this chapter you will learn how an algorithm is developed to write a program, how to enter a program into the computer and to correct programming errors. You will also be taught how to have the program perform simple calculations and display messages on the computer screen.

2.1 Steps in Problem Solving

Problem solving on the computer can be broken down into five steps:

1. **Analysis**: Determine whether the computer is the correct tool to solve the problem.
2. **Specification**: State the problem in a clear and unambiguous manner.
3. **Algorithm Design**: Construct a solution to the problem as a series of separate steps.
4. **Coding**: Translate these steps into a computer program and test the program to insure that it works properly.
5. **Interpretation**: Look at the results produced by the program. Are they consistent with the specification/problem statement? Do they answer the original questions? Do the results make sense?

Analysis

Before an algorithm can be designed, the programmer must first analyze the problem to be solved to answer the question:

> Is the computer the appropriate tool for solving this problem? Or would the problem be better solved using other means (e.g., the political process, human interaction, pencil and paper, etc.)?

Inefficiency and even serious errors can result when the computer is applied to a problem which is better suited to another mechanism. There are many examples of people who spend more time computerizing a task than the task would have taken without a computer. A favorite theme of science fiction writers is the misuse of computer decision making when human judgement would be preferred.

Specification

Once it has been determined that a computer program may be useful in solving a problem, a clear and unambiguous definition of the problem should be constructed. This step is crucial in developing a successful solution. To illustrate its importance, imagine that a friend calls and asks you to buy her a blue woolen sweater. At first these instructions appear simple enough, but upon reflection you realize that your friend has not told you what price range she is willing to pay or if she has a certain brand or style of sweater in mind. Your friend has not stated the problem in sufficient detail — her specification was weak. Her instructions would have been better if she had said:

> Buy me a small blue woolen sweater for a price not to exceed $70. Try to buy a Calvin Klein sweater, but if none is available any other well known designer label will do.

This specification is better because it includes sufficient information to cover most possibilities. Often the specification of a problem appears adequate at first glance but later is proven to have flaws. As problem-solving skills are developed, you will become better at anticipating these flaws and avoiding them.

Note that the specification does not discuss how the problem is to be solved. For example, it does not say where to buy the sweater — a mall or a mail order firm would be equally satisfactory. A specification tells *what* is to be done, while the *how* is left to the skills and creativity of the programmer.

In large projects the analysis and specification of a problem are not usually performed by the programmer, but are instead the job of a "systems analyst" in conjunction with the program's user. When errors or omissions in the specification are discovered by the programmer, the correct procedure to follow is to consult with the user or systems analyst to resolve the problem.

Algorithm Design

After the problem specification has been developed, the programmer must construct a method of solution as a series of steps — an algorithm. By definition an algorithm is a set of well defined rules and processes for solving a problem in a finite number of steps. Put more simply an algorithm is a *plan*.

Note that the algorithm design should be done before the programmer sits down at a computer to write the program. It is a crucial mistake to start writing program code before the algorithm has been carefully thought through.

An algorithm provides a detailed description of a method for solving the problem. They are often stated in simple phrases, leaving out minor details. For the above problem, a reasonable algorithm might be:

1. Go to the shopping center.
2. Find a store which sells sweaters.
3. Find the sweater department.
4. If the right sweater is found, purchase it;
   otherwise go back to step 2 and repeat until all stores selling sweaters have been checked.
5. Deliver sweater to your friend, or tell her that sweater could not be found.

Notice that each line of the algorithm is itself a new problem. For example, the fourth step, "If the right sweater is found" can be further broken down:

> a) check for blue sweater.
> b) check manufacturer.
> c) check size.
> d) check price.

It should be clear that this process can also be applied to each of these smaller steps so that any amount of detail can be included. Since the algorithm is being refined (made more specific) by adding a series of steps, this is called "stepwise refinement." During this process of refinement it sometimes becomes necessary to return to the problem's original specification and add additional detail.

In conjunction with the development of the algorithm, the programmer must determine what information (data) must be stored and how it should be organized. In the early part of this course, this is a simple task. As projects grow in complexity, however, organizing the data will occupy a greater portion of the time spent on design.

Coding   Writing a computer program is the next step in the refinement of an algorithm. This step is called "coding," and the actual lines of the program are called "code."

Because computers are not intelligent, the algorithm must be stated with almost all details given. An additional requirement is that the instructions must be written in a language that the computer understands. Common programming languages include Ada, BASIC, COBOL, C, FORTRAN and Pascal. Such languages tend to be restrictive in their vocabulary, requiring the programmer to use only words that are part of that language. For example, the two statements

```
Write 'Hello world'
```

and

```
PRINT "Hello world"
```

would seem to be similar, but only the second causes BASIC to display the message `Hello  world` on the computer screen. The coding process is not complete until the program has been thoroughly tested to insure that it works properly.

Interpretation   This is where the programmer takes a critical look at the results produced. Although the program may execute without obvious errors, it may not produce results which solve the problem. This may indicate errors in the specification or algorithm design steps.

2.2 How to Use This Text

Throughout this text new concepts are introduced in a two-step process. First the concept is discussed and then it is followed by a section titled *Review*. Reviews serve as reinforcement, and should only be performed after the preceding section has been carefully read. This chapter has several sections marked *Practice*. These Practices provide step-by-step directions and should be performed on the computer.

Review

1. Write an algorithm for making a trip by airplane from your home to a hotel in Paris, France. Start by phoning your travel agent to make reservations.

2. Write an algorithm for holding a birthday party. Start by making a list of those who will be invited.

GETTING STARTED ON THE COMPUTER

You are now ready to learn how to start the computer, enter the date and time, and run BASIC.

2.3 Using Disks

Disks will be used both to start the computer and to save the programs that you create. It is important to handle the disks carefully because they store large quantities of data in a magnetic format that is vulnerable to dirt and heat. Observing the following rules will help to insure that your disks give you trouble free service:

1. Keep disks away from electrical and magnetic devices such as computer, monitors, television sets, stereos and any type of magnet.

2. Make sure that your disks are not exposed to either extreme cold or heat. Being made of plastic they are sensitive to temperature.

3. Be careful not to allow dust, dirt, or moisture to penetrate the disk by keeping it in a safe place when not in use.

4. Never touch the disk except by the edges of its jacket. Touching the disk's magnetic surface will usually damage it, destroying valuable data.

5. Do not bend or crimp the disk and never place paper clips on it.

2.4 Starting the Computer

Before you are able to use BASIC, it is first necessary to load the disk operating system (DOS) into the computer's memory. DOS contains special programs that the computer needs in order to run. The process of transferring DOS from disk to computer memory is called "booting."

Practice 1

The following Practice explains how to turn on the computer, enter the current date and time, and then boot DOS and start BASIC. You should perform the Practice on a computer. (Instructions for network and hard disk users are slightly different — see your instructor for details.)

1) INSERT THE SYSTEM DISK

a. Place the DOS disk carefully in drive A: (the top or left hand drive) with its label up and towards you as shown in the diagram:

Carefully place the disk in the drive as shown

b. Close the drive door and then turn on both the computer and the monitor. After a few seconds, the red "in use" light on the disk drive comes on and the computer automatically loads DOS from the disk. Never open the drive door when this light is on because this may damage the disk.

2) ENTER THE DATE

When you see the message

```
Current date is Tue 1-1-1980  <Date may be different>
Enter new date (mm-dd-yy):
```

type today's date in the form *mm-dd-yy* and then press the key marked Enter. (Note that on some computers this key is marked "Return" or with the symbol ↵.) Pressing the Enter key enters whatever has been typed into the computer's memory. If you make a mistake typing the date, press the key marked Esc (the Escape key) and start over. The computer will not accept an invalid date.

3) ENTER THE TIME

When you see the message

```
Current time is 0:05.17        <Time may be different>
Enter new time:
```

type the current time in the form *hh:mm* and press the Enter key. If you make a mistake typing the time, press the key marked Esc and enter the time again. The computer will not accept an invalid time.

4) LOAD BASIC

After the date and time are entered, the computer will display a prompt (usually A>). When this "DOS prompt" is displayed, type BASIC and press the Enter key:

```
A> BASIC   ↵
```

BASIC is then loaded from the disk into the computer's memory and the following screen displayed:

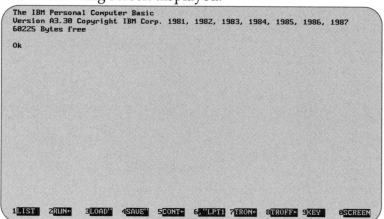

The BASIC screen

2.5 The Cursor

When the computer is first turned on, a small blinking underline appears which is called the cursor. The cursor can be moved around the screen by using the cursor control or "arrow" keys:

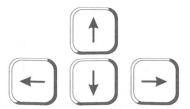

All the cursor keys are repeat keys which means that they continue to operate when they are held down. As long as a cursor key is depressed, the cursor will continue to move over anything written on the screen without erasing it. To move the cursor down the screen use the key marked with a down-arrow. Each time this key is pressed the cursor moves down one line. Similarly, to move the cursor up, left or right, use the keys marked with arrows pointing in these directions.

2.6 Immediate Mode

A computer does nothing without first being given instructions. It is possible to have the computer follow an instruction immediately by typing a BASIC statement and then pressing Enter (⏎); this is called using the computer in "immediate mode." It is also possible to give the computer instructions using a program which will be explained later in this chapter. After the computer has executed your instruction it displays "Ok". This indicates that BASIC is ready and waiting for you to enter another instruction.

Most BASIC statements can be used in immediate mode. However, it is best to use immediate mode only for simple calculations and to use programs to perform most other tasks.

2.7 The PRINT Statement

PRINT is the statement used in BASIC to display numbers, characters and words on the screen. Using immediate mode, the following example prints the result of a math operation (calculation) on the screen when Enter is pressed:

```
PRINT 12 + 5        <press Enter>
 17
Ok
```

PRINT followed by a math operation tells the computer to print the result of that operation. Notice that only the result is printed, and not the math expression itself. In immediate mode the computer carries out this operation as soon as Enter is pressed. The Ok means that BASIC has completed executing the PRINT, and is ready to accept another statement.

In BASIC the following symbols are used to produce calculations:

Operation	Sign
Addition	+
Subtraction	–
Multiplication	*
Division	/
Exponentiation	^ (raised to a power)

The computer can use both numbers and words. To the computer a number is something that can be used in a mathematical calculation; something that can be added, subtracted, multiplied or divided. A word or character, on the other hand, cannot be used to do any of those things.

Note that in this text we will enter all BASIC statements, such as PRINT, in uppercase letters to distinguish them from other code. You do not have to enter the statements in all upper-case — BASIC will convert them automatically.

2.8 PRINT with Quotation Marks

PRINT followed by quotation marks tells the computer to print whatever appears between the quotation marks. Using immediate mode, the following example prints a message on the screen:

```
PRINT "The computer is fast!"    <press Enter>
```

When Enter is pressed, the message The computer is fast! is printed on the screen. The word PRINT and the quotation marks are not printed.

A special use of PRINT is to print a blank line. When PRINT is used alone, without a message or calculation, it causes a blank line to be displayed.

2.9 Syntax Errors

The computer can act only when it recognizes a statement or instruction that is in its language. When the computer does not recognize an instruction, it prints an error message and stops what it is doing to allow the programmer to correct the error. One of the most common errors is the Syntax Error:

```
PRUNT "The computer is fast!"
Syntax Error
Ok
```

Since the computer cannot think for itself, it does not realize that the programmer meant "PRINT", and not "PRUNT". The BASIC language does not contain the statement PRUNT, so the computer displays an error message and halts its attempt to carry out the instruction.

2.10 Avoiding Syntax Errors with Alt

Most BASIC commands can be entered using the Alt key and a single letter. The advantage of this approach is that it helps to avoid simple syntax errors such as typing "PRUNT" instead of PRINT.

For example, to have the computer enter the BASIC statement PRINT, hold down the Alt key and press P (written as Alt-P). When you let both keys up, the word PRINT and a space are inserted at the current cursor position. Many commands and statements have an Alt key shortcut, which are listed in Appendix C.

Practice 2

If you have not already done so, boot DOS and start BASIC as described in Practice 1, and then follow these instructions:

1) USE PRINT TO DISPLAY THE RESULTS OF CALCULATIONS

Execute the following statements in immediate mode. Be sure to press Enter at the end of each statement. If you make a mistake in a statement, before pressing Enter, use the arrow keys to move the cursor to the error and then type the correction:

```
PRINT 5 + 3
PRINT 5 - 3
PRINT 5 * 3
PRINT 5 / 3
PRINT 5 ^ 3
```

2) USE PRINT TO DISPLAY A MESSAGE

Type the following statement and press Enter:

```
PRINT "I am 6 feet tall."
```

3) USE THE CURSOR KEYS TO EDIT THE STATEMENT

Using the arrow keys, move the cursor to the I in PRINT and type an O so that the statement now reads:

```
PRONT "I am 6 feet tall."
```

Press Enter. Note the message Syntax error.

4) CORRECT THE ABOVE STATEMENT

Move the cursor to the O in PRONT, type an I and press Enter. The message is now printed correctly.

5) USE AN ALT KEY SHORTCUT TO ENTER A PRINT STATEMENT

a. Hold down the Alt key and press P. BASIC displays PRINT and a space.

b. Type the message: "Alt key shortcuts are fast!" The statement should be displayed as:

```
PRINT "Alt key shortcuts are fast!"
```

Press Enter. BASIC displays the message.

2.11 Writing a Program

As we have noted, immediate mode allows the computer to execute a single statement at a time. A program, on the other hand, gives the computer a series of instructions written as numbered lines. These lines are stored in the computer's memory until it is given the command to execute the program. The computer then finds the lowest numbered line, executes the instruction on that line, and continues to the next line. This process is repeated until the highest numbered line is completed (usually an END statement as described in the next section).

2.12 The END Statement

The END statement is used to halt the program's execution, and should always be the last statement in any program. For example,

```
99 END
```

causes the run of a program to stop when line 99 is reached. It is a good programming practice to place an END statement in a program since it helps to ensure that the program will terminate properly.

2.13 Entering Program Lines

There are a few simple rules about program lines and line numbering which you should keep in mind when writing a program:

1. Programs lines must begin with a number. Any whole number from 0 to 65529 can be used as a line number.

2. When writing a program, use line numbers that are units of ten (10, 20, . . . 100, 110, 120, etc.). This leaves room to insert nine additional lines between any two lines in case it is necessary to add new lines later.

3. It is not necessary to enter the lines in order. Line 20 can be entered first, then line 10 and later line 30. BASIC automatically puts the lines in numerical order by line number. Any time a new instruction is to be added to a program, just type the line number, the instruction and press Enter. BASIC will then put the line into proper sequence.

4. To enter a program line into the computer's memory, press the Enter key when the line is completed:

   ```
   10 PRINT 2 + 2              <press Enter>
   ```

   If the Enter key is not pressed the line is ignored.

5. The END statement should be the last line in the program. Use a line number such as 99 or 999. This makes it stand out from other statements which are usually numbered by tens and also allows for the insertion of new lines before the END statement as explained in the next section.

6. Do not confuse the capital letter "O" with the number zero "0". Use the zero (0) when a number is needed and the character "O" when a letter is needed.

7. Do not use the Enter key or the space bar to move the cursor around the screen; instead use the cursor control keys to move up, down, left or right. Using Enter to move down the screen can cause lines to be entered or erased by accident, and using the space bar will erase characters by printing a space over them.

2.14 RUN

The RUN command tells the computer to begin executing the program stored in its memory — it finds the lowest numbered line, executes the instruction on that line, and continues to the next line until the highest numbered line is completed. It is important to realize that the RUN is not part of the program; it does not get a line number and is typed only after the program is complete.

BASIC instructions which are not included in a program, such as RUN, are called "commands." Instructions contained in a program line, such as PRINT, are called "statements."

Practice 3

If you have not already done so, boot DOS and start BASIC, then follow the instructions given below.

1) ENTER THE FOLLOWING PROGRAM INTO THE COMPUTER

Be sure to copy the program exactly as shown and remember to press Enter at the end of each line:

```
10 PRINT "Hello"
20 PRINT "I am a computer."
99 END
```

Note that no output has been produced. This is the difference between immediate mode and entering a program.

2) RUN THE PROGRAM

Type RUN and press Enter. You should see the following output:

```
RUN
Hello
I am a computer.
Ok
```

The computer executes the program lines that are stored in its memory, starting at line 10 in this example. When a line is executed, PRINT works the same as it does in immediate mode. The message "Hello" is printed because those characters are between quotation marks as is the message "I am a computer." on line 20. Notice that the words PRINT and the quotation marks are not printed when the program is executed.

3) ENTER THE FOLLOWING PROGRAM INTO THE COMPUTER

This program uses the PRINT statement to print the result of four mathematical operations:

```
10 PRINT 5 + 3
20 PRINT 5 - 3
30 PRINT 5 * 3
40 PRINT 15 / 3
99 END
```

4) RUN THE PROGRAM

Type RUN and press Enter. You should see the following output:

```
RUN
 8
 2
 15
 5
Ok
```

When line 10 is executed, the computer prints the sum of 5 and 3. Line 20 tells the computer to print the difference between 5 and 3. Line 30 tells the computer to print the product of 5 and 3, while line 40 prints the result of 15 divided by 3.

2.15 Printing Calculations and Messages

It is possible to use a single PRINT statement to display both the result of a calculations and to print a message. The rules for doing this are simple. Whatever words, numbers or characters are to be printed must be typed within quotation marks while any calculations that are to be carried out must be typed outside the quotation marks.

This following program prints numbers, words, and characters at the same time:

```
10  PRINT "Mathematics"
20  PRINT "5 * 3"
30  PRINT 5 * 3
40  PRINT "5 * 3 =" 5 * 3
99  END
```

```
RUN
Mathematics
5 * 3
 15
5 * 3 = 15
```

Line 20 prints 5 * 3 rather than the product of 5 and 3 because the computer understands the 5, * and 3 to be characters when they are inside quotation marks. Line 30 prints the product 15 since the 5, * and 3 are not inside quotation marks. Line 40 combines the printing of words and calculations in one PRINT statement. 5 * 3 = appears on the screen because it is inside quotation marks and the product 15 is printed because of the 5 * 3 that is outside the quotation marks.

2.16 LIST

The LIST command is used to display the program currently in the computer's memory. For instance, when an error is made and needs to be corrected, LIST shows the program lines enabling the programmer to see where the mistake is and correct it. The program from Section 2.15 is employed to demonstrate three ways that LIST can be used.

1. **LIST by itself:**

```
LIST
10  PRINT "Mathematics"
20  PRINT "5 * 3"
30  PRINT 5 * 3
40  PRINT "5 * 3 =" 5 * 3
99  END
```

Typing LIST and then pressing Enter displays the entire program on the screen.

2. **LIST a single line:**

```
LIST 40
40 PRINT "5 * 3 =" 5 * 3
```

It is possible to LIST a single line of a program by typing LIST followed by the line number of the desired line.

3. **LIST a range of lines:**

```
LIST 20 - 40
20 PRINT "5 * 3"
30 PRINT 5 * 3
40 PRINT "5 * 3 =" 5 * 3
```

This command tells BASIC to list all lines from line 20 to line 40, inclusive. This is useful for programs which have many lines, more than could fit on the screen at one time.

2.17 NEW

The NEW command is used to erase the program currently stored in the computer's memory. Before entering a new program it is a good practice to first type NEW. This ensures that program lines from any previous program will not affect the new program:

```
LIST
10 PRINT "Mathematics"
20 PRINT "5 * 3"
30 PRINT 5 * 3
40 PRINT "5 * 3 =" 5 * 3
50 END
Ok

NEW
Ok

LIST
Ok
```

After the NEW command is entered, the LIST command shows that there is no program in the computer's memory. Be sure that you really want your program erased from the computer's memory when you type NEW. Once it is erased it is lost forever unless it has been saved on disk as described in Section 2.21.

Practice 4

1) WRITE A MULTIPLICATION PROGRAM

Write and run a program that produces the following output. Be sure to use mathematical calculations to produce each result:

```
RUN
This program calculates large products.
358.7 * 312.21 = 111989.7
32767 * 0.0835 = 2736.045
2971 * 51.784 = 153850.3
```

2) **LIST THE PROGRAM**

Type LIST.

3) **ERASE THE PROGRAM**

Type NEW.

4) **LIST THE PROGRAM AGAIN**

Type LIST. What is displayed? Why? What has happened to the program?

2.18 Correcting Errors and Modifying Programs

Typing errors or other mistakes in a program can be corrected in several ways. The following examples use the mathematics program entered in Section 2.15:

1. **Retyping A Line**. A program line can be changed by simply typing a new statement using the same line number:

```
LIST
10 PRINT "Mathematics"
20 PRINT "5 * 3"
30 PRINT 5 * 3
40 PRINT "5 * 3 =" 5 * 3
99 END

10 PRINT "Math Magic"
```

```
RUN
Math Magic
5 * 3
 15
5 * 3 = 15
Ok
```

Notice that the output of line 10 only is changed. Instead of Mathematics, the program now displays Math Magic.

2. **Adding A New Line**. To add a line between other lines of a program, type the new line and press Enter. The computer will then put the line in its proper place. A new line can be added as shown below:

```
35 PRINT "Presto!"
```

```
RUN
Math Magic
5 * 3
  15
Presto!
5 * 3 = 15
Ok
```

3. **Erasing A Whole Line**. An entire line of a program can be erased by typing the line number and pressing Enter:

   20
   30

```
RUN
Magic Math
Presto!
5 * 3 = 15
Ok
```

Notice that the output produced by lines 20 and 30 in the original program does not appear since these lines have been erased from the computer's memory.

Changes to existing lines may be made by LISTing the program and using the arrow keys to move the cursor to the position of the modification. The following keys may then be used to edit the existing line:

4. **Deleting A Character**. The `Del` key (Delete) is used to erase one character at a time. Each time the Del key is pressed the character directly above the cursor is erased. When the modification is complete, press Enter to place the corrected line into the computer's memory.

5. **Inserting Characters**: The `Ins` key (Insert) allows new characters to be inserted into an existing line. To insert new characters, move the cursor to the location where the insertion is to be made and press the Ins key. The cursor will change into a blinking box. Each character now typed will be inserted into the current line. When you have completed the insertion, press the Ins key again to halt the insertion and then Enter to place the corrected line into the computer's memory.

6. **Replacing Characters**: Characters may be replaced in an existing line by typing new characters over top of them. When the cursor is its normal, blinking underline, any characters typed will replace existing characters. Pressing Enter places the modified line into the computer's memory.

Note that this technique requires that the Enter key be pressed to place the corrected line into the computer's memory. If the Enter key is not pressed, and another key (such as an arrow) used, BASIC will ignore the correction. To cancel a correction leaving the line unchanged, press the Escape key instead of Enter.

An error in a computer program is called a "bug", and the process of finding and removing errors "debugging." Using LIST and the editing techniques described above are powerful debugging techniques.

Practice 5

Boot DOS and BASIC if you have not already done so. In this Practice you will enter a program and then edit it using the techniques presented above.

1) ENTER AND RUN THE FOLLOWING PROGRAM

Start by entering the NEW command to clear any old programs from the computer's memory, and then enter and run this program:

```
NEW
10 PRINT "This is a test program."
20 PRINT "3 + 5 =" 3 + 5
30 PRINT "Watch this line disappear."
99 END
RUN
```

2) REPLACE LINE 20 AND LIST THE PROGRAM

Enter the line

```
20 PRINT "4 * 6 =" 4 * 6
```

and type LIST. Note how the new line 20 has replaced the original line 20.

3) DELETE LINE 30 AND RUN THE PROGRAM

Type:

```
30
RUN
```

Note that line 30 has been erased so that its output is no longer displayed.

4) ADD LINE 15 AND RUN THE PROGRAM

Enter:

```
15 PRINT "This is the new line."
RUN
```

The output from line 15 is displayed between lines 10 and 20.

5) LIST THE PROGRAM

Enter the LIST command. The program currently in the computer's memory is displayed in proper sequence.

6) **DELETE CHARACTERS IN LINE 15**

   a. Using the arrow keys, move the cursor to the "n" at the beginning of the word "new" in line 15.
   b. Press the `Del` key 4 times. The word "new" and the space following it are deleted.
   c. Press Enter to replace line 15 in the computer's memory with the modified line.
   d. Move the cursor to any blank line below the program using the down-arrow key and enter the RUN command. Note that the word "new" is removed from the output of line 15.

7) **INSERT CHARACTERS IN LINE 10**

   a. Use the arrow keys to move the cursor to the beginning of the word "test" in line 10 of the listed program.
   b. Press the `Ins` key to enter Insert mode. Note that the cursor becomes a blinking rectangle.
   c. Type "modified and edited" followed by a space.
   d. Press the `Ins` key to leave Insert mode.
   e. Press `Enter`.
   f. Move the cursor down to the RUN command.
   g. Press Enter. Note the change in the output of line 10.

2.19 The Home Key and CLS

After a program has been worked on for a while, the screen can become filled with program lines, error messages and old output. This can get in the way as you try to make changes, correct errors or run the program. Either the `Home` key or CLS command can be used to clear the screen of such unwanted characters.

Pressing the `Home` key places the cursor in the upper left corner of the screen, which is its "home" position. Holding down the `Ctrl` (control) key and pressing the `Home` key (`Ctrl-Home`) clears everything off the screen and also returns the cursor to its home position. Clearing the screen has no effect on the computer's memory. All program lines that have been entered remain in the memory of the computer; only the screen is erased.

CLS can be used within a program or in immediate mode to clear the screen. For example, the line

    50 CLS

clears the screen when line 50 is executed. It is important to remember that only the screen is erased, not the contents of the computer's memory. The CLS (CLear Screen) statement performs the same function as the `Ctrl-Home` keys except that it may be used within a program.

2.20 REM Statements

The REM statement is used in the body of a program to explain portions of code. These REMarks are ignored by the computer when the program is run. For example, the line

```
30 REM ** Calculate the Area of a Rectangle **
```

is displayed only when the program is LISTed. It is good programming style to use REM statements throughout a program to explain what different parts of the program do so that another programmer would be able to read and understand the program without difficulty.

REM statements may also be used to identify the program. It is a good idea to includes REMs at the beginning of a program which give your name and the purpose of the program:

```
10 REM   Bill Freitas
20 REM   Computer Programming I; Mr. Taylor
30 REM   Bank Teller assignment, #5
```

Practice 6

1) ENTER AND RUN THE FOLLOWING PROGRAM

Enter the lines:

```
NEW
10 REM ** This is a calculator program **
20 PRINT "35 / 18 =" 35 / 18
30 PRINT "45 * 107 =" 45 * 107
99 END
RUN
```

2) ADD A REMARK TO THE PROGRAM

Enter line 15 and then run the program:

```
15 REM ** Division and multiplication are
   performed **
RUN
```

Note that lines 10 and 15 produce no output.

3) CLEAR THE SCREEN

Hold down the CTRL key and press the HOME key to clear the screen.

4) LIST THE PROGRAM

Enter the LIST command. Note that lines 10 and 15 appear in the listing, but do not affect the output.

5) ADD A LINE TO CLEAR THE SCREEN

Enter the line

```
5 CLS
```

and RUN the modified program. The screen is cleared of all old information before the program's output is displayed.

6) **REMOVE LINE 5**

Type:

    5

and RUN the program. The old output now remains on the screen.

2.21 SAVE, LOAD and FILES

Saving your programs on disk is important because the computer's memory can only store information while the power is on; any data in memory is lost when the computer is turned off. However, if a copy of a program is saved on disk, the program can later be retrieved and loaded into memory. Unfinished programs, as well as those that might need future editing or will be re-run at a later time should always be saved.

Another important reason for saving programs is to prevent their accidental loss. A momentary power interruption can wipe everything out of the computer's memory. Even bumping the power cord can sometimes cause the memory to be cleared. It is therefore a good practice, especially when working on long programs, to save them periodically. Then should a power failure occur, the program can be restored from the disk at the point where it was last saved. It is also important to save a program on disk before you attempt to run it because programs containing errors may cause the computer to erase its memory. The SAVE command is used to store a program on a disk. Its form is:

    SAVE "<program name>"

For example,

    SAVE "EXER7A"

saves the program currently in memory on the disk and gives it the name EXER7A.BAS. The extension .BAS is added to the program name by the computer to indicate that the program is written in <u>BASIC</u>. If no disk drive is specified the computer assumes the default drive (usually drive A:). However, it is possible to save the program on another drive:

    SAVE "B:WORK1"

save the program currently in memory on the disk in drive B: under the name WORK1.BAS.

Note that the program name must be enclosed in quotation marks. Program names should begin with a letter and must be from one to eight characters in length. The characters should be only letters and digits.

Once a program has been saved on disk it may be retrieved and loaded back into the computer's memory using the LOAD command which takes the form:

    LOAD "<program name>"

For example,

```
LOAD "MYPROG"
```

transfers MYPROG.BAS from the disk in drive A: into the computer's memory. (LOAD "B:MYPROG" would cause the program to be loaded from the disk in drive B:.)

To list the names of programs stored on a disk the FILES command is used. Typing

```
FILES
```

lists the names of the files stored on the disk in drive A:. If a disk drive is specified FILES will list the programs stored on that disk (e.g., FILES "B:"). To list just those files which are BASIC programs, type:

```
FILES "*.BAS"
```

2.22 SYSTEM and BASIC

It is important to exit BASIC properly when you are finished writing programs to allow you to run some other application like word processing or to turn the computer off. Entering the command

```
SYSTEM
```

returns you to the disk operating system prompt at which point you can run another application or turn the computer off. It is important to realize that SYSTEM exits BASIC — no further BASIC commands may be entered, and any program currently in memory but not saved is lost.

To return to BASIC, enter the command

```
BASIC
```

at the DOS prompt (A>).

Practice 7

In this Practice you will save the program created in Practice 6, display a list of saved programs, load the program back into memory, and exit BASIC. Make sure that the program from Practice 6 is on the screen; if it is not type it in again.

1) SAVE THE PROGRAM ON DISK

Enter the proper command to save the program on your disk:

```
SAVE "MYPROG"
```
← if you have one disk drive

or

```
SAVE "B:MYPROG"
```
← to save on the disk in drive B:

The disk light should flash indicating that the program is being saved. Ok will be displayed when saving has been completed.

2) ERASE THE PROGRAM FROM THE COMPUTER'S MEMORY

Enter the command:

```
NEW
```

3) LIST THE CONTENTS OF THE COMPUTER'S MEMORY

Enter the command:

```
LIST
```

The program has been erased from memory so no lines are shown.

4) LIST THE FILES STORED ON DISK

Enter the command

```
FILES
```
← if you have one disk drive

or

```
FILES "B:"
```
← to see the files saved on drive B:

depending on which drive your disk is located in. A listing of all files on the disk, including MYPROG.BAS, is displayed.

5) LOAD MYPROG.BAS FROM DISK INTO THE COMPUTER'S MEMORY

Enter the command:

```
LOAD "MYPROG"
```
or
```
LOAD "B:MYPROG"
```

The disk light flashes indicating that the disk is being accessed. BASIC displays Ok when the file has been loaded.

6) LIST THE PROGRAM

Enter the command:

```
LIST
```

A listing of MYPROG is displayed, proving that it was loaded from the disk.

7) EXIT BASIC

Enter the command:

```
SYSTEM
```

The DOS prompt (A>) is displayed indicating that the computer can be turned off or another application (such as a word processor) run.

8) RETURN TO BASIC

Enter the command:

```
BASIC
```

The BASIC screen is again displayed.

9) EXIT BASIC

Enter the command

```
SYSTEM
```

The DOS prompt is displayed. The computer can now be turned off.

Chapter Summary

Five steps are employed in solving a problem on the computer. The first step, analysis, is to determine if the computer is the appropriate tool for solving a problem. The second step, specification, requires a clear and unambiguous definition of the problem. Algorithm design is the third step where the programmer constructs a method of solution as a series of steps (an algorithm). Coding is the fourth step and involves writing the computer program. The fifth step is interpretation where the programmer looks at the results produced by the program to determine if they solve the specified problem. Errors discovered during any step may require returning to an earlier step to add more detail, etc.

The first step in starting the computer is loading the disk operating system (DOS) which contains special programs needed by the computer in order to run. Transferring DOS from disk to the computer's memory is called "booting." BASIC is next loaded into memory.

The PRINT statement is used to display numbers, characters and words. The following symbols are used to produce calculations: addition (+), subtraction (–), multiplication (*), division (/), and exponentiation (^). BASIC statements are displayed in uppercase to distinguish them from other items in a program (such as the contents of a REM).

Anything appearing between quotation marks in a PRINT statement is displayed on the screen. For example,

```
10 PRINT "Smith"
RUN
Smith
Ok
```

The Ok is produced by BASIC to let you know that it is ready to accept another command. PRINT used alone, with no message or calculation, produces a blank line.

PRINT may be used to both display the results of a calculation and print a message. The message must be enclosed within quotation marks. For example,

```
10 PRINT "5 * 3 =" 5 * 3
RUN
 5 * 3 = 15
```

A Syntax Error is displayed whenever the computer does not recognize an instruction. To avoid such an error most BASIC commands can be entered using the Alt key and a single letter. For example, Alt-P is used to enter PRINT.

Errors in a program can be corrected by retyping a line, adding a new line, or erasing a line. To erase a line the line number is typed and Enter pressed. Changes to an existing line can be made by deleting characters (Del key), inserting characters (Ins key) or replacing characters. Enter is pressed to enter a modified line into memory. The process of finding and removing errors is called "debugging."

A program is a series of numbered instructions that are executed only after the RUN command is given. The END statement is used to halt program execution, and should be the last statement in a program. Program lines must begin with a number. It is best to use line numbers that are units of ten so that other lines can be inserted between lines and it is not necessary to enter lines in order. For example, line 30 may be entered before line 20, and when the program is run the computer will execute the lines in order.

The LIST command is used to display the program in memory. A single line can be listed (LIST 20) or a range of lines (LIST 20 – 50). The NEW command is used to erase the program in memory.

Pressing the Home key places the cursor in the upper left corner of the screen while holding down the Ctrl key and pressing the Home key clears the screen. The CLS statement can be used within a program to clear the screen.

Comments can be added to a program using the REM statement. These comments are ignored when the program is run.

The command SAVE "EXER5" saves the program currently in memory naming it EXER5.BAS. The program name must be enclosed in quotation marks, must begin with a letter and be from one to eight characters in length. To transfer EXER5 back into memory from disk the command LOAD "EXER5" is used. To list the names of files stored on disk the FILES command is used.

BASIC is exited by entering the SYSTEM command. Exiting BASIC clears all programs from the computer's memory, so they should be saved on disk before using the SYSTEM command.

Vocabulary

Algorithm - A plan or set of well defined rules and processes for solving a problem.
Algorithm design - Constructing a solution to a problem as a series of separate steps.
Analysis - Determining if the computer is the appropriate tool for solving a problem.

BASIC - Command entered to run BASIC. Also, the name of the computer programming language taught by this text.

Booting - Transferring DOS from disk to the computer's memory.

CLS - Statement that clears the screen.

Code - A program or part of a program.

Coding - Writing a computer program.

Command - BASIC instruction which is not included in a program such as RUN or LIST.

Cursor - Blinking underline indicating where data typed will appear on the screen.

Disk operating system (DOS) - Special programs needed by the computer in order for it to operate.

END - Statement used to terminate program execution, should be last statement in a program.

FILES - Command that lists the names of the files stored on disk.

Home **key** - Moves cursor to upper left corner of the screen.

Immediate mode - When the computer immediately executes commands after the Enter key is pressed.

Interpretation - Determining if the results produced by a program solve the specified problem.

LIST - Command used to display the program in memory.

LOAD - Command used to transfer a program from disk to memory.

NEW - Command used to erase the program in memory.

PRINT - Statement used to display information on the screen.

RUN - Command that executes the program stored in memory.

SAVE - Command used to save the program in memory on disk.

Specification - Definition of a problem.

Statement - BASIC instruction which is contained in a program line.

Stepwise refinement - Refining an algorithm by adding steps and detail.

Syntax error - A common error caused when the computer does not recognize an instruction.

SYSTEM - Command to exit BASIC and return to DOS.

Exercises

1. Perform each of the following computations on paper as the computer would. Check your answers using immediate mode:

    a) 5 + 16   d) 33 - 16   g) 2^2
    b) 13 * 3   e) 239 * 27   h) 4^2 + 5 - 12
    c) 250 / 5   f) 999 / 11   i) 18 / 6 + 5

2. Write a program that displays the following:

    ```
    RUN
    A
    B
    C
    D
    ABCD
    Ok
    ```

3. Write a program that draws a rectangle using the asterisk ("*") symbol:

    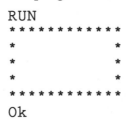

    ```
    RUN
    * * * * * * * * * * *
    *                   *
    *                   *
    *                   *
    * * * * * * * * * * *
    Ok
    ```

4. Write a program that first clears the screen and then draws a triangle using the "/", "\" and "_" symbols:

    ```
    RUN
          /\
         /  \
        /    \
       /      \
      /_____\
    Ok
    ```

5. Write a program that first clears the screen and then draws the following face:

    ```
    RUN
          * * * * *
         *         *
       *   o     o   *
      *        +        *
       *    \___/    *
         *         *
          * * * * *
    Ok
    ```

6. Write a program that adds the numbers 3, 5 and 7. Have BASIC perform the math:

    ```
    RUN
    3 + 5 + 7 = 15
    Ok
    ```

7. Write a program that first multiplies then divides 275 by 39. A run of the program should be similar to:

    ```
    RUN
    275 * 39 = 10725
    275 / 39 = 7.051282
    Ok
    ```

8. In the first week of the season, the jogging club ran the following number of miles each day: 2, 3, 5, 3, 5. Write a program to calculate and print the total mileage for the week:

    ```
    RUN
    Mileage for the first week is 18
    Ok
    ```

9. There are 5 gerbils, 6 mice and 3 birds in the biology lab. Write a program that lists these animals:

    ```
    RUN
    BIOLOGY LAB
    Gerbils: 5
    Mice: 6
    Birds: 3
    Ok
    ```

10. a) Change the biology lab program from Exercise 9 so that it also calculates and prints how many animals there are total. Have BASIC perform the math:

```
RUN
BIOLOGY LAB
Birds: 3
Gerbils: 5
Mice: 6

Total animals = 14
Ok
```

b) The mice had 5 babies. Edit the program to reflect the new number of mice and the new total:

```
RUN
BIOLOGY LAB
Birds: 3
Gerbils: 5
Mice: 11

Total animals = 19
Ok
```

c) The lab has acquired 2 new snakes. Edit the program to reflect this new addition and total:

```
RUN
BIOLOGY LAB
Birds: 3
Gerbils: 5
Mice: 11
Snakes: 2

Total animals = 21
Ok
```

11. Orange juice is on sale for $1.99 a gallon this week. Milk is $.89 a quart. Write a program that displays the following sign:

```
RUN
* * * * * * * * * * * * * * * * * * * * * * * *
*                                         *
*            BIG SALE!                    *
*                                         *
*     Orange Juice   $1.99                *
*     Milk (quart)   $ .89                *
*                                         *
* * * * * * * * * * * * * * * * * * * * * * * *
Ok
```

12. a) Write a program to calculate the cost of 2 gallons of orange juice and 3 quarts of milk using the prices from Exercise 11. The program's output should be similar to:

```
RUN
2 gallons Orange Juice = $ 3.98
3 quarts Milk = $ 2.67
Ok
```

b) Modify the program to calculate and print the total cost:

```
RUN
2 gallons Orange Juice = $ 3.98
3 quarts Milk = $ 2.67
Total cost is $ 6.65
Ok
```

13. Eggs sell for $0.06 each at a local store. Write a program to calculate and display the cost of a dozen eggs:

```
RUN
One dozen eggs cost $ .72
Ok
```

14. When travelling by car it is often useful to know how many miles the car travels per gallon of gasoline. Write a program that calculates the average miles per gallon (MPG) assuming that a car traveled 67.5 miles on 2.4 gallons of gas:

```
RUN
67.5 miles on 2.4 gallons = 28.125 MPG
Ok
```

15. You bicycle three miles every day to school. Assuming that you attend school 180 days every year, write a program which calculates the total number of miles you will bicycle in one school year:

```
RUN
3 miles per day for 180 days = 540 miles
total
Ok
```

Chapter 3

Using Variables

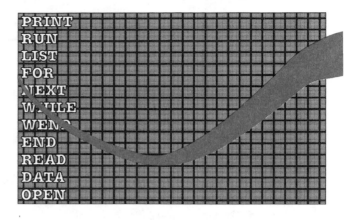

```
PRINT
RUN
LIST
FOR
NEXT
WHILE
WEND
END
READ
DATA
OPEN
```

INPUT

LINE INPUT

FOR...NEXT

READ...DATA

INPUT

LINE INPUT

FOR...NEXT

READ...DATA

Objectives

Chapter Three

After completing this chapter you will be able to:

1. Make use of numeric and string variables.

2. Print both messages and variables.

3. Enter numeric and string data from the keyboard using INPUT.

4. Use prompts and multiple variables with INPUT.

5. Input string data including commas using LINE INPUT.

6. Produce definite loops using FOR...NEXT.

7. Store data within a program using READ...DATA.

8. Employ a FOR...NEXT loop to execute a READ statement a fixed number of times.

9. Format PRINT output using commas and semicolons.

*A*s we have noted, a computer is a data processing machine which accepts data in the form of numbers, words, letters and symbols, which are called "input." When input is entered into a program, the result may be displayed on screen, saved on disk, or printed on paper. This information is known as "output." In general, then, a computer takes information as input, processes it according to the directions given in a program, and then provides new information as output.

There are many different ways in which data is used. The same information may be used repeatedly in a program or it may change each time the program is run. To allow for these different situations, BASIC uses "variables." This chapter will explain what variables are and how they are used within a program.

3.1 Variables

A variable is a name which is used to represent a value. For example,

```
NUM = 5
```

The number 5 is assigned to the variable NUM which can then be used in place of the number 5. Because variables stand for a value, they are one of the most useful ways to represent data into a program.

Variable names must start with a letter and may be up to 40 characters in length. The characters can be either letters or numbers, but spaces may not be used. All of the following are legal variable names:

```
NUMBER
CLASS45
TOTAL
YEAR1992
```

It is best to use descriptive variable names. For example, a variable used to store the radius of a circle should be named RADIUS. Note that when creating variable names there are reserved words which may not be used. These are words that the computer uses as part of the BASIC language. For example, the words PRINT, END, RUN and NAME may not be used to name variables. If they are a `Syntax error` will result. Appendix D lists BASIC's reserved words.

To the computer there are two kinds of data: numbers and characters. Therefore, in order to use variables, the computer must be told both the name of the variable and the data to be assigned to that variable.

3.2 Assigning a Numeric Variable

An assignment statement is one way of giving a value to a variable. For example:

```
10 NUM = 5
```

The computer's memory is like a post office, divided into many boxes with a variable name used to represent the address of a single box. When the computer executes the above assignment statement, it sets aside a box in its memory, names it NUM and puts 5 in it:

NUM

```
+-----+
|  5  |
+-----+
```

Whenever the computer is told to use NUM, it looks in the box named NUM and uses the value that NUM stores, in this case 5.

Variables can change in value as the name itself implies; however, it is important to realize that a variable can hold only one value at a time. Suppose a later statement such as

```
50 NUM = 7
```

is executed. Then at line 50 the value NUM will change from 5 to 7. Therefore, the value stored by NUM is now 7:

NUM

```
+-----+
|  7  |
+-----+
```

The old value of NUM is lost and may not be retrieved again.

The computer will not accept the value first and then the variable in an assignment statement because the "=" sign really means "is given the value." Therefore, it is not possible to have "value = variable":

```
10 5 = AGE

RUN
Syntax error in 105
Ok
105 = AGE
```

The computer assumes that the 5 in line 10 is part of the line number, making it line 105. Rewriting the line as

```
10 AGE = 5
```

fixes this problem. (Line 105 must also be deleted.)

Statements must be written exactly the way the computer has been programmed to understand them. If a statement is not understood by the computer because it is not in the correct form, the computer stops the program and prints the Syntax error message. The computer indicates in which line the error can be found and then automatically lists the line, placing the cursor at the beginning so that the line may be edited.

When a variable name appears in a statement, BASIC uses the value stored by that variable:

```
10 NUMBER = 27
20 PRINT "Number =" NUMBER
30 PRINT NUMBER * 2
99 END
```

```
RUN
Number = 27
 54
Ok
```

In line 20, the value stored by NUMBER, 27, is printed, not the name of the variable. In line 30, the value stored by NUMBER is multiplied by 2, resulting in 54 being printed.

3.3 Using Multiple Variables

A program may have many different variables, each with a unique variable name. This program shows how two variables can be used in a program:

```
10 NUM1 = 5
20 NUM2 = 3
30 PRINT "Product =" NUM1 * NUM2
99 END
```

```
RUN
Product = 15
Ok
```

Line 10 assigns 5 to the variable named NUM1, and line 20 assigns 3 to NUM2:

NUM1	NUM2
5	3

Line 30 prints the product of the values stored in NUM1 and NUM2. Remember that a variable can only store one value at a time. If a different number is assigned to that variable, the first number is erased and lost.

The following program shows how a variable's value is changed when a new value is assigned:

```
10 REM ** Changes a variable's value **
20 STUDENTS = 5
30 PRINT "Students =" STUDENTS
40 STUDENTS = 25
50 PRINT "Students =" STUDENTS
99 END
```

```
RUN
Students = 5
Students = 25
Ok
```

When line 20 is executed, a 5 is assigned to the variable named STU-DENTS. At line 40, STUDENTS is changed to 25 and the first value of STUDENTS is erased from the computer's memory. Therefore, when STUDENTS is printed for the second time at line 50, it prints a 25.

This program demonstrates how one variable may be used to give another variable its value:

```
10 REM ** Value of variable assigned
            to second variable **
20 FIRST = 3
30 PRINT "First =" FIRST
40 SECOND = FIRST + 5
50 PRINT "Second =" SECOND
60 PRINT "First =" FIRST
99 END
```

```
RUN
First = 3
Second = 8
First = 3
Ok
```

At line 40 SECOND is assigned the value 8 which is the value stored by FIRST (3) plus 5. Line 60 shows that FIRST is unchanged by this process.

Review

1. Write a program that assigns a variable named **FIRST** a value 45 and a second variable named **SECOND** a value 15 and then produces their difference:

```
RUN
First = 45
Second = 15
First - Second = 30
Ok
```

2. What output is produced by the following program?

```
10 NUM1 = 20
20 NUM2 = NUM1 + 10
30 PRINT NUM2
99 END
```

3. Find the errors in the following program. When you have found them, enter the corrected program and run it.

```
10 64 = NUM2
20 32 = NUM1
30 TOTAL = NUM1 + NUM2
40 PRINT Result = TOTAL
99 END
```

3.4 String Variables

A character is any letter, number, punctuation mark or mathematical sign which can be found on the computer's keyboard. For example, A, @, 5 and D are all characters. Even a blank space is a character. A "string" is a single character or series of characters that form a word, phrase or other sequence of symbols.

String variable names must end with a dollar sign ($). The dollar sign tells BASIC that this variable will store strings, not numeric values. The following are examples of legal string variable names:

```
WORD$
CLASS25$
STUDENTNAME$
```

As when naming numeric variables, it is important to give a string variable a name that describes the values it will store. Also, reserved words may not be used. (Note that NAME is a reserved word in BASIC so it is not possible to create a variable named NAME$. However, variables such as NAME1$ or STUNAME$ are legal.)

The characters that make up a string are enclosed in quotation marks ("):

```
10 PLAYER$ = "Harry"
```

This statement assigns the string "Harry" to the variable PLAYER$. If we think of mail boxes again, the computer names one of its boxes PLAYER$ and place the string "Harry" in that box when line 10 is executed:

PLAYER$

```
┌─────────────┐
│  Harry      │
└─────────────┘
```

The string stored by PLAYER$ may be changed. For example, executing

```
50 PLAYER$ = "Jill"
```

changes the value of PLAYER$ from "Harry" to "Jill":

PLAYER$

```
┌─────────────┐
│  Jill       │
└─────────────┘
```

This program shows a string variable being assigned and then changed:

```
10 REM ** Assigns a string to a
           string variable **
20 FIRSTNAME$ = "Judy"
30 PRINT "First Name = " FIRSTNAME$
40 FIRSTNAME$ = "George"
50 PRINT "First Name = " FIRSTNAME$
99 END
```

```
RUN
First Name = Judy
First Name = George
Ok
```

Note how line 40 changes the value of FIRSTNAME$ from Judy to George.

This program demonstrates the difference between numbers (digits) assigned to a string variable and numeric values assigned to a numeric variable:

```
10 REM ** Assigns numbers to string and
           numeric variables **
20 NUM1$ = "5"
30 NUM2$ = "10"
40 COUNT1 = 5
50 COUNT2 = 10
60 PRINT "Number 1 + Number 2 = " NUM1$ + NUM2$
70 PRINT "Count 1 + Count 2 =" COUNT1 + COUNT2
80 PRINT "Number 2 + Number 1 = " NUM2$ + NUM1$
90 PRINT "Count 2 + Count 1 =" COUNT2 + COUNT1
99 END
```

```
RUN
Number 1 + Number 2 = 510
Count 1 + Count 2 = 15
Number 2 + Number 1 = 105
Count 2 + Count 1 = 15
Ok
```

In line 60 the plus sign tells the computer to add NUM1$ and NUM2$. The dollar sign ($) indicates that these are not numeric variables but character strings, so it attaches NUM2$ to NUM1$. This causes the computer to print the string "510". In line 70, COUNT1 and COUNT2 are numeric variables which can be added mathematically, and 15 is printed. Line 80 puts NUM2$ first and then attaches NUM1$ to it so that the string "105" is printed. Adding 10 and 5 gives the same answer as adding 5 and 10, so 15 is printed by line 90.

3.5 PRINTing Messages and Variables

As shown in the previous examples, variables can be combined with messages in PRINT statements. This allows a programmer to display both the value of a variable an identifying message. It is important to note that when printing variables the computer places a space before and after a numeric value, whereas a string is printed with no leading or trailing spaces. Any spaces that are needed to keep the characters of a string separated from the characters of a PRINT message must be provided by the programmer. This is illustrated by the program below:

```
10 REM ** Demonstrates combining
          variables and messages **
20 NUMBER = 5
30 NUMBER$ = "five"
40 PRINT NUMBER "is alive"
50 PRINT NUMBER$ " is alive"
60 PRINT "John is" NUMBER "years old."
70 PRINT "John is " NUMBER$ " years old."
99 END
```

```
RUN
 5 is alive
five is alive
John is 5 years old.
John is five years old.
Ok
```

Because it is a numeric value, a space is printed before and after the 5 when line 40 is executed. In line 50 we must place a space within the quotes so that "five" and "is" are properly separated because NUMBER$ is a string. For the same reasons, line 60 does not require leading or trailing spaces within the quotes, but line 70 does. Note that NUMBER and NUMBER$ are two different variables. NUMBER is a numeric variable which may only store values and is separate in the computer's memory from the string variable NUMBER$.

Review

4. Find the errors in the following program, correct them and then run the program:

```
10 TEXT$ = COMPUTER
20 64 = NUMBER
30 PRINT TEXT$
40 PRINT NUMBER
99 END
```

5. Write a program that assigns the numbers 10 and 20 to numeric variables and the strings Tony and Sally to string variables. Using the variables produce the following output:

```
RUN
Sally is 20
Sally and Tony are friends.
 10 + 20 = 30
Sally + Tony = SallyTony
Ok
```

3.6 INPUT: a Number

Often the data used by a program to accomplish its task will be different each time the program is run. The INPUT statement is a good way to give a variable its value in such a situation. (The assignment statement, on the other hand, is best used when data will remain the same for each program run.) An INPUT statement takes the form:

```
10 INPUT <variable>
```

When the computer executes an INPUT statement, it prints a question mark and then waits for data to be typed on the keyboard. When the Enter key is pressed, the computer reads the data and assigns it to the <variable> listed. For example

```
20 INPUT GPA
```

assigns the data typed by the user to the variable GPA.

A savings account provides a good example of these two situations. Each time money is deposited or withdrawn from an account the amount is likely to be different, but the interest rate that the bank pays will change infrequently. Therefore, an assignment statement is best used for the interest rate and an INPUT statement for each deposit or withdrawal.

The following program shows how INPUT is used to get a value from the user. Note that in program runs we will show data input by the user as underlined. This is done to distinguish the input data typed by the user from other output produced by the program:

```
10 REM ** Multiplies an entered deposit
            times interest **
20 INTEREST = 0.05
30 PRINT "Enter a deposit"
40 INPUT DEPOSIT
50 PRINT "Deposit * interest = $" DEPOSIT *
INTEREST
99 END
```

```
RUN
Enter a deposit
? 600
Deposit * interest = $ 30
Ok
```

Note how the interest rate is assigned at line 20 and the deposit is entered by the user at line 40. (Remember that 0.05 is the decimal representation of 5%.) Each time the program is run the interest rate remains the same, but the deposit changes depending upon the number entered by the user. Running the program a second time illustrates this:

```
RUN
Enter a deposit
? 1895
Deposit * interest = $ 94.75
Ok
```

When entering program lines, the keyboard shortcut for INPUT is Alt-I.

3.7 INPUT with String Variables

An INPUT statement can also be used to enter a string of characters from the keyboard. For example:

```
10 INPUT WORD$
```

Letters, symbols or numbers can be stored by WORD$ because a string may contain any character on the keyboard. Numbers can be made part of a string, but they cannot later be used in mathematical operations since the computer considers them to be characters rather than values.

This program allows the user to enter a string from the keyboard:

```
10 REM ** Demonstrates string input **
20 INPUT WORD$
30 PRINT "This is what you typed: " WORD$
99 END
```

```
RUN
? Computers are fast
This is what you typed: Computers are fast
Ok
```

WORD$ stores the characters typed; Computers are fast. When line 30 is executed the contents of WORD$ are printed following the message (which must be enclosed in quotation marks).

3.8 The ?Redo from start Error

Commas may not be used when entering numeric INPUT values. Attempting to do so causes a ?Redo from start error. To demonstrate this we run the bank deposit program from Section 3.6 a third time:

```
RUN
Enter a deposit
? 4,500
?Redo from start
? 4500
Deposit * interest = $ 225
Ok
```

If a letter or word is typed by mistake when the computer is expecting a number, the computer will print a ?Redo from start error message:

```
RUN
Enter a deposit
? Thousand
?Redo from start
? 1000
Deposit * interest = $ 50
Ok
```

The ?Redo from start message does not mean start the program over again, but to reenter the input value from the start. Commas, dollar signs and other symbols cannot be assigned to a numeric variable. (The period is legal because it represents a decimal point.) Since the computer can accept any character as part of a string this error will not occur if symbols are entered for string input.

3.9 INPUT with Prompts and Multiple Variables

To prevent a ?Redo from start error, a message indicating the type of data expected should be given. This message, called a "prompt", can be made part of an INPUT statement by enclosing it in quotation marks before the variable name:

```
10 INPUT "Enter a number"; NUMBER
```

A semicolon (;) must follow the quotation mark that ends the message. If the semicolon is missing, a Syntax error will halt program execution.

This program shows how a prompt message can be made part of an INPUT statement:

```
10 INPUT "Enter a number"; NUMBER
20 PRINT "The number is" NUMBER
99 END
```

```
RUN
Enter a number? 25
The number is 25
Ok
```

It is possible to enter values for several different variables using a single INPUT statement by separating the variables with commas. For example, the statement

```
10 INPUT NUM1, NUM2, NUM3, NUM4
```

allows a single INPUT to get the values for 4 separate variables at one time. When this statement is executed the individual pieces of data input from the keyboard must be separated by commas.

This program asks the user for a student's name and three grades, then prints the name and the student's average:

```
10 REM ** Calculates student average **
20 INPUT "Student's name"; STUNAME$
30 INPUT "Enter three grades"; GRADE1,
   GRADE2, GRADE3
40 PRINT
50 AVERAGE = (GRADE1 + GRADE2 + GRADE3) / 3
60 PRINT "The average for " STUNAME$ " is"
   AVERAGE
99 END
```

```
RUN
Student's name? Mike
Enter three grades? 85, 87, 68

The average for Mike is 80
Ok
```

The blank PRINT statement at line 40 causes the computer to skip a line after displaying the two INPUT prompts. Line 50 calculates the average and assigns it to variable AVERAGE. Note how parentheses are used to add the three grades before dividing by 3. Without the parentheses only GRADE3 would be divided.

INPUT always displays a question mark as its prompt. This can be avoided by using a comma (,) instead of a semicolon to separate the prompt from the variable names. For example,

```
10 INPUT "Type your name here: ", N$
```

displays:

```
Type your name here:
```

No question mark is printed because of the comma before the N$. Note the space after the colon in the prompt which separates the prompt from the entered data.

3.10 LINE INPUT

As described in the previous section, the INPUT statement uses commas to separate the different pieces of information when reading multiple variables. This makes it difficult to INPUT strings which contain embedded commas, such as "Rob, Ruth, and I went home". For example, executing the statements

```
10 INPUT "Enter string: ", S$
20 PRINT S$
```

produces

```
Enter string: Rob, Ruth, and I went home
?Redo from start
```

One way to avoid this problem is to enclose the string in quotes as it is entered. Typing the quotes as part of the input

```
Enter string: "Rob, Ruth, and I went home"
Rob, Ruth, and I went home
```

eliminates the error.

A better approach is to use the LINE INPUT statement which terminates the string only when the Enter key is pressed. LINE INPUT stores the commas in the string. Executing

```
10 LINE INPUT "Enter string: "; S$
20 PRINT S$
```

produces

```
Enter string: Rob, Ruth, and I went home
Rob, Ruth, and I went home
```

The LINE INPUT statement does not supply a question mark to prompt the user as does the INPUT statement. If one is desired it may be included in the prompt. For example,

```
10 LINE INPUT "Your name? "; N$
```

will print "Your name?" as the prompt.

Review

6. Write a program that uses INPUT to get values for two numeric variables. Have the computer calculate their sum and product. A RUN of the program should be similar to:

```
RUN
Enter number 1? 45
Enter number 2? 10
 45 + 10 = 55
 45 * 10 = 450
Ok
```

7. Modify your answer to Review 6 above so that only one INPUT statement is used:

```
RUN
Enter two numbers: 45, 10
 45 + 10 = 55
 45 * 10 = 450
Ok
```

8. Write a program that allows you to input your name and a friend's name and print a message. The output should be similar to:

```
RUN
What is your name? Beth
What is your friend's name? Brian

Brian is a friend of Beth
Ok
```

3.11 FOR...NEXT Loops

Computers are able to perform repetitive tasks quickly and accurately. Looping statements which allow program lines to be executed numerous times take advantage of this. The FOR...NEXT loop is a looping structure which repeatedly executes a set of instructions a fixed number of times. This number is set when the loop is first started, and cannot be changed after it has begun. For this reason the FOR...NEXT loop is called a "definite" loop. The general form of a FOR...NEXT loop is:

```
FOR <variable> = <starting value> TO <ending value>
   .
   .
   .
NEXT <variable>
```

Note that the variable after FOR and NEXT must be the same and that a string variable cannot be used. In this form the values assigned to the variable increase by 1 each time the loop is executed.

This program uses a FOR...NEXT loop to print the numbers from 1 to 6:

```
10 REM ** Uses FOR loop to print numbers
           from 1 to 6 **
20 FOR NUM = 1 TO 6
30    PRINT "Number =" NUM
40 NEXT NUM
99 END
```

```
RUN
Number = 1
Number = 2
Number = 3
Number = 4
Number = 5
Number = 6
Ok
```

Note that line 30 is indented two spaces. Indenting the lines between the FOR and NEXT statements is done to show anyone reading the program where the loop begins, which lines are inside the loop and where the loop ends. It is a good practice to indent the bodies of all loops this way.

By adding STEP and an increment to the FOR statement the loop variable can be changed by values other than +1. For example, changing line 20 to:

```
20 FOR NUM = 2 TO 8 STEP 2
```

produces the set of even numbers starting with 2 and terminating with 8:

```
RUN
Number = 2
Number = 4
Number = 6
Number = 8
Ok
```

The addition of a FOR...NEXT loop to the program in Section 3.9 allows the program to calculate student averages for a predetermined number of students, in this case 3:

```
10 REM ** Calculates student averages **
15 FOR STUDENT = 1 TO 3
20    INPUT "Student's name"; STUNAME$
30    INPUT "Enter three grades"; GRADE1,
      GRADE2, GRADE3
40    PRINT
50    AVERAGE = (GRADE1 + GRADE2 + GRADE3) / 3
60    PRINT "The average for " STUNAME$ " is"
      AVERAGE
70    PRINT
80 NEXT STUDENT
90 PRINT "All averages have been calculated."
99 END
```

```
RUN
Student's name? Judy
Enter four grades? 78, 65, 88

The average for Judy is 77

Student's name? Carlos
Enter four grades? 87, 79, 95

The average for Carlos is 87

Student's name? Lee
Enter four grades? 82, 89, 91

The average for Lee is 87.33334

All averages have been calculated.
Ok
```

Note how the FOR...NEXT loop has been added between lines 15 and 80 and how the lines within the loop have each been indented 2 spaces. Line 70 prints a blank line after each student's average. It is a good programming practice to include a statement similar to line 90 which indicates that the program has completed its task.

There is one more change we can make to the program that will allow it to calculate the averages for any number of students. By adding an INPUT statement the user can be asked how many student averages will be calculated and this value then used to determine how many times the loop will be executed. To do this line 14 is added and line 15 changed to:

```
14 INPUT "How many averages"; NUMSTUS
15 FOR STUDENT = 1 TO NUMSTUS
```

```
RUN
How many averages? 2
Student's name? William
Enter four grades? 68, 95, 77

The average for William is 80

Student's name? Hortense
Enter four grades? 90, 98, 87

The average for Hortense is 91.66667

All averages have been calculated.
Ok
```

What would the output of this program be if line 14 were mistakenly placed within the loop at line 16?

When entering programs, the shortcut Alt-F can be used for FOR and Alt-N for NEXT.

Review

9. Write a program that asks for a name and then prints it 3 times spaced with blank lines:

```
RUN
What is your name? Bruce

Bruce

Bruce

Bruce
Ok
```

10. a) Write a program which asks the user to input a number. Have the computer calculate the value of the number plus 12 and times 12. The output should be similar to:

```
RUN
Input a number? 2
  2 + 12 = 14
  2 * 12 = 24
Ok
```

b) Add lines to the program to allow the user to determine how many times it will be executed:

```
RUN
How many numbers will be entered? 2
Input a number? 15
  15 + 12 = 27
  15 * 12 = 180

Input a number? 3
  3 + 12 = 15
  3 * 12 = 36

Calculations complete.
Ok
```

3.12 READ...DATA

So far we have given a value to a variable either using an assignment or INPUT statement. Another way is to use the READ and DATA statements. These two statements work together as a team to provide data to a program; one of them cannot be used without the other.

READ and DATA are useful because they allow data to be stored within a program. Unlike INPUT, the data need not be re-entered each time the program is run.

This program shows how to use READ and DATA to give a value to a variable:

```
10 REM ** READ...DATA example **
20 READ NUMBER
30 PRINT "The number is" NUMBER
99 END
1000 REM ** Numeric data
1010 DATA 125

RUN
The number is 125
Ok
```

The READ statement in line 20 tells the computer to assign NUMBER the first value it finds in a DATA statement. Since the first DATA statement is on line 1010, and it contains the number 125, NUMBER is assigned the value 125. Note that it is a good programming practice to place DATA statements at the end of a program and to separate them from the body of a program by numbering them starting with a high line number, such as 1000. They should be preceded with a REM which explains what the data is. Also, note that there is no problem in placing DATA statements after the END statement.

When READ is used with a numeric variable, the computer will only accept numbers. Any symbols used with the numbers cause an error message and halt the program. Therefore, data such as $2.75, or 2'6" cannot be read into numeric variables. Dollar signs, letters of the alphabet and any other characters can be read using READ and DATA only if the computer is told instead to read a string variable. For example,

```
20 READ WORD$
```

assigns variable WORD$ the value of a string stored in a DATA statement.

This program READs two strings from a DATA statement:

```
10 REM ** Reads string data **
20 READ NAME1$, NAME2$
30 PRINT "A famous philosopher was " NAME1$ "."
40 PRINT NAME2$ " often disagreed with him."
99 END
1000 REM ** Data: Name 1, Name 2
1010 DATA Plato, Aristotle
```

```
RUN
A famous philosopher was Plato.
Aristotle often disagreed with him.
Ok
```

When line 20 is executed, the computer locates the first piece of data, Plato, and assigns it to NAME1$. NAME2$ is assigned the second string, Aristotle. Both the variable names in the READ statement and the strings in the DATA statement are separated by commas, as illustrated by lines 20 and 1010.

Review

11. Write a program that READs two numbers from a DATA statement and then prints their difference:

```
RUN
 5 - 3 = 2
Ok
```

12. Write a program that READs the name of your favorite snack and your favorite drink from a DATA statement. The output of the program should be similar to:

```
RUN
A hamburger is my favorite snack.
A coke is my favorite drink.
Ok
```

3.13 FOR...NEXT and READ...DATA

A FOR...NEXT loop can be useful when used in conjunction with READ and DATA since the loop can execute the READ statement a fixed number of times until all of the data in the DATA statements has been read. It is important that the data be kept in proper sequence by the use of commas so that it matches the variables that will read it. It is also important to have the loop variable equal the number of sets of data in the DATA statement. Attempting to read beyond the end of the data will result in an Out of DATA message.

The following program reads a list of candies and their prices from DATA statements:

```
10 REM ** Reads and displays candies
            and prices **
20 FOR NUMBER = 1 TO 4
30    READ CANDY$, PRICE
40    PRINT "Candy: " CANDY$, "Price: $" PRICE
50    PRINT
60 NEXT NUMBER
99 END
1000 REM ** Candies and their prices
1010 DATA Hubba Bubba, .35, Hershey Bar, .45
1020 DATA Good and Plenty, .58, Mars Bar, .78
```

```
RUN
Candy: Hubba Bubba              Price: $ .35

Candy: Hershey Bar              Price: $ .45

Candy: Good and Plenty          Price: $ .58

Candy: Mars Bar                 Price: $ .78

Ok
```

Since there are four sets of data, a candy and a price, the ending value of the loop at line 20 is set to 4. Line 30 reads a value for the string variable CANDY$ and numeric variable PRICE from the DATA statements beginning on line 1010. Note how line 30 uses a comma to produce properly spaced output. This technique is covered in more detail in the next section.

If line 20 is changed to

```
20 FOR NUMBER = 1 TO 5
```

an Out of DATA in 30 message is produced when the program attempts to read a fifth set of data. If line 30 is changed to

```
30    READ PRICE, CANDY$
```

a Syntax error in 1010 is displayed because line 30 tells the computer to read a numeric value followed by a string, but the data is reversed in the DATA statement at line 1010.

Review

13. a) Write a program that reads a list of your favorite sports teams from DATA statements and outputs that list to the screen:

```
RUN
My favorite teams:
Boston Red Sox
Miami Dolphins
Philadelphia Flyers
Ok
```

b) Modify the program to include your favorite basketball team:

```
RUN
My favorite teams:
Boston Red Sox
Miami Dolphins
Philadelphia Flyers
Chicago Bulls
Ok
```

14. Write a program that reads the numbers 1, 30, 68, 350, 790, 1234 from a DATA statement and then prints every other number:

```
RUN
 1
 68
 790
Ok
```

15. a) How many lines of output does the following program produce?

```
10 READ A, B, C
20 PRINT (A + B + C) / 3
99 END
1000 DATA 11, 32, 42, 14, 25, 36
1010 DATA 58, 39, 50, 61, 22, 83
```

b) Modify the program to make use of all the data.

3.14 Formatting PRINT Output

The way in which data is displayed on the screen is an important part of good programming style. One way to affect the appearance of data on the screen is to use commas and semicolons. When used as part of a PRINT statement and outside of quotations marks, these punctuation marks are format instructions which give the computer instructions about where data should be displayed.

Commas are used in PRINT statements to move the cursor to one of the five print zones that divide the screen. The computer can print 80 characters on a single line which is divided into four print zones of 14 characters each and a fifth zone of 24 characters. The semicolon, on the other hand, is used to tell the computer to print in the next space to the right of the previous output.

The following program shows where the print zones are on the screen and the difference between using commas and semicolons in a PRINT statement:

```
10 REM ** Shows location of print zones **
20 A$ = "*"
30 PRINT A$, A$, A$, A$, A$
40 PRINT A$; A$; A$; A$; A$
50 NUM = 25
60 PRINT A$; NUM
70 PRINT A$, NUM
80 PRINT A$; NUM; A$
90 PRINT A$ NUM A$
999 END
```

```
RUN
*                *                *                *                *
* * * * *
*  25
*                         25
  25 *
*  25 *
*  25 *
Ok
```

Line 30 uses commas to print an asterisk (*) at the beginning of each of the five print zones. Because semicolons are used the asterisks are printed together by line 40. Note the spacing produced by lines 60 and 70. The first uses a semicolon to place the value of NUM next to A$, while the second uses a comma to place NUM at the beginning of the next print zone. Remember that BASIC always prints a single space before and after a numeric value. BASIC prints data next to each other when no punctuation is used (similar to using a semicolon). This is illustrated by lines 80 and 90.

The space before a numeric value is reserved for the minus sign on negative numbers. If NUM were -25, line 80 would print:

```
* - 25  *
```

There are certain times when semicolons must be used. For example the statement

```
10 PRINT "*"  - 5
```

causes a Syntax error because BASIC interprets this as an attempt to subtract a 5 from a character. The correct form is

```
10 PRINT "*"; -5
```

which prints:

```
* - 5
```

More precise formatting commands are given in later chapters.

3.15 End of Chapter Problems

From this point on, most chapters end by solving a problem which requires a carefully thought out algorithm. A problem is stated and then broken down into a series of smaller problems upon which the program will be based. The algorithm is developed by asking the following questions:

1. What data is to be input?
2. What calculations (processing) are to be performed?
3. What output is to be produced?

When the input and output is determined, variable names are given. You are urged to carefully study and analyze the techniques used in developing the algorithm and then in writing the program from the algorithm.

Problem: A teacher needs a program to calculate the term grades for each of her four students. Each student has three quiz grades and two exam grades with each exam grade to be given twice the weight of a quiz grade.

Algorithm: For each student
1. Read the student's name, quiz grades, and exam grades.
2. Compute the student's term grade by adding the exam grades multiplied by 2 to the sum of the quiz grades and then dividing the total by 7 to produce the properly weighted average.
3. Print each student's name and term average.

Input:

Number of students	STUNUM
Student name	STUDENT$
Quiz grades	QUIZ1, QUIZ2, QUIZ3
Exam grades	EXAM1, EXAM2

Output:

Student Name	STUDENT$
Term Average	AVERAGE

```
10 REM ** Calculates weighted term averages **
20 PRINT "Name", "Term Average"
30 PRINT
40 FOR STUNUM = 1 TO 4
50    READ STUDENT$, QUIZ1, QUIZ2, QUIZ3,
      EXAM1, EXAM2
60    AVERAGE = (2 * (EXAM1 + EXAM2) +
      (QUIZ1 + QUIZ2 + QUIZ3)) / 7
70    PRINT STUDENT$, AVERAGE
80 NEXT STUNUM
99 END
1000 REM ** Data: Name, 3 quiz grades, 2 exams
1010 DATA C.Tibbets, 82, 71, 60, 90, 85
1020 DATA M. Porter, 85, 40, 75, 80, 70
1030 DATA M. Bidwell, 70, 65, 63, 71, 65
1040 DATA H. Crane, 80, 85, 90, 82, 80
```

```
RUN
Name            Term Average

C. Tibbets      80.42858
M. Porter       71.42858
M. Bidwell      67.14285
H. Crane        82.71429
Ok
```

Study line 60 carefully to determine how the average is calculated. Note how parentheses are used to group the grades. Without the outermost set only the quizzes would be divided by 7. The PRINT statements at lines 20 and 70 make use of the comma to move to the next print zone.

Chapter Summary

A variable is a name used in a program to represent a value. Variable names must start with a letter and may be up to 40 characters in length. Spaces and other special characters may not be used. The value stored by a variable may change, but a variable can only store one value at a time. If a different value is assigned to a variable, the first is erased and lost. Only numeric values can be assigned to numeric variables:

```
AGE = 5
```

A string is made up of a single character or series of characters and must be enclosed by quotation marks. String values may only be assigned to string variables. All string variable names end with a dollar sign:

```
NAME1$ = "Jonathan"
```

Messages and variables can be printed by the same PRINT statement:

```
20 PRINT "The number ="; NUM
```

When printing variables the computer places a space before and after a numeric variable, but a string variable is printed with no leading or trailing spaces.

The INPUT statement is used to enter either numeric or string data directly from the keyboard into a program. When executed IN-PUT prints a question mark and then waits for data to be typed. If an attempt is made to enter non-numeric data into a numeric variable a ?Redo from start error will occur. Any type of data may be entered into a string variable without causing an error.

Prompts are messages included with INPUT to indicate the type of data that is expected from the user. The message must be enclosed in quotation marks:

```
20 INPUT "Enter a number"; NUMBER
```

A semicolon follows the quotation mark that ends the prompt. If a comma is used in place of the semicolon a question mark will not be displayed when the statement is executed.

It is possible to enter the values for a number of variables using a single INPUT statement by separating the variables with commas:

```
20 INPUT STUNAME$, GRADE, GPA
```

When the statement is executed the data input from the keyboard must be also separated by commas. The LINE INPUT statement allows string data to include commas when entered into a single string variable.

A FOR...NEXT loop repeatedly executes a set of instructions a fixed number of times. For this reason it is called a "definite" loop. The numeric variable after FOR and NEXT must be the same. To show where a loop begins and ends, the statements inside the loop are indented. Adding STEP and an increment to the FOR statement allows the loop variable to be changed by values other than +1.

The READ statement is used to read data stored in DATA statements and assign it to variables. The data in DATA statements is separated by commas. It is a good programming practice to place all DATA statements at the end of a program after the END statement.

A FOR...NEXT loop can be used to execute a READ statement a fixed number of times until all of the data contained in DATA statements has been read. The loop must execute a number of times equal to (or less than) the number of sets of data. Attempting to read more data than is present causes an Out of DATA error.

Commas are used in PRINT statements to move the cursor to one of five print zones. There are four print zones of 14 characters each and a fifth zone of 24 characters. A semicolon is used to print in the next space to the right of previous output.

Vocabulary

DATA - Statement which stores data which can be read by a READ statement.

Definite loop - Loop which executes a pre-defined number of times.

FOR . . . NEXT - Statements that produce a loop which executes statements a definite number of times.

Input - Data entered into the computer.

INPUT - Statement that allows data to be entered into a program directly from the keyboard.

LINE INPUT - Statement that allows string data including commas to be input into a string variable.

Numeric variable - Variable that stores a numeric value.

Output - Data produced by a computer program.

Prompt - A message indicating the type of data that is expected by a program.

READ - Statement which reads data stored in DATA statements and assigns it to variables.

String variable - Variable that stores a string of alpha-numeric characters. String variable names must end with a dollar sign ($).

Variable - Name used to represent a value that is stored in memory by a program. The value assigned to a variable may be changed.

Exercises

1. Which of the following are NOT valid BASIC variable names?

   a) `TODAYS DATE`   d) `PRINT`
   b) `CLASSOF2000`   e) `16TODAY`
   c) `AVERAGE'S`   f) `THEFUTUREISNOW`

2. Write a program that assigns the length in centimeters of one side of a cube to a numeric variable. Have the program compute and print the surface area and the volume of the cube. (Surface area is $6 \times length^2$; Volume is $length^3$.):

   ```
   RUN
   Side length = 10 centimeters
   Surface area of cube = 600 cm^2
   Volume of cube = 1000 cm^3
   Ok
   ```

3. Write a program in which the price of a loaf of bread and the number of loaves bought are INPUT from the keyboard. The total spent for the bread is to be printed:

   ```
   RUN
   Price of bread? .79
   Number of loaves? 5
   Total spent = $ 3.95
   Ok
   ```

4. Write a program in which you input your weight in pounds and height in inches. Have the program print the quotient weight/height followed by the phrase "pounds per inch":

   ```
   RUN
   Enter your weight in pounds? 135
   Enter your height in inches? 72
    1.875 pounds per inch
   Ok
   ```

5. Write a program in which you input your first name and your last name. Have the program then print your full name:

   ```
   RUN
   Enter your first name? Albert
   Enter your last name? Einstein
   Your name is: Albert Einstein
   OK
   ```

6. Write a program that allows a string to be entered. Have the computer print the string followed by the phrase "keep the doctor away.":

    ```
    RUN
    String? Trains, planes and cars
    Trains, planes and cars keep the doctor away.
    Ok
    ```

7. Using a single INPUT statement, write a program which produces the following output. Note that the program asks for two sets of numbers:

    ```
    RUN
    Enter two numbers? 2, 4
    X = 2       Y = 4       X * Y = 8

    Enter two numbers? -8, 70
     X =-8       Y = 70       X * Y =-560

    Ok
    ```

8. According to an educational expert the time a student spends on homework should equal 10 times the student's grade level. Write a program which inputs a student's grade level and then prints the time to be spent on homework:

    ```
    RUN
    Enter grade level? 9
    Time to be spent on homework: 90 minutes
    Ok
    ```

9. Write a program in which you input a number and a bar graph of "$"s is produced:

    ```
    RUN
    Enter a number? 10
    $$$$$$$$$$
    OK
    ```

10. A piece of pizza contains about 375 calories. Jogging one mile uses about 100 calories. Write a program that asks how many pieces of pizza you have eaten and tells you how far you must jog to burn up the calories:

    ```
    RUN
    How many pieces did you eat? 4
    You must run 15 miles.
    Ok
    ```

11. Write a program which displays percents and their decimal equivalent for 10%, 20% and so on up to 100%:

```
RUN
 10 %              .1
 20 %              .2
 30 %              .3
      .  .  .
 90 %              .9
100 %             1
Ok
```

12. Write a program using DATA statements to have the computer evaluate the expression 12x + 7y for the following values:

X	Y
3	2
7	9
12	-4

13. Write a program to compute the areas (in cm²) of circles with radii of 5.0, 3.0 and 8.0 cm. Use a DATA statement to store the radii and have the output in the form "Area of circle =", with two blank lines between each.

14. Using INPUT statements, write a program that will compute the volume of a room given its length, width and height in feet:

```
RUN
Length of room? 25
Width of room? 13
Height of room? 10
Room volume = 3250 ft^3
Ok
```

15. Just as three-dimensional objects are measured by volume, so four-dimensional objects are measured by "tesseracts". Write a program which asks the user how many objects will be calculated, and then for the dimensions of each four-dimensional object (height, width, length and "presence"). Have the program calculate and print the object's tesseracts (in cm⁴):

```
RUN
How many four dimensional objects? 2

Enter height and width (in cm): 1, 3
Enter length and presence (in cm): 9, 27
The tesseract is 729 cm^4.

Enter height and width (in cm): 5, 7
Enter length and presence (in cm): 12, 15
The tesseract is 6300 cm^4.

The 2 tesseracts have been calculated.
Ok
```

16. With the equation $E = MC^2$, Einstein predicted that energy could be produced from matter. If the average human hair weighs a tenth of a gram and the town of Woodsylvania uses 2×10^{11} units of energy per day, find out how many hairs from Einstein's head would be required to supply the town with energy for a day ($C = 3 \times 10^{10}$). Remember that numbers are raised to a power in a calculation by using the caret symbol (^):

17. Help your town library by writing a program that calculates overdue book fines. Start by asking the user how many fines are to be calculated. For each fine have the user enter the fine per day and the number of days the book is late:

```
RUN
How many fines are to be calculated? 3

Enter fine/day? .22
Enter number of days late? 12
The fine is $ 2.64

Enter fine/day? .15
Enter number of days late? 5
The fine is $ .75

Enter fine/day? 1.01
Enter number of days late? 4
The fine is $ 4.04

Calculations completed.
Ok
```

18. a) The perimeter of a triangle is equal to the sum of the lengths of the three sides of the triangle. One triangle has sides of lengths 13, 8 and 11 cm. A second triangle has sides of 21, 16 and 12 ft. Write a program that reads these measurements from DATA statements and then prints the perimeter of each triangle, showing the correct units. The output should be similar to:

```
RUN
Perimeter of first triangle: 32 cm.

Perimeter of second triangle: 49 ft.
Ok
```

b) The "semiperimeter" is one-half of the perimeter. Modify the program to include this measurement:

```
RUN
Perimeter of first triangle: 32 cm.
Semiperimeter of first triangle: 16 cm.

Perimeter of second triangle: 49 ft.
Semiperimeter of second triangle: 24.5 ft.
Ok
```

19. Professional athletes have succeeded in making staggering sums of money through careful negotiations. Of course, the real winner is the Internal Revenue Service, which does not negotiate at all. Write a program which asks for a player's earnings and then prints the take-home pay and taxes if the tax rate for that income bracket is 44%:

```
RUN
What are the player's earnings? 150000
The player keeps $ 84000
The player pays $ 66000 in taxes.
Ok
```

20. A state has a 7% sales tax. Write a program which allows you to INPUT the names and prices (before taxes) of different items found in a department store and then prints the item, tax and the price of the item including tax. First ask how many items will be calculated:

```
RUN
How many items will be calculated? 2

Item's name? Coat
What is the price? 65

Coat has a tax of $ 4.55 and costs $ 69.55

Item's name? Tennis racket
What is the price? 23

Tennis racket has a tax of $ 1.61 and costs $
24.61

Calculations completed
Ok
```

21. Sale prices are often deceptive. Write a program to determine the original price of an item, given the sale price and the discount rate (%):

```
RUN
Sale price? 3.78
Discount rate (%)? 10

The original price was $ 4.2
Ok
```

22. Candidate Smith ran against candidate Jones in an election for mayor. Below is a listing of the number of votes each candidate received in each ward. Write a program to determine the total number of votes for each candidate and what percentage of the total votes each received:

Ward	Smith	Jones
1	528	210
2	313	721
3	1003	822
4	413	1107
5	516	1700

23. a) Given the assumption that you sleep a healthy eight hours a night, have the computer print the number of hours in your life which you will have spent sleeping. Input the date of your birth and today's date in numeric form (e.g., 9, 27, 61). Assume 365 days in each year and 30 days in a month to simplify your calculations.

b) Modify the program to determine the number of full days that you have slept (24 hours in a day).

24. a) Using INPUT statements, write a program which averages each of the following sets of numbers. Note that each set does not contain the same number of elements:

```
(2, 7, 15, 13)
(8, 5, 2, 3)
(12, 19, 4)
(15, 7, 19, 24, 37)
```

b) Rewrite the above problem using DATA statements to store the numbers.

Chapter 4

Making Decisions

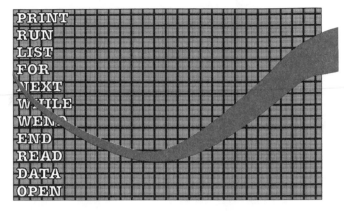

```
PRINT
RUN
LIST
FOR
NEXT
WHILE
WEND
END
READ
DATA
OPEN
```

IF...THEN

AND

OR

IF...THEN...ELSE

WHILE...WEND

PRINT USING

PRINT TAB

RESTORE

Objectives

Chapter Four

After completing this chapter you will be able to:

1. Use the IF...THEN statement to program decisions.

2. Compare strings alphabetically using IF...THEN.

3. Join two or more comparisons in an IF...THEN statement using AND and OR.

4. Join a series of statements on a single line to form compound statements.

5. Extend the IF...THEN statement by the addition of ELSE clauses.

6. Produce indefinite loops using WHILE...WEND.

7. Use a counter to determine how often an event occurs.

8. Use an accumulator to add amounts that vary.

9. Format output with the PRINT USING and PRINT TAB statements.

10. Use flags to indicate that a condition has been met.

*T*he previous chapters introduced statements that allow the computer to accept data and perform simple calculations. Though useful, these statements do not take advantage of the computer's ability to make decisions. To allow a program to make decisions we will introduce the IF...THEN statement.

Chapter Three produced FOR...NEXT loops which execute a predetermined number of times. These are called definite loops. In this chapter we introduce WHILE...WEND loops that execute until a specified condition is met and are called "indefinite" loops.

4.1 IF...THEN

The IF...THEN statement has the form:

```
IF <condition> THEN <statement>
```

In the <condition> a comparison is made. If the comparison is true, the computer executes the statement following THEN; if false, it ignores the statement. By using the symbols shown below, two quantities can be compared:

SYMBOL	MEANING
=	equal to
>	greater than
<	less than
>=	greater than or equal to
<=	less than or equal to
<>	not equal to

The IF...THEN statement is a "conditional" statement — when the condition is met the statement is executed; when the condition is not met, the statement is ignored. This is in contrast to the statements introduced so far (PRINT, INPUT, FOR...NEXT, etc.) which are always executed whenever they are found.

An example of an IF...THEN statement is:

```
50 IF X > 5 THEN PRINT "X greater than 5"
```

When the condition X > 5 is true, the computer prints the message "X greater than 5." When the condition is false, (X is less than or equal to 5), the computer ignores the PRINT statement and proceeds to the next line in the program. When entering IF...THENs in program lines, Alt-T is a shortcut for typing THEN.

This program demonstrates how an IF statement can be used to compare two numbers. A FOR...NEXT loop is employed to allow three numbers to be tested:

```
10 REM ** Compares input numbers to a
           specified number **
20 NUM1 = 115
30 FOR COUNT = 1 TO 3
40    INPUT "Enter a number"; NUM2
50    IF NUM2 < NUM1 THEN PRINT NUM2 "is less
      than" NUM1
60    IF NUM2 > NUM1 THEN PRINT NUM2 "is
      greater than" NUM1
70    IF NUM2 = NUM1 THEN PRINT NUM2 "is equal
      to" NUM1
80    PRINT
90 NEXT COUNT
999 END
```

```
RUN
Enter a number? 17
 17 is less than 115

Enter a number? 115
 115 is equal to 115

Enter a number? 234
 234 is greater than 115

Ok
```

Line 20 assigns the value 115 to the variable NUM1. This allows us to easily change the comparison by editing only this line. The computer performs comparisons at lines 50 (<), 60 (>) and 70 (=). Since only one of the three conditions can be true at a time, the PRINT statement on only one of these lines is executed. Note in the run how we have checked each of the three possibilities (less than, greater than, equal to) by the numbers we chose to enter. It is always a good practice to check each possible result that a program might produce.

4.2 Comparing Strings

The IF...THEN statement can also compare strings. When using strings, the comparison symbols refer to alphabetic order rather than numeric order. Strings can be compared using variables or constants. For example:

```
30 IF A$ < B$ THEN PRINT "less than"
40 IF A$ > "M" THEN PRINT "Maximum"
50 IF NOW$ = "Noon" THEN PRINT "Lunchtime!"
```

Strings are compared left to right, until two characters differ. The result of the entire comparison is based on these two characters. In general, numbers (digits) are less than letters, and upper-case letters are less than lower-case ones. Therefore, the string "McMahon" is greater than "MCMAHON".

This program determines whether two words entered from the keyboard are the same, or if the first is greater or less than the second alphabetically:

```
10 REM ** Determines the alphabetic
           relationship between two words **
20 FOR COUNT = 1 TO 3
30   INPUT "Enter word 1"; WORD1$
40   INPUT "Enter word 2"; WORD2$
50   IF WORD1$ = WORD2$ THEN PRINT WORD1$
     " equals " WORD2$
60   IF WORD1$ > WORD2$ THEN PRINT WORD1$
     " comes after " WORD2$
70   IF WORD1$ < WORD2$ THEN PRINT WORD1$
     " comes before " WORD2$
80   PRINT
90 NEXT COUNT
999 END
```

```
RUN
Enter word 1? Sky
Enter word 2? Blue
Sky comes after Blue

Enter word 1: Rat
Enter word 2: Snake
Rat comes before Snake

Enter word 1: Computer
Enter word 2: Computer
Computer equals Computer

Ok
```

Review

1. Write a program that allows a string to be entered as input. If the string is the password, "Aviatrix", have the computer print "Password approved", otherwise have it print "Access denied!":

```
RUN
Enter password please? Jumbo
Access denied!
Ok

RUN
Enter password please? Aviatrix
Password approved
Ok
```

2. Write a program that allows the user to enter two numbers and then prints the numbers in descending order:

```
RUN
Enter first number? 27
Enter second number? 32

The numbers in order are: 32   27
Ok
```

3. Write a program that allows two names to be entered and then outputs the names in alphabetical order. Include a loop that allows the program to execute two times:

```
RUN
Enter first name? Smith
Enter second name? Jones
The names in order are: Jones Smith

Enter first name? Jane
Enter second name? Mary
The names in order are: Jane Mary
Ok
```

4.3 AND & OR

AND and OR are used in an IF...THEN statement to join two or more comparisons together as one condition. AND and OR combine comparisons differently to decide whether a condition is true or false. Because of this, the decisions that a program makes can be made more complex.

AND: When AND is used to join two comparisons, all comparisons must be true for the entire condition to be true. For example,

```
40 IF X > 5 AND Y = 3 THEN PRINT "Both are
   true"
```

prints Both are true only when both comparisons are true. The value of X must be greater than 5 and the value of Y must also equal 3.

OR: When OR is used to join two comparisons, the condition will be true when either or both comparisons are true. The condition is false when both comparisons are false. For example,

```
50 IF X > 5 OR Y = 3 THEN PRINT "One or
   both is true"
```

prints One or both is true if one or both of the comparisons is true. When both comparisons are false, the message is not printed.

This program uses AND to determine if a number is within a certain range, and then OR to see if it is a multiple of 5 in that range:

```
10 REM ** Checks number using AND and OR **
20 INPUT "Enter a number (1-10)"; NUM
30 IF NUM >= 1 AND NUM <= 10 THEN PRINT
   "Number within range"
40 IF NUM = 5 OR NUM = 10 THEN PRINT
   "Multiple of 5"
99 END
```

```
RUN
Enter a number (1-10)? 6
Number within range
Ok
```

```
RUN
Enter a number (1-10)? 10
Number within range
Multiple of 5
Ok
```

In line 30 the number must be greater than or equal to 1 and less than or equal to 10 for the message to be printed. Note how the prompt indicates that numbers entered should be between 1 and 10. In line 40 the message is printed if NUM is 5 or 10, the multiples of 5 between 1 and 10.

More than one AND and OR may be placed in a statement. For example, adding line 50

```
50 IF NUM = 3 OR NUM = 6 OR NUM = 9 THEN
   PRINT "Multiple of 3"
```

prints the message for the multiples of 3 between 1 and 10.

4.4 Compound Statements

BASIC allows a series of statements to be entered on a single program line by separating them with colons (:), forming a "compound statement." Compound statements are especially useful when used with IF...THEN, allowing more than one operation to be performed when the condition is true. For example, line 30 in the program in Section 4.3 can both print the message "Number within range" and assign a value to RANGE$:

```
30 IF NUM >= 1 AND NUM <= 10 THEN PRINT
   "Number within range" : RANGE$ = "Yes"
```

Adding the line

```
50 IF RANGE$ <> "Yes" THEN PRINT "Number out
   of range"
```

and running the program demonstrates how this works:

```
RUN
Enter a number (1-10)? 15
Number out of range
Ok
```

```
RUN
Enter a number (1-10)? 7
Number within range
Ok
```

Remember that the symbol <> means "not equal to."

Another good use for compound statements is to include a REMark on the same line as a complex or possibly confusing statement. For example,

```
80 RATE = 0.056 : REM 5.6% interest rate
```

helps the reader of this program know that RATE represents the interest rate, and that 0.056 is 5.6 percent.

A compound statement may be used anywhere a regular statement may appear. For example,

```
70 PRINT "This" : PRINT "is" : PRINT "it!"
```

prints

```
This
is
it!
```

If one part of a compound statement is executed, then all parts are executed. Therefore, use compound statements to group only related statements — statements that belong together.

4.5 IF...THEN...ELSE

The IF...THEN statement can be extended with an ELSE clause to include a statement which is executed only when the condition is false:

```
IF <condition> THEN <statement1> ELSE <statement2>
```

Statement1 is executed when the condition is true, and statement2 when it is false. When the statement

```
40 IF NUMBER > 50 THEN PRINT "Larger" ELSE
   PRINT "Smaller or equal"
```

is executed, Larger is printed if X is greater than 50; otherwise Smaller or equal is printed. When entering program lines, Alt-E is a shortcut for typing ELSE.

It is important to note that if the IF...THEN...ELSE statement is longer than 80 characters it will wrap around onto the next line on the screen. This is perfectly valid. When entering long statements the Enter key should only be pressed after the statement is complete. Pressing

Enter before the statement is complete will cause it to be improperly divided into two statements.

It is possible to use multiple IF...THEN...ELSE statements on a single program line. The following line uses two IF...THEN...ELSE statements to determine if NUM is less than, greater than, or equal to 35 and then prints the appropriate message:

```
30 IF NUM < 35 THEN PRINT "Low" ELSE IF NUM
   > 35 THEN PRINT "High" ELSE PRINT "Equal"
```

If NUM is less than 35 then Low is printed and the rest of the statement ignored. If NUM is greater than or equal to 35 the ELSE portion of the line is executed and the second IF is checked to determine if NUM is greater than 35. If it is, High is printed, if it is not then NUM must equal 35 and Equal is printed. In typing this line Enter was pressed only at the end of the complete statement, after "Equal". The only restriction on the use of multiple IF...THEN...ELSE statements is that the total length of a single program line may not exceed 255 characters.

The tremendous flexibility of the IF...THEN...ELSE statement should be apparent. Using this statement properly can substantially reduce both the size and complexity of a program.

This program uses an IF...THEN...ELSE statement similar to the one shown above as part of a number guessing game. The user enters a number and is told whether the guess is low, high or correct. The game allows five guesses:

```
10 REM ** The user is given 5 chances to
            guess a number **
20 NUMBER = 35
20 FOR COUNT = 1 TO 5
30    INPUT "What is your guess"; GUESS
40    IF GUESS < NUMBER THEN PRINT "Low" ELSE
      IF GUESS > NUMBER THEN PRINT "High" ELSE
      PRINT "Correct!"
50    PRINT
60 NEXT COUNT
999 END
```

```
RUN
What is your guess? 10
Low

What is your guess? 50
High

What is your guess? 33
Low

What is your guess? 35
Correct!

What is your guess? 35
Correct!

Ok
```

The variable NUMBER, assigned at line 20, allows the number being guessed to be easily changed. Note that the program asks the user for a fifth guess even though the correct number was entered for the fourth guess. It would be much better if the program continued to ask for guesses until the correct number was entered and then immediately terminated execution. In the next section we will introduce the statements needed to correct this deficiency.

Review

4. a) Rewrite your answer to Review number 1 using an IF...THEN...ELSE statement.
    b) Rewrite your answer to Review number 3 using an IF...THEN...ELSE statement.

5. Write a program that asks for two names as input. If the first name is Smith and the second Jones print `Smith and Jones are friends`. If the first name is Smith and the second not Jones print `Where is Jones?` If the first name is not Smith and the second is Jones print `Where is Smith?` For all other possibilities print nothing:

```
RUN
Enter name 1? Smith
Enter name 2? Presley
Where is Jones?
Ok

RUN
Enter name 1? Freitas
Enter name 2? Jones
Where is Smith?
Ok
```

6. Write a program which asks for a student's grade average and then prints the message `High Honors` if the average is 90 or above, `Honors` if it is between 80 and 89, `Passing` if between 60 and 79 and `Failing` if below 60. Use a properly structured multiple IF...THEN...ELSE statement to print the messages:

```
RUN
What is your average? 75
Passing
Ok
```

4.6 WHILE...WEND Loops

The only method we have had for repeating the execution of program lines has been the FOR...NEXT loop. This is called a definite loop since it executes a predetermined number of times. Often it is desirable to execute statements as long as a given condition is true. This may be done using the WHILE...WEND loop which takes the form:

```
WHILE <condition>
   <statements>
   .  .  .
WEND
```

When the WHILE statement is encountered, the <condition> is evaluated and if it is true, the statements between WHILE and WEND are executed. The computer then returns to the WHILE statement and evaluates the condition again. If the condition is still true, the process is repeated, otherwise execution resumes with the statement immediately following WEND. Since the number of executions of the loop is not predetermined this is called an "indefinite loop."

This program is a rewrite of the guessing game program in Section 4.5. The FOR...NEXT loop has been replaced by a WHILE...WEND so that the loop is executed only the number of times necessary for the user to guess the correct answer:

```
10 REM ** The user is given as many chances
             as needed to guess a number **
20 NUMBER = 35
30 INPUT "What is your guess"; GUESS
40 WHILE GUESS <> NUMBER
50    IF GUESS < NUMBER THEN PRINT "Low" ELSE
      PRINT "High"
60    PRINT
70    INPUT "What is your guess"; GUESS
80 WEND
90 PRINT "Correct!"
999 END
```

```
RUN
What is your guess? 12
Low

What is your guess? 60
High

What is your guess? 33
Low

What is your guess? 37
High

What is your guess? 34
Low

What is your guess? 35
Correct!
Ok
```

This program contains a number of important concepts and should be studied carefully. The user has taken 6 guesses to get the answer correct, but would have been allowed as many as was necessary. Each time the program encounters line 40 it evaluates the condition GUESS <> NUMBER. If it is true that GUESS is not equal to NUMBER the loop is executed. When GUESS equals NUMBER program execution is sent to the line proceeding the WEND statement; in this case line 90 where `Correct!` is printed.

Note the use of the INPUT statement at line 30 to get a value for GUESS before the loop is encountered. This is called "priming" the loop. If the first guess is correct the loop will not be executed at all and the program will immediately go to line 90 and print `Correct`.

The location of the INPUT statement at line 70 is critical. If it were placed at the beginning of the loop, say at line 45, it would ask for input before line 50 could print `Low` or `High` for the original guess input at line 30. For a WHILE...WEND loop to operate properly some condition within the loop must make it possible for the loop to terminate execution. In this program line 70 serves this function. If line 70 were not included, the value for GUESS would never change and the loop would continue forever. This is called an "infinite loop" and is clearly undesirable. Should you encounter an infinite loop, hold down the key marked `Ctrl` and press the `Break` key (`Ctrl-Break`). This terminates the loop so that you can fix the error. Here we erase line 70 and run the program:

```
70
RUN
What is your guess? 12
Low

Low

Low
^C
Break in 60
Ok
```

Low will continue to be printed until `Ctrl-Break` is pressed (shown as ^C on the computer screen) to terminate the infinite loop.

Review

7. Write a program that continues to ask for a name until the name "Brown" is input. Print `Wrong name` after each incorrect attempt.

```
RUN
Enter a name? Jones
Wrong name

Enter a name? Kwolsky
Wrong name

Enter a name? Brown
Correct
Ok
```

4.7 Counting in a Loop

If the programmer decides to keep score for the number guessing game in Section 4.6 some technique will have to be devised to keep count of the number of guesses taken. One way is to use a "counter" statement such as this:

```
60 COUNT = COUNT + 1
```

Algebraically this statement makes little sense. However, in BASIC the = sign means "is given the value of" rather than "equals." Therefore, this statement means "COUNT is given the value of COUNT + 1." Each time the computer executes this line, 1 is added to the current value of COUNT and this new value assigned back to COUNT.

The number of guesses taken can be displayed by adding lines 35, 75 and 100 to the program in Section 4.6:

```
10 REM ** The user is given as many chances
            as needed to guess a number **
20 NUMBER = 35
30 INPUT "What is your guess"; GUESS
35 COUNT = 1
40 WHILE GUESS <> NUMBER
50    IF GUESS < NUMBER THEN PRINT "Low" ELSE
      PRINT "High"
60    PRINT
70    INPUT "What is your guess"; GUESS
75    COUNT = COUNT + 1
80 WEND
90 PRINT "Correct!"
100 PRINT "The number of guesses taken is "
      COUNT
999 END
```

```
RUN
What is your guess? 45
High

What is your guess? 25
Low

What is your guess? 35
Correct!
The number of guesses taken is 3
Ok
```

At line 35 COUNT is assigned an initial value of 1. At line 75 COUNT is increased by 1 each time the loop is executed. Line 100 displays the final value of COUNT after the correct number has been guessed.

A counter does not have to count by 1. The following statements

```
150 ODD = ODD + 2
200 SETS = SETS - 1
```

make a program count by twos, or decrease by 1.

To make our guessing game program more interesting we could replace the counter with one that gives a score at the end of the game. We start by assigning the variable SCORE a value of 100 points and then subtract 10 points for each incorrect guess the user takes:

```
10 REM ** The user is given as many chances
            as needed to guess the number and a
            score is printed **
20 NUMBER = 35
30 INPUT "What is your guess"; GUESS
35 SCORE = 100
40 WHILE GUESS <> NUMBER
50    IF GUESS < NUMBER THEN PRINT "Low" ELSE
      PRINT "High"
55    SCORE = SCORE - 10
60    PRINT
70    INPUT "What is your guess"; GUESS
80 WEND
90 PRINT "Correct!"
100 PRINT "Your score ="; SCORE; "points"
999 END
```

```
RUN
What is your guess? 12
Low

What is your guess? 60
High

What is your guess? 33
Low

What is your guess? 37
High

What is your guess? 34
Low

What is your guess? 35
Correct!
Your score = 50 points
Ok
```

Line 35 initializes the counter SCORE to 100. Line 55 subtracts 10 points from SCORE for each wrong guess taken.

Review

8. Write a program which uses WHILE and a counter to print the numbers from 1 to 10:

```
1
2
. . .
10
Ok
```

9. Add a counter to the program written for Review 7 which keeps count of the number of names entered and prints the count after Brown is input:

```
RUN
Enter a name? Munger
Wrong name

Enter a name? Andrews
Wrong name

Enter a name? Brown
Correct!
 3 names entered
Ok
```

4.8 Accumulating a Total

Often a problem requires some sort of running total to produce the desired output. One way of calculating a total is through the use of a special type of counter known as an "accumulator." An accumulator adds an amount that may vary each time the statement is executed. For example, the statement

```
50 TOTAL = TOTAL + NUMBER
```

is an accumulator, where NUMBER is a changing value added to TOTAL.

This program incorporates an accumulator to calculate the value of a savings account into which an initial deposit of $2,000 is made. The annual interest rate is 5.8% and the program calculates the account's balance after 30 years:

```
10 REM ** Calculates interest for 30 years **
20 BALANCE = 2000
30 FOR YEAR = 1 TO 30
40   BALANCE = BALANCE + (0.058 * BALANCE)
50 NEXT YEAR
60 PRINT "After 30 years the account contains
   $"; BALANCE
99 END
```

```
RUN
After 30 years the account contains $ 10854.26
Ok
```

The variable BALANCE stores the total amount of money in the savings account. It is initially set to $2,000 at line 20. Each time line 40 is executed the current value of BALANCE is added to 0.058 (5.8%) times the value of BALANCE, and this new value assigned back to BALANCE. This process is repeated 30 times, once for each of the 30 years. Note how much the original $2,000 has grown in this time.

10. a) Write a program which asks a user to enter 5 numbers and then prints the sum of the numbers. You may use only a single INPUT statement:

```
RUN
Enter number 1? 12
Enter number 2? 28
Enter number 3? 32
Enter number 4? 15
Enter number 5? 71
The sum of the five numbers is 158
Ok
```

b) Modify the program written in part (a) to also calculate the average of the entered numbers:

```
RUN
Enter number 1? 12
Enter number 2? 28
Enter number 3? 32
Enter number 4? 15
Enter number 5? 71
The sum of the five numbers is 158
The average is 31.6
Ok
```

11. a) Write a program which asks the user to enter several numbers and then prints the sum of the numbers:

```
RUN
Enter number (0 to stop)? 12
Enter number (0 to stop)? 28
Enter number (0 to stop)? 32
Enter number (0 to stop)? 15
Enter number (0 to stop)? 71
Enter number (0 to stop)? 0
The sum of the numbers is 158
Ok
```

b) Modify the program written in part (a) to also calculate the average of the entered numbers:

```
RUN
Enter number (0 to stop)? 12
Enter number (0 to stop)? 28
Enter number (0 to stop)? 32
Enter number (0 to stop)? 15
Enter number (0 to stop)? 71
Enter number (0 to stop)? 0
The sum of the numbers is 158
The average is 31.6
Ok
```

4.9 Formatting Output: PRINT USING

We stated earlier that producing easy to read output is an important objective of a good program. A useful statement that allows us to determine what our output will look like is PRINT USING. It formats a line of output into zones of variable length. These zones may contain numbers, strings, or a combination of both. The general form of PRINT USING is:

```
PRINT USING "<format>"; <variables>
```

The <format> describes how the <variables> are to appear when printed. Backslash characters (\) are used to indicate strings. To format the space for numbers, pound signs (#) are used with each pound sign reserving space for a single digit. Any spaces included in the format are also printed. For example,

```
30 PRINT USING "\              \   $###.##
   ##"; NAME1$, SALARY, AGE
```

formats a line to print a 14 character string, 3 spaces, a five digit number which includes a dollar sign and two decimal places, 4 spaces, and a two digit number with no decimal places. The value of NAME1$ is printed between the slash marks, the value of numeric variable SALARY in the first set of pound signs preceded by a dollar sign, and the value of numeric variable AGE in the second set of pound signs. The output produced by this statement for the data Crangi, 78.7, 21 would be:

```
Crangi          $ 78.70       21
```

Note the dollar sign used in printing SALARY. All that need be done is to include the dollar sign in the output is to place it in the <format>. Also, note that a space is printed between the dollar sign and the money amount leaving room for a fifth digit, and that a zero is automatically added to make 78.7 read 78.70. If a number is larger than the space given in the format, a percent sign is printed before the number.

This program reads data and then formats it with PRINT USING:

```
10 REM ** Formats output with PRINT USING **
20 PRINT "Name            Salary        Age"
30 FOR COUNT = 1 TO 5
40    READ NAME1$, SALARY, AGE
50    PRINT USING "\            \   $###.##
      ##"; NAME1$, SALARY, AGE
60 NEXT COUNT
99 END
1000 REM ** Data: Name, Salary, Age
1010 DATA Presley, 78.78, 45.6
1020 DATA Freitas, 192.15, 29
1030 DATA Brown, 83.45, 25
1040 DATA Crane, 76, 32
1050 DATA Porter, 81.29, 26
```

```
RUN
Name            Salary        Age
Presley         $ 78.80        46
Freitas         $192.20        29
Brown           $ 83.45        25
Crane           $ 76.00        32
Porter          $ 81.29        26
Ok
```

Even though the DATA statement at line 1010 contains Presley's age as 45.6 it is printed rounded to two places as 46. We will continue to make use of this rounding feature of PRINT USING. Notice that zeros are added to any salary which does not contain a sufficient number of decimal places and that all numbers are printed in even columns lined up by decimal points.

Numbers can be formatted with both commas and decimal points. For example,

```
30 PRINT USING "$###,###.##"; BUDGET
```

prints

```
$305,298.00
```

when BUDGET stores the value 305298.

Any text that is included within a PRINT USING statement, but not within formatting symbols is printed just as it appears:

```
30 PRINT USING "The budget is $###,###.##";
   BUDGET
```

prints

```
The budget is $305,298.00
```

The following program prints the yearly earnings for five large corporations:

```
10 REM ** Prints the yearly earnings for
           five corporations **
20 PRINT "             Corporate yearly
   earnings"
30 PRINT
40 FOR COUNT = 1 TO 5
50   READ CORP$, EARNINGS
60   PRINT USING "Yearly earnings for \
     \ is $###,###,###.##"; CORP$, EARNINGS
70 NEXT COUNT
999 END
1000 REM ** Corporate name, yearly earnings
1010 DATA Hildreth Inc., 568345.9
1020 DATA International, 678234523.8
1030 DATA Boca Tools, 45678.12
1040 DATA Jones Realty, 214568.76
1050 DATA Delmar Travel, 89345.12
```

```
RUN
                Corporate yearly earnings

Yearly earnings for Hildreth Inc.   is $    568,345.90
Yearly earnings for International    is $678,234,523.80
Yearly earnings for Boca Tools      is $     45,678.12
Yearly earnings for Jones Realty     is $    214,468.76
Yearly earnings for Delmar Travel    is $     89,345.12
Ok
```

The dollar signs are all printed in a row regardless of the length of the numeric amount. It is possible to print the dollar sign immediately to the left of the numeric amount by using two dollar signs ($ $) in the PRINT USING statement:

```
60    PRINT USING "Yearly earnings for \
      \ is $$###,###,###.##"; CORP$, EARNINGS
```

This is called a "floating" dollar sign. When the program is run with this change, the dollar signs are floating:

```
RUN
                Corporate yearly earnings

Yearly earnings for Hildreth Inc.   is     $568,345.90
Yearly earnings for International    is $678,234,523.80
Yearly earnings for Boca Tools      is      $45,678.12
Yearly earnings for Jones Realty     is     $214,468.76
Yearly earnings for Delmar Travel    is      $89,345.12
Ok
```

When entering program lines, the shortcut Alt-P may be used for PRINT and Alt-U for USING. PRINT USING contains a number of other formatting options which are listed in Appendix B.

Review

12. Write a program which contains a PRINT USING statement to produce the following table. The necessary data should be stored in DATA statements:

```
RUN
Salary for Jones:      $45,830.20 Bonus:  $3,271.14
Salary for Crane:      $53,712.18 Bonus:    $214.18
Salary for Wagy:      $123,419.27 Bonus:  $7,840.00
Salary for Freitas:    $79,841.00 Bonus:  $4,705.18
Salary for Hotchkiss:   $9,540.18 Bonus: $12,478.15
Ok
```

4.10 PRINT TAB

The PRINT TAB statement, which works similarly to the Tab key on a typewriter, provides an easy way to format output. The left edge of the screen is located at TAB(1), while the right edge is at TAB(80). For example, the following statement prints information at screen positions 13, 25 and 32:

```
PRINT TAB(13); "This"; TAB(25); "is"; TAB(32); "TAB"
         This          is       TAB
```

It is necessary to include a semicolon (;) or space after each TAB in a PRINT statement.

A TAB may not move the cursor to the left, only to the right. If a TAB position is specified which is to the left of the current position, it will be printed on the next line. TABs with negative numbers or 0 are treated as TAB(1).

Variables may also be used in the TAB function. This program uses TAB to draw a triangle on the screen:

```
10 REM ** Displays a triangle using TAB **
20 PRINT "*******"
30 FOR X = 2 TO 6
40   PRINT TAB(X); "*"; TAB(7); "*"
50 NEXT X
60 PRINT TAB(7); "*"
99 END
```

```
RUN
* * * * * * *
  *         *
    *       *
      *     *
        *   *
          * *
            *
Ok
```

Line 20 prints the top of the triangle while line 30 initiates the loop which prints the two sides. Line 40 prints two points on the screen. Notice how the variable X is incorporated with the TAB function to draw a diagonal line; because X increases by one each time, the first asterisk is printed one more position to the right. Line 60 completes the triangle by plotting the final point.

Review

13. Determine the output of the following program:

```
10 REM ** Review #13 **
20 FOR COUNT = 1 TO 4
20   PRINT TAB(COUNT); COUNT
30 NEXT COUNT
40 FOR COUNT = 1 TO COUNT
50   PRINT TAB(COUNT), COUNT
60 NEXT COUNT
99 END
```

14. Using TABs, write a program which draws the following triangle:

```
RUN
              *
            *   *
          *       *
        *           *
      *               *
    *                   *
  *   *   *   *   *   *   *

Ok
```

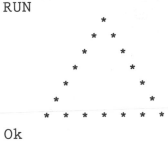

4.11 Using Flags

A computer "flag" uses an IF...THEN statement to determine if a certain condition has been met. The flag is actually a variable that stores a value which indicates the current status of the condition. For instance, a flag can be used to keep the computer from halting a program with an error message when the end of the data in a DATA statement has been reached.

This program searches a list of names stored in a DATA statement to determine whether an input name is in the list. Two flags are used; one to signal if the name has been found and the second to indicate the end of the data:

```
10 REM ** Searches list for entered name **
20 INPUT "Name to search for"; NAME1$
30 FLAG$ = "Not found"
40 WHILE FLAG$ = "Not found" AND SEARCH$ <>
   "EOD"
50   READ SEARCH$
60   IF NAME1$ = SEARCH$ THEN PRINT NAME1$
     " found" : FLAG$ = "Found"
70 WEND
80 IF FLAG$ = "Not found" THEN PRINT NAME1$
   " not on list"
99 END
1000 DATA Attis, Crangi, Freitas
1010 DATA Jones, Presley, Wagy, EOD
```

```
RUN
Name to search for? Attis
Attis found
Ok
```

```
RUN
Name to search for? Zamboni
Zamboni not on list
Ok
```

This program contains a number of important concepts. First, note how the string variable FLAG$ is used. It is initially set to Not found at line 30 and is reset to Found at line 60 only if the input name matches one of the names stored in the DATA line. A string makes a good flag variable because it is easy to tell the status of the program by printing the string (in this case "Found" or "Not found"). Second, note how the value EOD (for End Of Data) is the last data item in line 1000. Checking for this value in the WHILE's condition guarantees that an attempt will not be made to read past the end of the data, which would cause an error. Third, note how the WHILE statement operates at line 40. The loop is only executed if both FLAG$ equals "Not found" *and* SEARCH$ is not equal to "EOD". If either condition is not met program execution is sent to line 80 where the message is printed only if FLAG$ has remained equal to Not found.

4.12 RESTORE

The computer keeps track of the items read from DATA statements, and attempting to READ more data than is present results in a Out of DATA error. There are times when a set of data statements must be read more than once. This may be accomplished using the RESTORE statement which tells BASIC to start reading from the beginning of the data again. RESTORE takes the form:

```
120 RESTORE
```

The next READ statement executed after a RESTORE will read the first item in the DATA statements. RESTORE may be executed unlimited times in a program, and is of particular use when searching the same list of DATA for different items.

Review

15. Write a program which reads a person's name, hours worked and pay rate from a DATA statement and then computes and prints their weekly salary. Use a WHILE...WEND loop to control the processing with the terminating condition being the name equals "END OF DATA", which will be placed in the last DATA statement. <u>Hint:</u> Remember not to print the last set of data.

```
RUN
Name            Hours        Pay rate       Salary
Chin            23.0         $ 4.50         $103.50
Doucette        14.0         $ 6.75          $94.50
Gould           17.5         $ 8.00         $140.00
Ok
```

16. Write a program which reads a music store's inventory from the following DATA statements:

```
1000 REM ** Item name, Quantity, Price
1010 DATA Grand Piano, 4, 12795.95
1020 DATA Bass Fiddle, 7, 784.95
1030 DATA Electric Guitar, 15, 398.95
1040 DATA Mandolin, 6, 235.95
1050 DATA EOD, 0, 0
```

Print a chart showing all the information plus the value of each item:

```
RUN
Item              Quantity  Price         Total value
Grand Piano          4      $12,795.95    $51,183.80
Bass Fiddle          7      $    784.95   $ 5,494.65
Electric Guitar     15      $    398.95   $ 5,985.25
Mandolin             6      $    235.95   $ 1,415.70
Ok
```

4.13 End of Chapter Problem

To review the material covered in this chapter we will design a program that allows the user to search for a student by entering the student's identification number. Each student's identification number, name and four grades are stored in DATA statements. If a student is found, his or her name, grade average and the words Honors, Passing or Failing are printed depending upon the average.

Algorithm

1. Enter student ID.
2. Search through data to find student.
3. If student is found:
   calculate average.
   print name, average and rating.
   If student not found:
   print message.

Input   Student I.D. to find   ID

Output   Student Name   STUNAME$
          Grade average   AVERAGE
          Rating message   RATING$

```
10  REM ** Searches list for input student ID **
20  REM ** If found, calculates average and
          prints rating message **
30  FOUND$ = "NO"
40  INPUT "Enter student I.D. #"; ID
50  READ STUID, STUNAME$, GRADE1, GRADE2,
    GRADE3, GRADE4
60  WHILE FOUND$ = "NO" AND STUID <> -1
70     AVERAGE = (GRADE1 + GRADE2 + GRADE3 +
       GRADE4) / 4
80     IF AVERAGE > = 85 THEN RATING$ = "Honors"
       ELSE IF AVERAGE >= 60 THEN RATING$ =
       "Passing" ELSE RATING$ = "Failing"
90     IF ID = STUID THEN PRINT USING "\
       \        ##.#          \            \";
       STUNAME$, AVERAGE, RATING$ : FOUND$ =
       "YES"
100     READ STUID, STUNAME$, GRADE1, GRADE2,
        GRADE3, GRADE4
110 WEND
120 IF FOUND$ = "NO" THEN PRINT "No student
    found with entered I.D."
999 END
```

```
1000 REM ** Student data - I.D., Name,
               Grade1, Grade2, Grade3, Grade4
1010 DATA 313, Presley, 67, 89, 90, 78
1020 DATA 472, Freitas, 79, 90, 89, 92
1030 DATA 625, Brown, 65, 78, 55, 45
1040 DATA 636, Crane, 78, 76, 65, 70
1050 DATA 756, Sechton, 65, 50, 54, 70
1060 DATA -1, End of Data, 0, 0, 0, 0
```

```
RUN
Enter student I.D. #? 756
Sechton                    59.8              Failing
Ok
```

```
RUN
Enter student I.D. #? 257
No student found with entered I.D.
Ok
```

The searching technique employed in this program is similar to that used by the program in Section 4.11. Note the structure of line 50. It is important that six variables be used to read the six items of data for each student. The data for each student has been placed on a separate line (1010 to 1060). This is not necessary, but makes it easier to locate and modify the data for an individual student. Also note how the data on line 1060 is needed to avoid an error message, even though the data will not be used. At line 90 the student name, average and message is only printed if the identification number input at line 40 is equal to the I.D. number read from the data statements.

Chapter Summary

The IF...THEN statement has the form IF <condition> THEN <statement>. If the comparison made in the condition is true, the statement following THEN is executed, if false, the statement is ignored. In the statement

```
30 IF X < 20 THEN PRINT "Small"
```

"Small" is printed only if X is less than 20. If X is equal to or greater than 20 nothing is printed.

IF...THEN can be used to compare strings where the comparison refers to alphabetic rather than numeric order:

```
30 IF N1$ > N2$ THEN PRINT N1$ " is after " N2$
```

AND and OR are used in an IF...THEN statement to join two or more comparisons as one condition. When AND is used to join two comparisons both comparisons must be true for the condition to be true:

```
40 IF X > 10 AND Y < 5 THEN PRINT "Both are
   true"
```

When OR is used, the condition is true when either or both comparisons are true:

```
40 IF X > 10 OR Y < 5 THEN PRINT "One or both
   is true"
```

A series of statements, called a compound statement, can be entered on a single program line by separating them with colons. When used with IF...THEN compound statements allow more than one operation to be performed when the condition is true:

```
50 IF AGE > 12 AND AGE < 20 THEN PRINT
   "Teenager" : SCHOOL$ = "Yes"
```

An ELSE clause can be added to an IF...THEN statement and is executed only when the IF...THEN condition is false:

```
60 IF AGE > 12 AND AGE < 20 THEN PRINT
   "Teenager" ELSE PRINT "Not a teenager"
```

A WHILE...WEND loop is called an indefinite loop since the number of executions of the loop is not predetermined. When a WHILE statement is encountered its condition is evaluated and if it is true, the statements between WHILE and WEND are executed. If the condition is false the loop is skipped.

It is important that a WHILE...WEND loop contain a condition that will terminate loop execution to avoid producing an infinite loop. An infinite loop is one which continues to execute until interrupted by pressing `Ctrl-Break`.

A counter statement is used to keep count of the number of times an event occurs:

```
40 COUNT = COUNT + 1
```

Each time this statement is executed 1 is added to the old value of COUNT to produce the new value of COUNT.

An accumulator statement is used to add an amount that may vary each time the statement is executed:

```
50 TOTAL = TOTAL + NUMBER
```

Each time this statement is executed NUMBER is added to the old value of TOTAL to produce the new value of TOTAL.

PRINT USING formats a line of output into zones of variable length. These zones may contain numbers, strings, or a combination of both. The statement

```
60 PRINT USING "$###.##  \                \
   ##"; RENT, NAME1$, AGE
```

formats a line to print a five digit number which includes a dollar sign and two decimal places, 2 spaces, a 15 character string, 1 space, and a two digit number. Note that if AGE = 19.8 it will be properly rounded to two places and displayed as 20.

PRINT TAB is used to move the cursor to the right a specified number of spaces to format output. The statement

```
30 PRINT TAB(10); "Hello"; TAB(20); "how are";
   TAB(40); "you"
```

prints the data at screen positions 10, 20 and 40.

A flag uses an IF...THEN statement to signal that a certain condition has been met. A flag is often used to signal when the end of the data in a DATA statement has been reached.

Vocabulary

Accumulator - A variable used to store a total which changes by a different amount.

Compound statement - A series of statements that are separated by colons and entered on a single program line.

Counter - A variable that keeps count of an event by changing its value by a specific amount each time the event occurs.

ELSE - Clause added to IF...THEN which is executed when the condition is not true.

Flag - Variable used to signal that a certain condition has been met.

IF . . . THEN - Statement which performs an action only if a condition is true.

Indefinite loop - A loop for which the number of executions is not predetermined. See WHILE...WEND.

Infinite loop - A loop which continues to execute until interrupted by pressing Ctrl-Break.

Priming the loop - Asking the user to input the first value which determines if a WHILE...WEND loop is to be executed.

PRINT TAB - Statement that moves the cursor a specified number of spaces to the right to format a line of output.

PRINT USING - Statement that allows output to be formatted in a variety of ways.

WHILE . . . WEND - Statements which produce an indefinite loop.

Exercises

1. Using a loop, have the computer print the letter "I" using asterisks as follows:

    ```
    RUN
    * * * * * * *
        * * *
        * * *
        * * *
        * * *
        * * *
        * * *
    * * * * * * *
    Ok
    ```

2. Use a loop to print a horizontal line of 40 asterisks:

    ```
    RUN
    * * * * * * * * * * * * * * * * * * * * * * * * * * * * * * * * * * * * * * * *
    Ok
    ```

3. Use only one PRINT statement to produce the following rectangle:

    ```
    RUN
    * * * * * * * * * * * *
    * * * * * * * * * * * *
    * * * * * * * * * * * *
    Ok
    ```

4. Write a program to print the cubes of the odd integers from 11 to -11, inclusive, in descending order.

5. Write a program to print all the integers which end in 4 from 4 to 84, inclusive.

6. Write a program to print all the integers in the series 10, 13, 16, 19, . . ., 94, 97.

7. Write a program to draw a straight diagonal line (composed of asterisks) starting at the upper left hand corner and moving one space down and one space to the right until the line hits the bottom of the screen.

8. Use CLS and a WHILE...WEND loop to display an advertising sign on the screen. Store the text for the sign in DATA statements:

RUN

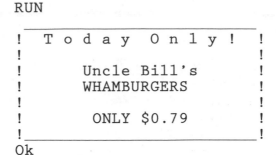

Ok

9. The Happy Holiday Campground has 10 cabins. Have the computer print a label for each cabin's door indicating the room number. For example:

RUN

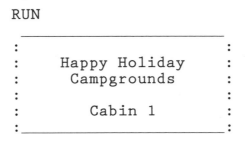

. . .

10. Using only two PRINT statements, write a program to print a triangle that is NUMBER lines high and NUMBER columns wide. For example:

```
RUN
Enter a number? 5
*
* *
* * *
* * * *
* * * * *
Ok
```

11. An investor purchased some stock and now wants to use the computer to calculate any profit or loss. The portfolio consists of 200 shares of Consolidated Technologies purchased at $85.58 per share and 400 shares of American Amalgamated Securities at $35.60 per share. Today CT is worth $70.82 a share and AAS is worth $47.32 a share. What is the total profit or loss?

```
RUN
Stock symbol? CT
Number of shares? 200
Purchase price per share? 85.58
Current price per share? 70.82
Loss on CT = $ -2,952.00

Another calculation (y/n)? y
Stock symbol? AAS
Number of shares? 400
Purchase price per share? 35.60
Current price per share? 47.32
Profit on AAS = $ 4,688.00

Another calculation (y/n)? n
Total profit/loss = $ 1,736.00
Ok
```

12. Write a program that allows two numbers to be entered. Have the computer compare them and print a message stating whether the first number is less than, equal to, or greater than the second:

```
RUN
Enter two numbers? 23, 45
 23 is less than 45
Ok
```

```
RUN
Enter two numbers? 50, -12
 50 is greater than -12
Ok
```

13. Write a program which allows two names to be entered. Have the computer print the names in alphabetic order on separate lines:

```
RUN
What is name 1? Machado
What is name 2? Li

The names in order are:
Li
Machado
Ok
```

14. Write a program which asks for a person's age. If the person is 16 years or older, have the computer print "You are old enough to drive a car!". Otherwise, have the computer indicate how many years the person must wait before being able to drive.

```
RUN
How old are you? 16
You are old enough to drive a car!
Ok

RUN
How old are you? 12
You can drive a car in 4 years.
Ok
```

15. Write a program in which the user inputs a number. Print "In the interval" if the number satisfies the inequality $25 < X < 75$, otherwise print "Not in the interval". Only one AND and one IF...THEN statement are to be used.

16. Below is a list of various creatures and the weapon necessary to destroy each:

Creature	Weapon
Lich	Fire Ball
Medusa	Sharp Sword
Mummy	Flaming Torch
Triffid	Fire Hose
Vampire	Wooden Stake
Werewolf	Silver Bullet

Using READ and DATA, have the computer state what weapon is to be used to destroy a given creature. For example:

```
RUN
Creature? King Kong
King Kong not found
Ok

RUN
Creature? Vampire
A Vampire can be destroyed with a wooden
stake
Ok
```

17. As candidate for mayor, you are very busy. Write a program using DATA statements to print thank-you letters to people who have contributed money to your election campaign. Be sure to mention the exact amount each person has contributed. Store the contributors' names and the amounts of their contributions in DATA statements, and have the program work for any number of contributors:

```
RUN
Dear Rich Bryburry,

Thank you for your generous contribution of
$25,000 to my election campaign. Maybe next
year we will have better luck!

Sincerely,

Smiley R. Politico

Dear Heidi Crane,

Thank you for your generous contribution of $
20 to my election campaign. Maybe next year
we will have better luck!

Sincerely,

Smiley R. Politico


        . . .
```

18. a) Write a program to produce the following table:

```
RUN
 X                    X^2                  X^3
 -                    - - -                - - -
 2                      4                    8
 4                     16                   64
 6                     36                  216
 8                     64                  512
10                    100                 1000
Ok
```

b) Modify the program to allow the user to enter the starting, ending, and step (increment) values for X.

19. The Bored Auto Company has done it again! Some models of their cars may be difficult to drive because their wheels are not exactly round. Cars with model numbers 102, 119, 189 through 195, 229, and 780 have been found to have the defect. Write a program that allows customers to enter the model number of their car to find out whether or not it is defective.

```
RUN
Enter model number of your car? 119
Your model is defective!

Do you want to enter another model (y/n)? y
Enter model number of your car? 337
Your model is not defective.

Do you want to enter another model (y/n)? n
Ok
```

20. The following table contains employee performance data for the Tippecanoe Typing Company:

Employee	Performance
Oakley	69%
Howe	92%
Anderson	96%
Wolley	88%
Goerz	74%

Tippecanoe Typing is suffering from financial difficulties and needs to cut back on its staff. Using READ..DATA and a loop, have the computer print notices of dismissal for any employee whose production is below 75 percent:

```
RUN
Dear Oakley,

I am deeply sorry that I must fire you. You
have been such a fine employee, with a per-
formance rating of 69%.

Sincerely,
G. Schwabb

   . . .
```

21. a) The Crude Oil Company uses the computer to determine the weekly wages of its employees. If an employee works over 40 hours, he or she is paid one and a half times the hourly rate for each additional hour:

```
RUN
Hours worked? 45
Hourly wage? 10.00
The wage for the week is $ 475.00
Ok
```

b) Taxes must be deducted from every paycheck. If the wage is $400 or more, deduct 28% for taxes. If less than $400, deduct 18%:

```
RUN
Hours worked? 45
Hourly wage? 10.00
The wage for the week is $ 475.00
The taxes are $ 133.00
The employee takes home $ 342.00
Ok
```

22. You have $200.00 to spend on a buying spree. Write a program that, as you purchase merchandise, subtracts the cost and the appropriate sales tax (5%) from your remaining money and shows your present total. The program should prevent you from buying items that cost more than you have. Entering a 0 for price terminates the program:

```
RUN
You have $ 200.00
How much does the item cost? 10.00
Your total is now $189.50

How much does the item cost? 250.00
You don't have enough money.
How much does the item cost? 25.00
Your total is now $163.25

How much does the item cost? 0
Ok
```

23. Have the computer find all odd integers from 5 to 25 which are simultaneous solutions of the inequalities $X^3 > 500$ and $X^2 + 3X + 2 < 700$. Print only the solutions.

24. The Lawrenceville National Bank needs a program to assist its customers with mortgage calculations. It wants the customer to be able to walk up to a terminal, enter the loan amount, interest rate and length of the loan, and have the monthly payment displayed. The formula for a monthly payment is:

$$\text{Payment} = \frac{\text{Amount} * \text{Interest}}{1 - (\text{Interest} + 1)^{-\text{Length}}}$$

Write a program that displays the monthly payment when the total amount borrowed, monthly interest rate and length of the loan (in months) are input.

25. A factorial (written as **N!**) is a number which is the product of all integers from 1 to N. For example, 4! = 1 * 2 * 3 * 4 = 24. Write a program to calculate factorials:

```
RUN
Enter a number? 5
5! = 120

Do you want another (y/n)? y
Enter a number? 3
3! = 6

Do you want another (y/n)? n
Ok
```

26. Write a program that allows the user to guess a 3 letter word. Ask the user to input each letter. The computer should respond by telling the user if the letter is correct or incorrect. If the letter is incorrect have the computer state whether the correct letter is above or below the letter guessed. Allow the user to make as many guesses as necessary. When the word has been correctly guessed print it out along with the number of guesses used:

```
        Word Guess Game
Guess 3 letters: J, A, N
First letter is correct
Second letter is greater than guess
Third letter is less than guess

Guess 3 letters: J, O, E
Correct — Word is JOE
You used 2 guesses
```

27. Write a program that plays a game of trivia. The computer asks a question and the user inputs the answer. If the answer is correct, the player gets 10 points. Have the computer continue to ask questions until the player does not answer correctly or the computer is out of data. Have the player's score double for every correct answer. If the player answers all available questions print "You are a genius" otherwise just print the final score:

```
     Answer These Trivia Questions
How many feet in a yard? 3
Correct! You have 10 points.

How many centimeters in an inch? 2.54
Correct! You have 20 points.

What is the square root of 1? 2
Incorrect. Your score: 20 points.
```

Advanced Exercise

The following exercise requires the development of a detailed algorithm. The program should not be written until all details of the algorithm have been worked out.

28. A car dealer orders cars by entering the name of the car, followed by a list of options from 4 categories: body style, seat type, sound system and engine. These options are simplified by using the following codes:

Body Style
1) 2 door
2) 4 door
3) hatchback
4) convertible

Seat Type
1) bench
2) bucket
3) split bench
4) reclining

Sound System
1) AM radio
2) AM/FM
3) AM/FM/tape
4) AM/FM/disk

Engine
1) 4 cylinder
2) 6 cylinder
3) 8 cylinder
4) diesel

Write a program to accept the orders from a dealer and display the list of options based on the codes entered:

```
RUN
Enter car model? Capri
Enter body style? 4
Enter seat type? 2
Enter sound system? 4
Enter engine? 3

Description of ordered car:
Model: Capri
Options:
Convertible
Bucket Seats
AM/FM/Disk
8 cylinder engine
Ok
```

Computer Arithmetic

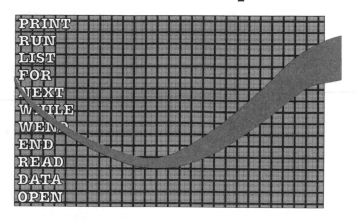

INT

RND

RANDOMIZE TIMER

INT

RND

RANDOMIZE TIMER

INT

RND

RANDOMIZE TIMER

Objectives

Chapter Five

After completing this chapter you will be able to:

1. Use the order of operations in performing calculations.

2. Take the integer value of a number using INT.

3. Generate random numbers with in a specified range using RND and INT.

4. Display numbers in scientific notation.

5. Round numbers to a specified number of decimal places.

*O*ne of the first things that comes to mind when people think of a computer is mathematics. The word "compute" means to calculate or figure mathematically, and computers are excellent "number crunchers." However, a programmer must still tell the computer which calculations to perform and when. This chapter describes how the computer performs mathematical operations, and how it uses both large and small numbers. The chapter also explains how the computer can be made to pick a random number and some of the situations where the computer's calculations are not accurate.

5.1 The Order of Operations

What value is assigned to variable A when the computer evaluates the following expression?

```
A = 3 + 12 / 3
```

Will the computer add 3 and 12 and then divide by 3? If it does, the answer will be 5. Or will the computer first divide 12 by 3 and then add 3? Entering the expression in immediate mode,

```
PRINT 3 + 12 / 3
 7
```

shows that the answer is 7. The computer divided first and then added 3 to the result. When evaluating mathematical expressions the computer always follows a specific order of operations. As a programmer you must know the order in which math operations will be executed to create proper expressions.

The computer uses the following priorities when evaluating a mathematical expression:

FIRST

Exponents: Any numbers raised to a power, i.e., 2^2, are calculated first. The caret symbol "^" is used by the computer for raising to a power:

```
PRINT 3 + 2 ^ 2
 7
```

The computer first calculates 2^2, which is 4, even though 3+2 appears first when reading the statement from left to right. Then 3 is added to the 4 to get 7.

SECOND   <u>Multiplication & Division</u>: Next, are multiplication or division which are of equal priority:

```
PRINT 2 + 5 * 6 / 3
 12
```

First the computer would evaluate any exponents. Finding none, it then performs any multiplications or divisions. Since these operations have a higher priority, the computer ignores the plus sign between 2 and 5, and proceeds to multiplication between the 5 and the 6, which is 30. The computer then divides 30 by 3 with a result of 10. Only after all the multiplications and divisions are done is the addition performed, adding 2 to 10 to get the final result of 12. Remember, when there is more than one operation of the same priority in a statement, they are performed in order from left to right.

THIRD   <u>Addition and Subtraction</u>: After exponentiation and multiplication/ division, the computer performs any additions or subtractions, which are of equal priority:

```
PRINT 3 * 2 + 5
 11
```

Since multiplication and division are done before addition, the computer first calculates the product of 3 and 2, which is 6. To get the final result, 5 is added to 6 to produce 11. Because multiplication is always done before addition, the statement

```
PRINT 5 + 3 * 2
 11
```

produces the same result, 11.

Parentheses may be used to change the order of operations. When parentheses are used, " (" and ")", the computer performs the operations within the parentheses first. If a programmer wants 5 added to 3 and the result of that divided by 2, parentheses can be used to tell the computer to follow that order:

```
PRINT (5 + 3) / 2
 4
```

If parentheses are used within parentheses, the computer will execute the operation within the inner-most set first:

```
PRINT 6 * ((5 + 3) / 2)
 24
```

First the computer adds 5 and 3 and then that result is divided by 2 to get 4. Finally the computer multiplies 4 by 6 to get the answer, 24. What would this statement print if all parentheses were removed?

When the number of left parentheses do not match the number of right parentheses, the computer prints a `Syntax error` message and halts the program:

```
10 PRINT 6 * ((5 + 3) / 2
RUN
Syntax error in 10
```

Review

1. Solve the following by hand using the computer's order of operations and then check your answers in immediate mode:

    a) 6 - 9 / 3   e) 5 * 15 - 5
    b) 3 ^ 2 + 1   f) 3 * (5 + 6)
    c) 25 / 5 + 3 * 12   g) (13 - 3) / (10 / 2)
    d) (2 + 1) ^ (8 / 4)   h) 3 * (2 + (5 - 2))

5.2 Numeric Accuracy

BASIC displays all numbers as decimals, including fractions and mixed numbers. This use of decimal numbers is most obvious with division, since any result other than a whole number is expressed as a decimal fraction:

```
PRINT 10 / 4
  2.5
```

BASIC prints the answer as a mixed decimal, 2.5. Often, the result of a division results in a repeating decimal:

```
PRINT 10 / 3
  3.333333
```

Since the computer can only store up to 6 decimal places it stopped dividing when the number of places reached 6.

If the last digit in a repeating decimal is equal to or greater than 5, it is rounded to the next highest digit:

```
PRINT 10 / 6
  1.666667
```

Since 6 is greater than 5, the last 6 is rounded up to 7.

Review

2. Predict the result of the following expressions and then use immediate mode to check your prediction:

    a) 100 / 8   d) 37 / 2
    b) 22 / 7   e) 11 / 3
    c) 5 / 6 - 1 / 8   f) 5 * 2 / 10

3. Perform each of the following computations on paper. Check your results using immediate mode:

    a) 3^2^3   e) 5 - 4^2
    b) 3 * (5 + 16)   f) 5 + 3 * 6 / 2
    c) 640 / 10 / 2 * 5   g) 5 + 3 * 4 - 1
    d) 2^3^2   h) 2^(3^2)
    i) 64 / 4 * 0.5 + ((1 + 5) * 2^3) * 1 / (2 * 4)

5.3 Producing INTegers

An integer is a whole number without decimal places. Therefore, the numbers 1, 2, 10 and 100 are all integers, but 3.14 is not. Often, only the integer part of a number is important. For instance, if you have 30 golf balls and you need to know how many dozen you have, only the whole number part of your division is used:

```
PRINT 30 / 12
   2.5
```

By using the INTeger function, the computer can be told to use only the whole number part of any value:

```
INT (<value>)
```

<value> can be a number (e.g., 5), a variable or a mathematical expression such as 10/3. The computer looks at the value within the parentheses and then uses only the whole number portion, discarding any decimals :

```
PRINT INT(30 / 12)
   2
```

INT() does not round a number off; instead, it drops any fractional part no matter what its value. For example:

```
INT(4.769) = 4        INT(5.99999) = 5
INT(0.41) = 0         INT(12.098) = 12
```

The value that the integer function returns is always equal to or smaller than the original value. Therefore, when INT() is used with negative numbers, the value returned is always one less than the whole number portion of the mixed number:

```
INT(-4.769) = -5      INT(-5.99999) = -6
INT(-0.41) = -1       INT(-12.098) = -13
```

The Skyhook International Company wants to pack 3 skyhooks in a box. They have written this program to tell them how many boxes they need and how many skyhooks will be left over:

```
10 REM ** Calculates number of boxes to
           hold skyhooks **
20 PERBOX = 3
30 INPUT "Number of skyhooks"; NUMHOOKS
40 BOXES = INT(NUMHOOKS / PERBOX)
50 PRINT "Boxes needed:" BOXES
60 LEFT = NUMHOOKS - (PERBOX * BOXES)
70 PRINT "Skyhooks left over:" LEFT
99 END
```

```
RUN
Number of skyhooks? 14
Boxes needed: 4
Skyhooks left over: 2
Ok
```

In the example shown, PERBOX is 3 and NUMHOOKS is 14. The result of 14/3 is 4.666667 so BOXES is assigned a 4 at line 40 because of the INT(). The number of skyhooks left over is equal to the total number of hooks minus those in the boxes, 14 - 12, or 2, as calculated at line 60.

Review

4. Predict the outcome of each of the following and then use immediate mode to check your prediction:

a) `INT(199.99999)`   d) `INT(22 / 7)`
b) `INT(-3.001)`   e) `INT(0.005)`
c) `INT(-0.999)`   f) `INT(-5.55)`

5.4 Random Numbers – RND

We can pick random numbers in a number of ways such as rolling dice, drawing a card from a deck or picking numbers from a hat. The computer can also be told to pick a random number. Random numbers have many uses, especially in producing computer games and simulations. The statement

```
NUMBER = RND
```

assigns NUMBER a random number that has a value greater than 0 but less than 1.

This program prints 5 random numbers. It is run twice. Note that it produces the same set of random numbers each time. (Your numbers may be different.)

```
10 REM ** Produces 5 random numbers **
20 FOR NUMBER = 1 TO 5
30    PRINT RND,
40 NEXT NUMBER
99 END
```

```
RUN
 .1213501    .651861    .8688611    .7297625    .798853
Ok
```

```
RUN
 .1213501    .651861    .8688611    .7297625    .798853
Ok
```

In many cases a value less than 1 is not very helpful. Therefore, the computer can be told to create a number that is greater than 1 by using multiplication:

```
30    PRINT RND * 10,
```

This statement generates a number that is greater than 0 and less than 1 and then multiplies it by 10. When the program above is run with this new line 30 it produces:

```
RUN
 1.213501  6.51861  8.688611  7.297625  7.98853
Ok
```

There are several things to notice about these numbers. First, the numbers are all decimal fractions, which can be a problem when a programmer would prefer whole numbers. Second, the computer never picked 10 as one of the numbers. 10 will not be picked because RND always generates a number less than 1, and only 10 * 1 will produce a result of 10.

5.5 More Useful Random Numbers

By using the INT function, it is possible to generate only whole numbers. When line 30 of the program in Section 5.5 is replaced by

```
30    PRINT INT(RND * 10),
```

it produces:

```
RUN
 1          6          8          7          7
Ok
```

The value of each of these integers is between 0 and 9. By adding 1 we can generate whole numbers from 1 to 10, inclusive:

```
30    PRINT INT(RND * 10 + 1)
```

If 0 is the integer picked, adding 1 will give 1. If 9 is picked, adding 1 will give 10. Now when the program is run again, it may pick 10 but it will not pick 0:

```
RUN
 2          7          9          8          8
Ok
```

Review

5. Write a program that picks ten random integers from 1 to 100:

```
RUN
 12         65         87         73         80
 25         59         1          33         100
Ok
```

6. Write a program that picks two random integers between 1 and 25 and then adds them:

```
RUN
 17 + 3 = 20
Ok
```

5.6 Choosing Numbers from a Range

BASIC can also be told to create random numbers that are within a specific range. For example, picking numbers that are between 5 and 10 or 100 and 200 is done by using the following formula:

```
LOW + INT((HIGH - LOW + 1) * RND)
```

In this formula, the variable LOW stands for the lowest number in the range, and HIGH for the highest number in the range. To pick a number that is greater than or equal to 10 and less than or equal to 20, the formula is:

```
10 + INT((20 - 10 + 1) * RND)
```

or

```
10 + INT(11 * RND)
```

Note that the part of the formula (HIGH - LOW + 1) is really the number of integers in the set from which a random number can be selected. In the example above there are 11 integers in the set of 10 to 20, inclusive. Therefore, we can express the formula as:

```
<low value> + INT(<number in set> * RND)
```

This program produces addition problems by picking two random numbers. The computer then waits for the user to enter an answer:

```
10 REM ** Creates addition problems **
20 MORE$ = "y"
30 WHILE MORE$ = "y"
40   NUM1 = 100 + INT(901 * RND)
50   NUM2 = 1 + INT(100 * RND)
60   SUM = NUM1 + NUM2
70   PRINT NUM1; " + "; NUM2; " = ";
80   INPUT ANSWER
90   WHILE ANSWER <> SUM
100      PRINT "Wrong answer, try again."
110      PRINT
120      PRINT NUM1; " + "; NUM2; " = ";
130      INPUT ANSWER
140   WEND
150   PRINT "Correct!"
160   PRINT
170   INPUT "Try another problem (y/n)"; MORE$
180 WEND
999 END
```

```
RUN
 221 + 66 = ? 287
Correct!

Try another problem (y/n)? y
 968 + 73 = ? 1290
Wrong answer, try again.

 968 + 73 = ? 1041
Correct answer

Try another problem? n
Ok
```

Line 40 selects a random integer between 100 and 1000, inclusive, and line 50 one between 1 and 100, inclusive. Note how the WHILE loop at lines 90 through 140 continues to ask the user for another answer until the correct one is entered.

Review

7. Write a program that outputs 15 random integers from 10 to 20.

8. Write a program that selects one random integer from 25 to 50 and another from 1 to 25 and outputs their difference:

```
RUN
 37 - 17 = 20
Ok
```

5.7 Making RND More Random - RANDOMIZE TIMER

Each time a program is run it generates the same numbers in the same order. For anyone writing a game program, this is a problem because game players will quickly figure out the pattern of the numbers. To eliminate this problem, the following statement should be added to any program using random numbers:

```
RANDOMIZE TIMER
```

This statement "randomizes" the numbers that are picked so that the numbers will be different each time the program is run. The statement can be placed anywhere in a program, but it must be executed before the program begins choosing random numbers. Therefore, it is best to place it near the beginning of the program.

This game program selects a random number from 1 to 100 and then gives the player an unlimited number of chances to guess the number. After each guess the computer tells the player whether the guess is too high, too low or correct:

```
10 REM ** Allows user to guess random number
            between 1 and 100 **
20 RANDOMIZE TIMER
30 PRINT "I'm thinking of a number between 1
   and 100."
40 NUMBER = 1 + INT(100 * RND)
50 INPUT "What is your guess"; GUESS
60 WHILE GUESS <> NUMBER
70    IF GUESS < NUMBER THEN PRINT "Low...try
      again" ELSE PRINT "High...try again"
80    PRINT
90    INPUT "What is your guess"; GUESS
100 WEND
110 PRINT "You are correct!"
999 END
```

```
RUN
I'm thinking of a number between 1 and 100.
What is your guess? 50
High...try again

What is your guess? 25
You are correct!
Ok
```

```
RUN
I'm thinking of a number between 1 and 100.
What is your guess? 50
Low...try again

What is your guess? 75
High...try again

What is your guess? 65
High...try again

What is your guess? 60
Low...try again

What is your guess? 63
You are correct!
Ok
```

In the first run the number to be guessed is 25, and in the second run it is 63. This is caused by the RANDOMIZE TIMER statement at line 20. Lines 60 through 100 create a loop which is executed until the user enters the correct number. The number to be guessed is selected only once, at line 40.

5.8 Rounding Errors

The computer may make a slight error during a calculation, called a "rounding error." For example,

```
PRINT 1 / 3
.3333334
```

The result of this calculation is not accurate. Dividing 1 by 3 should give .3333333, not .3333334. Because it cannot store an infinite number of digits, BASIC rounds the last decimal place. This error is small and will usually not cause a difficulty. However, problems can arise when the computer is asked to compare values in an IF...THEN statement:

```
10 IF 1 / 3 = .3333333 THEN PRINT "Equal"
```

The computer will not consider the two values equal and therefore, no message will be printed. To overcome this problem, numbers being compared should be rounded off to less than 7 places before the IF...THEN comparison is made. The technique required to round numbers is explained later in the chapter.

5.9 Scientific Notation (E Notation)

When numeric values have more than seven digits, BASIC displays them in scientific or "E" notation:

```
PRINT 12345 * 12345
1.52399E+08
```

To work with such large numbers BASIC rounds off the number and uses scientific notation. Scientific notation uses the letter E followed by a sign and a number. If the E is followed by a plus sign, the number shown is multiplied by 10 raised to that power:

$$1.524138E+09 = 1.524138 * 10^9 = 1,524,138,000.0$$

This really means that the decimal point on the number shown is moved 9 places to the right. A minus sign means multiplying by 10 raised to that negative power:

$$3.567879E-04 = 3.567879 * 10^{-4} = 0.0003567879$$

Because it is negative, the decimal point is moved 4 places to the left. E notation may be used wherever a number is expected, including DATA statements. The E in DATA 5.8943E+06 will not cause an error.

Review

9. Change the following from E notation to standard notation:

    a) `1.42E-02`   d) `4.321E+05`
    b) `4.56231E+08`   e) `5.0E-03`
    c) `6.7087E+06`   f) `6.7896E-05`

10. What will be the output of the following program? Make your prediction, then type it in to see if you were correct:

```
10 REM ** Converts scientific notation **
20 FOR COUNT = 1 TO 3
30    READ NUMBER
40    PRINT NUMBER
50 NEXT COUNT
60 PRINT "All data read"
99 END
1000 DATA 0.5E-02, 1.234E+05, 1.9845E-05
```

5.10 Rounding Off Numbers

There are many situations where a program does not need or want numbers that are carried out to seven places. For example, it makes little sense to calculate a paycheck to the thousandth of a cent. Since the computer automatically calculates to seven places, it must be given specific instructions to round numbers.

To illustrate the proper method of rounding, we will round 5.4356 to the nearest hundredth. The result should leave us with 5.44. The first step of the rounding process is to multiply the number by 10 for each decimal place required. For example, to round to two decimal places (i.e., the nearest hundredth), we should multiply by 100 (10×10):

5.4356 * 100 = 543.56

Once this is done, the last required digit is rounded to its proper value by adding 0.5:

543.56 + 0.5 = 544.06

To attain the desired number of digits, INT is used to "chop off" the part of the number that is unwanted:

INT(544.06) = 544

Finally, the decimal point must be moved back where it belongs, by dividing by the number that was multiplied originally. In this example, since we multiplied by 100 at the beginning of the process, we must now divide by 100. This yields

544 / 100 = 5.44

which is the desired result. All of these steps can be incorporated into one statement:

```
ROUNDNUM = INT(5.4356 * 100 + 0.5) / 100
```

More generally, to round any number N to D decimal places, the formula is:

$$\text{INT}(N * 10^D + 0.5) / 10^D$$

If numbers are to be rounded on the left side of the decimal point, for example to the nearest hundred or ten, the D in the formula should be negative:

$$\text{INT}(N * 10^{-D} + 0.5) / 10^{-D}$$

For example, to round to the nearest thousand (e.g., 5845 rounds to 6000), use the statement:

$$\text{INT}(5845 * 10^{-3} + 0.5) / 10^{-3}$$

It should be noted that the PRINT USING statement, described in Chapter Four, displays numbers rounded to a specified number of places, but it does not actually change the number. To round a number, the technique described above must be employed.

This program asks the user to input a number and then state how many places it should be rounded to:

```
10 REM ** Rounds numbers to desired decimal
           places **
20 MORE$ = "y"
30 WHILE MORE$ = "y"
40    INPUT "Number to be rounded"; NUMBER
50    INPUT "How many decimal places"; PLACES
60    ROUND = INT(NUMBER * 10^PLACES + 0.5) /
      10^PLACES
70    PRINT NUMBER "rounded to" PLACES "places
      =" ROUND
80    PRINT
90    INPUT "Another (y/n)"; MORE$
100 WEND
999 END
```

```
RUN
Number to be rounded? 29.452
To how many decimal places? 1
 29.452 rounded to 1 places = 29.5

Another (y/n)? y
Number to be rounded? 376.344
To how many decimal places? -2
 376.344 rounded to-2 places = 400

Another (y/n)? n
Ok
```

Note how the second number is rounded to the nearest hundred by instructing the computer to round to -2 decimal places.

This program rounds off baseball batting averages to the nearest thousandth of a point:

```
10 REM ** Batting average calculator **
20 MORE$ = "y"
30 WHILE MORE$ = "y"
40    INPUT "Enter times at bat"; TIMES
50    INPUT "Enter number of hits"; HITS
60    AVERAGE = HITS / TIMES
70    RNDAVG = INT(AVERAGE * 1000 + 0.5) / 1000
80    PRINT USING "Batting average is: #.###";
      RNDAVG
90    PRINT
100   INPUT "Calculate another (y/n)"; MORE$
110 WEND
999 END
```

```
RUN
Enter times at bat? 12
Enter number of hits? 4
Batting average is: 0.333

Calculate another? y
Enter times at bat? 15
Enter number of hits? 6
Batting average is: 0.400

Calculate another? n
Ok
```

The PRINT USING statement at line 80 makes sure that the average has leading and trailing zeros. All rounding is performed in line 70.

Review

11. Write a program that accepts a number and rounds off to the nearest tenth:

```
RUN
What number is to be rounded? 25.9234
 25.9234 to the nearest tenth is 25.9
Ok
```

5.11 End of Chapter Problem

Since frogs are in short supply, the Calaveras County Frog Jumping Race has decided to use a computer to simulate this year's race. Allow the user to input the number of races that two championship frogs should compete in. Each jump is between 0.1 and 1.0 meter in length. The first frog who jumps over the finish line at 10 meters wins the race.

Algorithm:

1. Ask how many races will be run.
2. Begin a race
   a. Let each of the frogs jump.
   b. Add the jump to the total distance the frog has travelled.
   c. Check if the finish line at 10 meters has been crossed.
   d. If not, return to step (a).
3. Determine which frog won and print the result.
4. Return to step 2 and race again until input number of races has been run.

Input: Number of races to be run   NUMRACES

Output: Print the winning frog and the distance by which it won the race.

```
10 REM ** Simulates frog jumping contest **
20 RANDOMIZE TIMER
30 INPUT "How many races"; NUMRACES
40 FOR RACE = 1 TO NUMRACES
50    LENGTH1 = 0
60    LENGTH2 = 0
70    WHILE LENGTH1 < 10 AND LENGTH2 < 10
80       LENGTH1 = LENGTH1 + INT(10 * RND + .5) / 10
90       LENGTH2 = LENGTH2 + INT(10 * RND + .5) / 10
100   WEND
110   IF LENGTH1 > LENGTH2 THEN PRINT USING "Frog
      1 wins by #.# meters."; 10 - LENGTH2 ELSE
      PRINT USING "Frog 2 wins by #.# meters.";
      10 - LENGTH1
120 NEXT RACE
130 PRINT "All races completed!"
999 END
```

```
RUN
How many races? 2
Frog 1 wins by 2.5 meters.
Frog 2 wins by 0.1 meters.
All races completed!
Ok
```

```
RUN
How many races? 5
Frog 2 wins by 0.2 meters.
Frog 1 wins by 3.4 meters.
Frog 2 wins by 1.1 meters.
Frog 1 wins by 2.0 meters.
Frog 1 wins by 0.4 meters.
All races completed!
Ok
```

At line 30 the user enters the number of races to be run. Lines 40 through 120 create a FOR loop which executes that number of times, once for each race to be run. Note lines 50 and 60. The lengths that the frogs have jumped must be set to 0 at the beginning of each race. The WHILE loop at lines 70 through 100 controls the individual races. Lines 80 and 90 determine how far each frog has jumped. A random number between 0.1 and 1.0 is added to each length to determine a new value of the length so far. When either of the lengths exceeds 10, the WHILE loop is exited and the winner is determined. Line 110 prints the distance of the losing frog from the finish line (which is at 10 meters).

Review

12. A careless programmer forgot lines 50 and 60 in the End of Chapter program above. What is the result of running the program without these lines?

13. a) A very rare occurrence is that both frogs will reach the finish line at exactly the same time, and the race will be a tie. Modify the End of Chapter program to account for this.

    b) Modify the program to keep track of how many races each frog wins and the number of ties:

    ```
    RUN
    How many races? 10
    Frog 1 wins by 1.2 meters.
     . . .
    All races completed!
    Frog 1 won 6 races.
    Frog 2 won 4 races.
     0 races were ties.
    Ok
    ```

Chapter Summary

When evaluating mathematical expressions the computer employs an specific order of operations. First it carries out exponentiation operations, then multiplication and division, and finally addition and subtraction. Operations of the same priority are performed in order from left to right. The order of operations may be changed by using parentheses; the operations within parentheses are performed first. When parentheses are used within parentheses, the computer executes the operation within the innermost set first.

BASIC displays all numbers as decimals, including fractions and mixed numbers. Numbers are displayed to 7 decimal places, only 6 of which are precise.

An integer is a whole number without decimal places. The INT function returns only the whole number portion of a number, discarding any decimals. For example, INT(35.9) returns 35. The value that the integer function returns is always equal to or smaller than the original value, therefore, INT(-5.8) = -6.

The RND function returns a random number greater than or equal to zero but less than one. Random numbers can be generated within a specified range using the formula:

    <low> + INT(<number in set> * RND)

For example, to generate random numbers in the range 75 to 90, inclusive the formula is:

    75 + INT(16 * RND)

Including the statement RANDOMIZE TIMER at the beginning of a program guarantees that a different set of random numbers is generated each time the program is run.

When numeric values exceed seven digits, the computer displays them in scientific or "E" notation (i.e., 5,632,181 is displayed as 5.63218E+06).

Because the computer can store only a finite number of places, it may make a slight error called "rounding error" when storing numbers of more than six decimal places. For example, the number 0.6666666 is stored as 0.6666667.

In many instances a programmer does not want numbers carried out to seven places. To round any number N to D decimal places, the formula is:

    ROUNDNUM = INT(N * 10^D + 0.5) / 10^D

Vocabulary

Floating point number - Number with a decimal point and decimals. Also called "real" numbers.

INT ( ) - Function that returns the integer portion of a floating point number.

Integer - A whole number or the whole number part of a mixed number.

Numeric accuracy - The number of decimals used to express a number.

Order of operations - The order in which the computer carries out math operations beginning with exponents, then multiplication and division, and finally addition and subtraction.

Random number - A number picked by chance.

RANDOMIZE TIMER - Statement that causes the computer to pick a different set of random numbers each time a program is run.

RND - A function that returns a random number greater than or equal to zero but less than one.

Rounding error - An error that may be made by the computer in storing numbers containing more than 6 decimal places.

Scientific notation - Displaying large numbers as a decimal times a specified power of ten (e.g., 345.68 = 3.4568E+02). Also called "E" notation.

Exercises

1. Write a program that prints ten random integers from -10 to 10, inclusive.

2. Write a program which generates three random numbers between 0 and 1, and prints their sum.

3. Write a program which generates 50 random numbers between 0 and 1, but prints only those numbers which are greater than 0.5.

4. Write a program that generates 50 random numbers between 1 and 5000. Print out only the lowest and highest number in the set.

5. Write a program that generates 10 random integers between 8 and 25, inclusive, and prints them on the same line. The output should be similar to:

    ```
    RUN
    17   12   22   25   8   17   19   11   21   23
    Ok
    ```

6. Write a program that generates 25 random integers between 1 and another random number between 5 and 20, inclusive:

    ```
    RUN
    Between 1 and 17:  5
    Between 1 and  5:  1
     . . .
    Between 1 and 11: 11
    Ok
    ```

7. Write a program that allows the user to input numbers. Have the computer indicate which numbers are integers and which are not. (Hint: Compare the number with INT(number).)

    ```
    RUN
    Enter a number? 56.3
     56.3 is not an integer
    Ok
    ```

8. Allow a user to guess a random integer between -3 and 4, inclusive, picked by the computer. Have the program print whether the guess is correct or not. If the guess is wrong, print the correct value:

    ```
    RUN
    Enter your guess (-3 to 4)? 2
    Wrong! The number is 1.
    Ok

    RUN
    Enter your guess (-3 to 4)? -2
    Correct!
    Ok
    ```

9. Have a program randomly determine how many coins you have in your pocket. You may have from 2 to 5 nickels, 1 to 4 dimes and 0 to 3 quarters. Lunch costs 99 cents. The program is to report the amount that you have and whether you are able to buy lunch with it:

    ```
    RUN
    You have $0.45
    Sorry, you can't buy lunch.
    Ok

    RUN
    You have $1.25
    You can buy lunch.
    Ok
    ```

10. a) Write a program which prints the sum of X random numbers between 0 and 1. Have the user enter a value for X:

    ```
    RUN
    How many numbers? 6
    The sum is 4.3276
    Ok
    ```

    b) Modify the program written in part (a) to round the sum to 2 decimal places:

    ```
    RUN
    How many numbers? 6
    The sum is 4.33
    Ok
    ```

11. You have applied for a job with an unusual pay scale. On the first day you are paid one penny. Every day thereafter your salary is double that of the previous day. Write a program which calculates your earnings after working for 30 days.

12. A child puts pennies into a piggy bank once a week. The bank initially contains 11 pennies. Write a program to allow pennies to be added each week and to print the dollar value of the bank's contents after each addition. The input of a 0 should halt the program:

```
RUN
Enter number of pennies? 7
Total value = $ 0.18

Enter number of pennies? 35
Total value = $ 0.53

Enter number of pennies? 0
Calculations completed
Ok
```

13. a) Have the computer simulate a game of dice between 2 players. Each player rolls 5 dice. If a five is showing on any of the die, the player's turn continues. The player's turn ends when a roll contains no 5's. The winner is the first player whose total score reaches 500 or greater.

    b) Modify the program so that before a total can begin accumulating the player must achieve a score of at least 50 in a single turn.

14. Write a program to flip a coin 50 times and print the total number of heads and tails. Run the program several times to get a comparison among the runs:

```
RUN
Number of heads = 26
Number of tails = 24
Ok

RUN
Number of heads = 23
Number of tails = 27
Ok
```

15. Input a positive integer and print all positive integers that are factors of that integer. The output should be similar to:

```
RUN
A positive integer, please? 1.4
Your number is not a positive integer.
A positive integer, please? 12

Factors of 12 are 1 2 3 4 6 12
Ok
```

16. a) Write a program that allows the user to enter an integer greater than 1 and then tells the user whether the integer is prime. A prime number is any integer that is evenly divisible only by itself or 1. For example, the numbers 2, 3, 5 and 7 are prime, but 4 and 9 are not. Test the integer by repeatedly dividing it by integers smaller than itself but larger than 1 and checking whether the quotient is whole. If so, the integer is not prime. The output should be similar to:

```
RUN
Integer > 1 please? 12
That integer is not prime.
Ok

RUN
Integer > 1 please? 17
That integer is prime.
Ok
```

b) Modify the program written above to print all the prime integers between 1 and 100.

17. Generate 1000 random integers between 1 and 9, inclusive, and print how many are even and how many are odd. The output should be similar to the following:

```
RUN
There are 577 odd integers.
There are 423 even integers.
Ok
```

18. Write a program that plays a numbers game. Allow the user to enter 3 integers, each between 1 and 5, and an amount to be bet. Have the computer then generate three random numbers, also between 1 and 5. Calculate the sums of both sets of numbers. The payoff for matching the sums is calculated by multiplying the sum times 21.50:

```
RUN
Enter 3 integers from 1 to 5: 2, 4, 3
Enter a bet: 10
The computer picks:  1  3  5
Your sum: 9     Computer's sum: 9
Match! You win $ 193.50
Ok
```

19. Write a program that allows the user and computer to alternately select integers between 3 and 12, inclusive. Keep a sum of all the integers selected and declare the winner to be the one who selects that integer which makes the sum greater than 50. Have the user pick again if a number out of the proper range is entered:

```
RUN
Enter a number (3 to 12)? 12
The computer picks 9
You: 12      Computer: 9

Enter a number (3 to 12)? 15
 15 is not a proper number, pick again
Enter a number (3 to 12)? 10
The computer picks 6
You: 22      Computer: 15

. . .

Enter a number (3 to 12)? 11
The computer picks 7
You: 49      Computer: 51

The computer wins!
Ok
```

20. A bank pays interest once a year at a yearly rate of 5%. A man deposits $1000 on January 1, 1992 and wishes to leave it there to accrue interest until the balance is at least $2000. Compute the balance on January 1 of each year, starting with 1993 and ending in the year when the balance exceeds $2000. The output should be similar to:

```
RUN
Date              Balance
Jan 1, 1993       $ 1050.00
Jan 1, 1994       $ 1102.50
. . .                . . .
. . .             $ 1979.93
. . .             $ 2078.93
Ok
```

Advanced Exercises

Each of the following exercises requires the development of a detailed algorithm. The program should not be written until all details of the algorithm have been worked out.

21. Write a program to simulate a simplified version of the game "21." A deck of cards numbered from 1 to 10 are used and any number can be repeated since the deck contains many cards. The computer starts by asking you how many cards you want. It then deals you the cards, which are randomly picked, and totals their value. If the value exceeds 21, you automatically lose. If your value is under 21, the computer deals itself three randomly picked cards. The winner is the one with the

highest score equal to or less than 21. Write your program so that the game can be played 10 consecutive times with the winner of each game winning one point. At the end of the 10 games print out the total winnings for you and the computer. The example below shows only the last four of the ten games:

```
RUN
. . .
How many cards do you want? 3
You: 8  5  1
Me:  8  3  3
I have 14 and you have 14 so we draw.

How many cards do you want? 2
You: 7  2
Me:  8  7  4
I have 19 and you have 9 so I WIN!

How many cards do you want? 3
You: 8  7  4
Me:  2  1  7
I have 10 and you have 19 so YOU WIN!

How many cards do you want? 3
You: 2  2  9
Me:  1  7  9
I have 17 and you have 13 so I WIN!

My winnings = 5
Your winnings = 3
Draws = 2
Ok
```

22. Design a program that will act as a computerized cash register for a school book store. The book store inventory is as follows:

ITEM	CODE #	PRICE
Note Book	100	$1.59
Folder	101	$0.79
Black Pen	202	$0.29
Text Book	300	variable
Ruler	400	$0.59
Calculator	500	$21.00
Miscellaneous	600	variable

The program should allow a salesperson to enter the product code and quantity of an item. If the item has a variable price, (code 300 or 600), the program asks for the price. When all the items have been entered, the salesperson enters 0 in response to the item code. The program then calculates and displays a total, including tax at 6%, rounded to the nearest cent. It also calculates and displays the amount of change the customer receives:

```
RUN
                  SCHOOL BOOK STORE
Item code? 100
Quantity? 3
  3 Note Book(s)          @ $  1.59           $4.77

Item Code? 300
Quantity? 1
Price? 15.00
  1 Text Book(s)          @ $ 15.00          $15.00

Item Code? 0

Bill of Sale
  3 Note Book(s)          @ $  1.59          $4.77
  1 Text Book(s)          @ $ 15.00          $15.00

      SUBTOTAL                               $19.77
      TAX                                     $1.19
      TOTAL                                  $20.96
Amount tendered $? 21.00
      CHANGE                                  $0.04
Ok
```

Chapter 6

Programming and Debugging Techniques

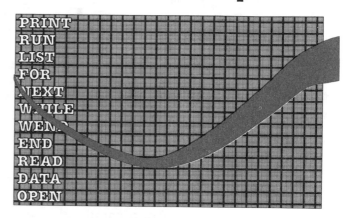

GOSUB

RETURN

ON . . . GOSUB

STOP

CONT

TRON

TROFF

Objectives

Chapter Six

After completing this chapter you will be able to:

1. Simplify a long program by dividing it into subroutines using GOSUB and RETURN.

2. Branch to a number of separate subroutines using ON...GOSUB.

3. Solve a problem using top-down planning to produce a program that flows logically and is easy to understand .

4. Use debugging techniques to locate errors and correct in a program.

5. Hand trace through a program using test data.

6. Debug a program by using additional PRINT statements.

7. Halt program execution with STOP and resume execution with CONT.

8. Follow the sequence in which program lines are executed using TRON and TROFF.

*W*riting programs that work properly and are easy to modify and correct requires planning and organization. Because the computer must be given many specific instructions to carry out even simple tasks, a program can easily become long and complex, increasing the opportunity for error. Therefore, writing a program is made easier if time is first spent carefully planning it. This is done by first developing a detailed algorithm which then acts as an outline for creating the computer program.

This chapter will explain new techniques and statements that help to simplify lengthy and complex programs. In addition, a series of techniques is presented that can be employed to find and correct programming errors.

6.1 GOSUB and RETURN

To simplify longer, more complex programs it is good programming practice to divide programs into sections called "subroutines." These subroutines can be activated or "called" from anywhere in the program. For instance, a long program can be divided into a main section followed by a series of subroutines. The main section describes the order in which the subroutines will be called, while each subroutine is written as if it were a short program that had only a simple task to perform. Another important use of subroutines is to reduce the size of a program by allowing a routine that is used several times to be written only once. Each time the programmer wants the computer to perform that task, the program simply tells the computer to call that subroutine.

GOSUB is the instruction that calls a subroutine. The computer is told to execute the statements in a subroutine by

    GOSUB <line number>

where <line number> is the number of the first line in the subroutine. When the subroutine has completed its task, the statement

    RETURN

returns to the line immediately following the one which called the subroutine. For example:

```
10 REM ** Demonstrates subroutines **
   . . .
100 REM ** Main program
110 GOSUB 2000 : REM ** Subroutine 1
120 . . .
   . . .
240 GOSUB 2000 : REM ** Subroutine 1
250 . . .
   . . .
999 END
1990 REM
2000 REM ** Subroutine 1 - Performs a task
2010  . . .
2020  . . .
2030 RETURN
```

When line 110 is executed, it calls the subroutine at line 2000. Lines 2000, 2010 and 2020 are then executed and the RETURN at line 2030 sends the program back to line 120. When line 240 calls the subroutine, lines 2000, 2010 and 2020 are again executed, and the RETURN sends the program back to line 250.

The "main" program (lines 100 - 999) contains the statements which call subroutines as needed. As a matter of style we will number the main program lines beginning at 100. Subroutines are placed at the end of a program following the main program. It is important to place the END statement before those used for the subroutines to avoid executing the subroutines without calling them.

To make a subroutine stand out as part of the program structure it is a good practice to place a blank REM before the subroutine and then begin the subroutine with a REM statement that describes its function. Note how the subroutine above begins at line 2000. We will number each subroutine in our programs beginning at 1000, 2000, etc. to make them stand out.

Subroutines may contain any number of lines — the example above was kept short for demonstration purposes. However, each subroutine should perform only one well-defined task. A subroutine with 40 or 50 lines is probably performing too much work and should be broken down into two or more subroutines.

GOSUB can be used in many situations. For instance, GOSUB can be used to call a subroutine from an IF...THEN statement

```
50 IF NETPAY > 500 THEN GOSUB 2000 : REM **
   Print taxes
```

or in a WHILE loop:

```
80 WHILE GUESS <> NUMBER
90   GOSUB 1000 : REM ** Get user guess
   . . .
```

Note the style used in the last two examples. Placing a REM after each GOSUB helps the reader understand the program, and makes it easier to debug.

Although it is possible to have more than one RETURN statement in a subroutine, this is a bad programming practice that can lead to confusion. Therefore, we will use only one RETURN in a subroutine.

This program shows how a single subroutine may be reused to perform slightly different tasks. Given the numbers of pennies, nickels, dimes and quarters as input, it calculates the total amount of money represented by the coins. One subroutine processes and reports the amount of money involved for each of the four types of coins:

```
10 REM ** Computes value of coins **
100 REM ** Main program
110 COIN$ = "pennies" : VALUE = .01
120 GOSUB 1000 : REM ** Inputs and totals pennies
130 COIN$ = "nickles" : VALUE = .05
140 GOSUB 1000 : REM ** Inputs and totals nickles
150 COIN$ = "dimes" : VALUE = .1
160 GOSUB 1000 : REM ** Inputs and totals dimes
170 COIN$ = "quarters" : VALUE = .25
180 GOSUB 1000 : REM ** Inputs and totals quarters
190 PRINT USING "Value of coins = $$#.##"; TOTAL
999 END
1000 REM ** Subroutine to input and total coins
1010 PRINT "How many "; COIN$;
1020 INPUT NUMCOINS
1030 PRINT NUMCOINS; COIN$; " =";
1040 PRINT USING "$$#.##"; NUMCOINS * VALUE
1050 TOTAL = TOTAL + (NUMCOINS * VALUE)
1060 PRINT
1070 RETURN
```

```
RUN
How many pennies? 5
 5 pennies = $0.05

How many nickles? 8
 8 nickles = $0.40

How many dimes? 12
 12 dimes = $1.20

How many quarters? 7
 7 quarters = $1.75

Value of coins =   $3.40
Ok
```

The subroutine at line 1000 is called four times (by lines 120, 140, 160, 180). Just before each call, the value of COIN$ which stores the name of the coin and VALUE which is the monetary value of the coin, is changed. Lines 1000 through 1070 input the number of each coin, calculate its value and add it to the total. Using a subroutine has avoided repeating these lines four times.

Note lines 1010 and 1020. An INPUT prompt cannot contain a variable. However, it is useful to print the name of the coin (COIN$) in this prompt. To do this, a PRINT is used before the INPUT. The semicolon (;) at the end of the PRINT statement keeps the cursor on the same line, so that when the INPUT is executed the question mark appears directly after the name of the coin.

Review

1. Modify the program in Section 6.1 so that 50 cent and dollar coins can also be used:

    ```
    RUN
    How many pennies? 3
     3 pennies = $0.03

       . . .

    How many quarters? 5
     5 quarters = $1.25

    How many 50 cent pieces? 3
     3 50 cent pieces = $1.50

    How many dollar coins? 4
     4 dollar coins = $4.00

    Value of coins = $7.98
    Ok
    ```

2. Write a program which contains 4 subroutines. Each subroutine prints one of the following comments:

    ```
    is a fantastic person.
    is tough to get along with.
    is growing older day by day.
    is one of my best friends.
    ```

    When a name is entered have the program randomly choose one of the comments to be printed along with the name:

    ```
    RUN
    Enter a name? Matilda
    Matilda is growing older day by day.
    Ok
    ```

    ```
    RUN
    Enter a name? Hortense
    Hortense is one of my best friends.
    Ok
    ```

3. Write a program that asks for a student's name and four grades, and then computes the average grade. Use a subroutine to enter the data from the keyboard (only valid grades) and a second subroutine to calculate the average rounded to 1 decimal place:

```
RUN
Enter student name? Johnson
Enter grade 1? 75
Enter grade 2? 83
Enter grade 3? 72
Enter grade 4? 91
The average for Johnson is 80.2
Ok
```

6.2 ON...GOSUB

The ON...GOSUB statement is like a special type of IF...THEN statement. It allows a program to branch to a number of separate subroutines based on the value of a variable:

```
ON <variable> GOSUB <line1>, <line2>, . . .
```

When the value of the <variable> is 1, the program branches to the first subroutine starting at line number <line1>. When the value is 2, it branches to the second subroutine, and so on. For example,

```
140 ON CHOICE GOSUB 1000, 3000, 4000
```

When CHOICE is 1 it calls the subroutine at line 1000. When CHOICE is 2 it calls the subroutine at line 3000 and when it is 3, it calls the third at line 4000. If the value of CHOICE is less than 1 or greater than the number of subroutines listed, execution moves directly to the next statement in the program ignoring the ON...GOSUB. ON...GOSUB saves both time and space because it allows a program to branch to a specific subroutine without having to write a long list of IF...THEN statements.

This program uses ON...GOSUB to deliver a synopsis of a selected Shakespearean play:

```
10 REM ** Prints synopsis of chosen
           Shakespearean play **
100 REM ** Main program
110 PRINT "Choose a Shakespearean play:"
120 PRINT "  1 - Hamlet     2 - MacBeth
    3 - Othello"
130 GOSUB 1000 : REM ** Input and check data
140 ON CHOICE GOSUB 2000, 3000, 4000
150 PRINT "** End of synopsis **"
999 END
1000 REM ** Input and check data
1010 INPUT "Enter number"; CHOICE
1020 WHILE CHOICE < 1 OR CHOICE > 3
1030    PRINT "Number must be 1, 2, or 3"
1040    INPUT "Enter number"; CHOICE
1050 WEND
1060 RETURN
1990 REM
```

```
2000 REM ** Hamlet Subroutine
2010 PRINT "Hamlet has a fight with his mother"
2020 PRINT "and makes a very long speech."
2030 PRINT "He also has a disagreement with"
2040 PRINT "his step-father."
2050 RETURN
2990 REM
3000 REM ** MacBeth Subroutine
3010 PRINT "MacBeth and Mrs. MacBeth plot to
      kill"
3020 PRINT "most of the other people in the
      play."
3030 PRINT "Witches confuse the plot by singing"
3040 PRINT "and boiling pots of foul smelling
      liquid."
3050 RETURN
3990 REM
4000 REM ** Othello Subroutine
4010 PRINT "Othello is in love with Desdemona,"
4020 PRINT "but he is very jealous."
4030 PRINT "He murders Desdemona, believing her"
4040 PRINT "to love another."
4050 RETURN
```

```
RUN
Choose a Shakespearean play:
  1 - Hamlet    2 - MacBeth    3 - Othello
Enter number? 3
Othello is in love with Desdemona,
but he is very jealous.
He murders Desdemona, believing her
to love another.
** End of synopsis **
Ok
```

```
RUN
Choose a Shakespearean play:
  1 - Hamlet     2 - MacBeth     3 - Othello
Enter number? 27
Number must be 1, 2, or 3
Enter number? -12
Number must be 1, 2, or 3
Enter number? 1
Hamlet has a fight with his mother
and makes a very long speech.
He also has a disagreement with
his step-father.
** End of synopsis **
Ok
```

The subroutine at line 1000 checks to determine if the user has entered a proper number (1, 2 or 3). If a proper number is entered at line 1010, the WHILE loop is skipped. If an improper number is entered the INPUT statement at line 1040 continues to ask for a new number until a proper one is entered. Note how the ON...GOSUB statement at line 140 then sends the program to the desired subroutine. After the subroutine is complete, execution returns to line 150 and a message is printed.

Review

4. Rewrite Review 2 using an ON...GOSUB statement

5. Write a program that asks the user to enter two numbers and then indicate whether the numbers are to be added, subtracted, multiplied or divided. Use an ON...GOSUB statement and four subroutines, one for each of the processes:

```
RUN
Enter first number: 75
Enter second number: 83
A)dd  S)ubtract  M)ultiply  D)ivide? M
 75 * 83 = 6225
Ok

RUN
Enter first number: 259
Enter second number: 3748
A)dd  S)ubtract  M)ultiply  D)ivide? S
 259 - 3748 = -3489
Ok
```

6.3 Planning a Program

Now that you are familiar with most of the BASIC statements it is important to spend time refining your programming techniques. As problems become more sophisticated and the programs to solve them longer, the development of a clear and unambiguous algorithm becomes increasingly important. You should review the steps given in Chapter 2 for planning a program. A useful technique in developing an algorithm is to first determine what the input, processing and output of the program will be. After this the details needed to produce the desired output can be filled in.

Proper planning enables the programmer to avoid the common mistake of writing the program before the problem or its solution is fully understood. Premature coding frequently results in a program which must be drastically modified by adding or deleting lines until the desired output is achieved, with the consequence that the final program is usually a jumble of statements which do not flow logically from one to another. Moreover, the code itself will lack clarity and will be less easily understood by other programmers. Therefore, one should plan a program as thoroughly as possible before using the computer. As the computer pioneer R.W. Hamming declared, "Typing is no substitute for thinking."

The correct method for planning the solution to a lengthy problem is called "top-down" planning, which involves working on the major portions of the solution first and leaving specifics until later. The problem is first broken down into large blocks with details of the blocks filled in afterwards. We will use subroutines to code each of the large blocks.

Most problems can be broken down into three broad areas: input, processing and output. Input is where needed data is entered. Processing is the steps required to take the input and produce the desired output, and output is the new data produced by the program.

As an example of this approach we are going to solve again the end of chapter problem from Chapter Four. By breaking the problem down into separate parts and using subroutines to program the parts, we will be able to produce a better solution.

The program allows the user to enter a student identification number and then searches DATA statements to determine if the student's data is stored. If it is, the student's name, grade average and status (Honors, Passing or Failing) are displayed.

We start by outlining the three major operations of our solution:

Algorithm:

1. **Input** - The ID number of the student to be found. Since student identification numbers are three digit (100 to 999) we must check to make sure that a proper number is input.

2. **Process** - Search the data to determine if a student with the input ID number exists. If found, calculate the average and determine the status. If not found print an appropriate message.

3. **Output** - If the ID is found, display the student name, average and status. If not found print a message. Ask if another search is desired and, if so, return to step 1.

The next step is to give names to the input and output variables:

Input: Student ID # to find   ID

Output: Student Name   NAME1$
              Grade average   AVERAGE
              Message   MESSAGE$

The completed program is shown on the next page. Note how each problem outlined above is solved by a separate subroutine:

```
10 REM ** Searches list for input student ID **
20 REM ** If found, calculates average and
           prints status **
100 REM ** Main program
110 MORE$ = "Y"
120 WHILE MORE$ = "Y" OR MORE$ = "y"
130    GOSUB 1000 : REM ** Input and check data
140    FOUND$ = "NO"
150    GOSUB 2000 : REM ** Search data
160    IF FOUND$ = "NO" THEN PRINT "Student # "
       ID "not found" ELSE GOSUB 3000 : REM **
       Display average and message
170    PRINT
180    INPUT "Check another student (Y/N)"; MORE$
190 WEND
999 END
1000 REM ** Input and check data
1010 INPUT "Enter student ID #"; ID
1020 WHILE ID < 100 OR ID > 999
1030    PRINT "Improper ID!"
1040    PRINT "ID must be between 100 and 999"
1050    INPUT "Enter student ID #"; ID
1060 WEND
1070 RETURN
1990 REM
2000 REM ** Search data
2010 RESTORE
2020 READ STUID, NAME1$, GRADE1, GRADE2,
     GRADE3, GRADE4
2030 WHILE STUID <> ID AND STUID <> -1
2040    READ STUID, NAME1$, GRADE1, GRADE2,
        GRADE3, GRADE4
2050 WEND
2060 IF STUID = ID THEN FOUND$ = "YES"
2070 RETURN
2990 REM
3000 REM ** Display average and message
3010 AVERAGE = (GRADE1 + GRADE2 + GRADE3 +
     GRADE4) / 4
3020 IF AVERAGE >= 80 THEN MESSAGE$ = "Honors"
     ELSE IF AVERAGE >= 60 THEN MESSAGE$ =
     "Passing" ELSE MESSAGE$ = "Failing"
3030 PRINT USING " \              \ ##.#        \
     \"; NAME1$, AVERAGE, MESSAGE$
3040 RETURN
8990 REM
9000 REM ** Student data - ID#, Name, Grade1,
            Grade2, Grade3, Grade4
9010 DATA 313, Presley, 67, 89, 90, 78
9020 DATA 472, Freitas, 79, 90, 89, 92
9030 DATA 625, Brown, 65, 78, 55, 45
9040 DATA 636, Crane, 78, 76, 65, 70
9050 DATA 756, Sechton, 65, 50, 54, 70
9060 DATA -1, End of Data, 0, 0, 0, 0
```

```
RUN
Enter student ID #? 313
Presley           81.0        Honors

Check another student (Y/N)? Y
Enter student ID #? 47
Improper ID!
ID must be between 100 and 999
Enter student ID #? 636
Crane             72.3        Passing

Check another student (Y/N)? Y
Enter student ID #? 222
Student # 222 not found

Check another student (Y/N)? Y
Enter student ID #? 756
Sechton           59.8        Failing

Check another student (Y/N)? N
Ok
```

Study the program carefully and check the output to determine how the program handles the different possible results: found ID, invalid ID, and not found ID as well as Honors, Passing and Failing averages. Each subroutine performs one of the major operations — input (1000), processing (2000), and calculations and output (3000). Note the RE-STORE statement at line 2010. As discussed in Chapter 4, this causes the READing to return to the first item in the DATA statements.

6.4 Finding Errors - Debugging

No matter how carefully planned, the longer a program the more likely it is to contain errors. Debugging is the process of locating errors or "bugs" in a program and correcting them. Obviously, when a program has been broken down into well-defined subroutines, it is easier to locate and correct errors. There are two basic types of errors which cause a program to work improperly; syntax and logic errors.

A syntax error is caused by entering a statement improperly.

```
10 REED X, Y
```

produces a `Syntax error in 10`. The statement should be:

```
10 READ X, Y
```

A second type of syntax error is caused by an instruction that is not in agreement with the computer's rules of operation. For example,

```
10 READ AGE
20 DATA Smith
```

causes the computer to halt execution with the error message `Syntax error in 20` because an attempt has been made to read the string "Smith" into the numeric variable AGE.

An error that produces an output different than what is desired is called a logic error, and frequently results from an incorrect analysis of the program's task. The Skyhook International Company wrote this short program to keep track of the number of skyhooks it has in inventory. There are initially 145 hooks:

```
10 REM ** Skyhook inventory **
20 MORE$ = "Y"
30 WHILE MORE$ = "y" OR MORE$ = "Y"
40    HOOKS = 145
50    INPUT "Hooks sold"; ORDER
60    HOOKS = HOOKS - ORDER
70    PRINT "Hooks now on hand:"; HOOKS
80    PRINT
90    INPUT "Another order (y/n)"; MORE$
100 WEND
110 PRINT "Calculations complete"
999 END
```

```
RUN
Hooks sold? 45
Hooks now on hand: 100

Another order (y/n)? y
Hooks sold? 30
Hooks now on hand: 115

Another order (y/n)? n
Calculations complete
Ok
```

The program appears to work at first, but the output is obviously incorrect since the company cannot have more hooks left after filling the second order than it had after filling the first. The programmer has made a logic error by placing line 40, which set the initial value of HOOKS, inside the loop. This causes the computer to keep resetting the value of HOOKS to 145 each time the loop is repeated. Moving line 40 outside the loop corrects this logic error:

```
15 HOOKS = 145
40
```

```
RUN
Hooks sold? 45
Hooks now on hand: 100

Another order (y/n)? y
Hooks sold? 30
Hooks now on hand: 70

Another order (y/n)? n
Calculations complete
Ok
```

Take careful note of line 30. The loop will execute if the user types an uppercase "Y" or lowercase "y". This small detail does not take much code, yet makes the program easier to use, which is a goal of all good programs.

6.5 Testing a Program: Hand Tracing

One way to create confidence in a program's output is to manually trace through the program using test data. This is called "hand tracing." It is best to use test data that covers the range of anticipated program input. For example, the program in Section 6.3 had five possible inputs: invalid ID, ID not found, and ID found with Honors, Passing or Failing status. If the program produces the same results as those obtained by hand tracing for each of these cases, the program can usually be considered reliable.

This program calculates the sum of the integers from 1 to an input number. For example, if a 3 is input the sum should equal 1 + 2 + 3, or 6. The program is repeated as many times as the user requests:

```
10 REM ** Prints sum of the first N integers **
20 MORE$ = "y"
30 WHILE MORE$ = "y" OR MORE$ = "Y"
40    INPUT "How many integers"; NUMBER
50    FOR COUNT = 1 TO NUMBER
60       SUM = SUM + COUNT
70    NEXT COUNT
80    PRINT "The sum of 1 to" NUMBER "=" SUM
90    PRINT
100   INPUT "Calculate another sum (y/n)"; MORE$
110 WEND
999 END
```

```
RUN
How many integers? 3
The sum of 1 to 3 = 6

Calculate another sum (y/n)? y
How many integers? 2
The sum of 1 to 2 = 9

Calculate another sum (y/n)? n
Ok
```

If the output is checked by hand for NUMBER = 3, 6 is the correct value for SUM (1 + 2 + 3 = 6). However, if the programmer relies only on this test data, then a serious logic error will be overlooked. In checking the result for the second input, NUMBER = 2, SUM should equal 3, (1 + 2 = 3), but instead the program shows SUM as 9. This program contains a logic error.

To find the bug, we make a table that shows the value of each variable line-by-line. We record only lines for which a variable changes value or is printed:

Line	NUMBER	COUNT	SUM	
30	0	0	0	
40	3	0	0	User enters 3
50	3	1	0	
60	3	1	1	
50	3	2	1	
60	3	2	3	
50	3	3	3	
60	3	3	6	
80	3	–	6	Prints 3 and 6
40	2	–	6	← Error!
50	2	1	6	
60	2	1	7	
50	2	2	7	
60	2	2	9	
80	2	–	9	Prints 2 and 9

When the program begins execution all variables have an initial value of 0. A value is not changed unless there is an assignment statement. The error becomes apparent when the computer returns to line 40 a second time to have a new value entered for NUMBER. At line 50 COUNT properly returns to a value of 1, but SUM still contains the value 6 when it should be 0. At line 60 1 is added to 6 rather than 0. This is a common error which can be easily corrected by adding a line which resets SUM to 0 inside the loop:

```
35 SUM = 0
```

```
RUN
How many integers? 3
The sum of 1 to 3 = 6

Calculate another sum (y/n)? y
How many integers? 2
The sum of 1 to 2 = 3

Calculate another sum (y/n)? n
Ok
```

Note that the sum of 2 integers is now correctly shown to be 3.

Review

6. Trace the execution of the following and determine its output:

```
10 REM ** Review 6: Trace this program **
20 FOR COUNT = 1 TO 5 STEP 2
30   READ NUM1, NUM2
40   SUM1 = SUM1 + NUM1 - NUM2
50   SUM2 = SUM2 - NUM1 + NUM2
60 NEXT COUNT
70 PRINT SUM1, SUM2
99 END
1000 DATA 1, 3, 2, 4, 3, 5
```

7. The following program has a logic error (i.e, the program runs, but the output is incorrect). Find and correct the error:

```
10 REM ** Prints the sum of three numbers **
20 FOR COUNT = 1 TO 3
30 READ NUM1, NUM2, NUM2
40 NEXT COUNT
50 PRINT "Sum = " NUM1 + NUM2 + NUM3
99 END
1000 REM ** Number 1, Number 2, Number 3
1010 DATA 5, 12, 7, 9, 8, 3, 32, 71, 34
```

8. The following program has a logic error. Find and correct the error:

```
10 REM ** Determines which of two numbers is
            smaller **
20 INPUT "Enter two numbers"; NUM1, NUM2
30 IF NUM1 > NUM2 THEN NUM3 = NUM1 : NUM4 =
   NUM2
40 IF NUM1 < NUM2 THEN NUM3 = NUM2 : NUM4 =
   NUM1
50 PRINT NUM3 "is smaller than" NUM4
99 END
```

6.6 Debugging with Additional PRINT Statements

When debugging, it is often useful to place additional PRINT statements at different program locations to check the value of variables. For example, the addition of the line

```
65 PRINT "NUMBER = "; NUMBER, "COUNT = ";
   COUNT, "SUM = "; SUM
```

to the original program in Section 6.5 will trace the variables as the program runs:

```
RUN
How many integers? 3
NUMBER = 3        COUNT = 1        SUM = 1
NUMBER = 3        COUNT = 2        SUM = 3
NUMBER = 3        COUNT = 3        SUM = 6
The sum of 1 to 3 = 6

Calculate another sum (y/n)? y
How many integers? 2
NUMBER = 2        COUNT = 1        SUM = 7
NUMBER = 2        COUNT = 2        SUM = 9
The sum of 1 to 2 = 9

Calculate another sum (y/n)? n
Ok
```

This can be quicker than hand-tracing, and shows that SUM is 7 at the start of the second sum (when it should be 1). When the additional PRINT statement is no longer needed for debugging purposes it can be removed. If the PRINT might be useful later in the debugging process, it is easy to turn it into a REM which may be restored later:

```
65 REM PRINT "NUMBER = "; NUMBER, "COUNT = ";
   COUNT, "SUM = "; SUM
```

6.7 STOP and CONTinue

Deliberately halting a program using the STOP statement can be a helpful debugging technique. STOP displays the line number where the break occurs. At this point the current value of any variable can be displayed using PRINT in immediate mode. A program halted by a STOP can be resumed at the point of the interruption by typing CONT.

In the section above we added a PRINT statement at line 65 to determine the value of the variables for the program in Section 6.5. We could instead have placed a STOP statement at line 65:

```
65 STOP
```

```
RUN
How many integers? 2
Break in 65
Ok
PRINT NUMBER, SUM, COUNT
 2             1              1
Ok
CONT
Break in 65
Ok
PRINT NUMBER, SUM, COUNT
 2             3              2
Ok
CONT
The sum of 1 to 2 = 3

Calculate another sum (y/n)? n
Ok
```

Note that each of the underlined lines are entered by the user. The results of this technique of debugging is similar to that achieved by adding a PRINT statement at line 65. When using this technique, the Alt-P shortcut for typing PRINT is useful. The CONT command may be entered by pressing the F5 function key.

6.8 Tracing Program Execution: TRON and TROFF

To follow the sequence in which the lines of a program are executed, type the command TRON (which stands for TRace ON) before typing RUN. Each line number is then printed as the line is executed thus allowing the programmer to trace program flow. To stop the tracing use the command TROFF (TRace OFF). TRON may be entered using the F7 function key and TROFF with the F8.

This is the result of entering the TRON command and then running the original program in Section 6.5. The TROFF command is entered when the run is complete:

```
TRON
Ok
RUN
[10][20][30][40]How many integers? 2
[50][60][70][60][70][80]The sum of 1 to 2 = 3
[90]
[100]Calculate another sum (y/n)? n
[110][999]
Ok
TROFF
Ok
```

6.9 End of Chapter Problem

We want to write a program that allows a student to be tested on addition, subtraction or multiplication problems. Once the student selects the type of problem, five problems are presented. The student is given three chances to get each problem correct. A score of 20 points is awarded if the answer is correct on the first try, 10 points if the second try is correct and 5 points for the third. If three incorrect attempts are made, the correct answer is printed and no points are awarded.

Algorithm:

1. Enter type of problem (addition, subtraction, multiplication).
2. Produce 5 problems of selected type:
   a) Pick 2 numbers.
   b) Give user 3 chances on each problem.
   c) After 3 incorrect answers give correct answer.
   d) Calculate score.
3. Print score.

Input:

Type of problem	SELECT$
User answer	ANSWER

Output:

Correct answer	CORANS
Score	SCORE

This problem can be solved in many different ways, but it is important to realize that the only difference between the three types of problems is the mathematical operator used: +, -, or *. We will break the problem down into subroutines which perform the following functions taking this fact into account:

1. Select type of problem.
2. Produce problems:
   a) addition.
   b) subtraction.
   b) multiplication.

This solution requires 5 subroutines with the Produce problems subroutine able to call one of 3 subroutines based upon the type of problem being produced (add, subtract, multiply). In reviewing the program note how the same instructions are used by the Produce problems subroutine to create any problem. The only changes made are the calculation of CORANS and the symbol assigned to SIGN$.

```
10 REM ** Presents 5 math problems of a
            selected type **
100 REM ** Main program
110 RANDOMIZE TIMER
120 GOSUB 1000 : REM ** Make selection
130 GOSUB 2000 : REM ** Produce problems
140 PRINT "Your score ="; SCORE
999 END
1000 REM ** Select type of problem
1010 INPUT "A)ddition, S)ubtraction,
      M)ultiplication"; SELECT$
1020 WHILE SELECT$ <> "A" AND SELECT$ <> "S"
      AND SELECT$ <> "M"
1030   PRINT "You made an improper selection.
      Must be A, S or M."
1040   INPUT "A)ddition, S)ubtraction,
      M)ultiplication"; SELECT$
1050 WEND
1060 RETURN
1990 REM
2000 REM ** Produce problems
2010 FOR PROBLEM = 1 TO 5
2020   NUM1 = INT(99 * RND) + 1
2030   NUM2 = INT(99 * RND) + 1
2040   IF SELECT$ = "A" THEN GOSUB 3000 : REM
      Add
2050   IF SELECT$ = "S" THEN GOSUB 4000 : REM
      Subtract
2060   IF SELECT$ = "M" THEN GOSUB 5000 : REM
      Multiply
2070   PRINT "What is" NUM1; SIGN$; NUM2 "= ";
2080   INPUT ANSWER
2090   TRY = 1
2100   WHILE ANSWER <> CORANS AND TRY < 3
2110     INPUT "Wrong answer, try again";
          ANSWER
2120     TRY = TRY + 1
2130   WEND
2140   IF TRY = 1 THEN PRINT "Correct!" :
      SCORE = SCORE + 20
2150   IF TRY = 2 THEN PRINT "Correct!" :
      SCORE = SCORE + 10
2160   IF TRY = 3 AND ANSWER = CORANS THEN
      PRINT "Correct!" : SCORE = SCORE + 5
2170   IF TRY = 3 AND ANSWER <> CORANS THEN
      PRINT "Wrong. The answer is " CORANS
2180   PRINT
2190 NEXT PROBLEM
2200 RETURN
```

```
2990 REM
3000 REM ** Addition
3010 SIGN$ = "+"
3020 CORANS = NUM1 + NUM2
3030 RETURN
3990 REM
4000 REM ** Subtraction
4010 SIGN$ = "-"
4020 CORANS = NUM1 - NUM2
4030 RETURN
5000 REM ** Multiplication
5010 SIGN$ = "*"
5020 CORANS = NUM1 * NUM2
5030 RETURN
5990 REM
```

```
RUN
Enter A)ddition, S)ubtraction, M)ultiplication:
Enter selection? C
You made an improper selection. Must be A, S or M.
Enter selection? A
What is 32 + 33 = ? 62
Wrong answer, try again? 65
Correct!

What is 94 + 37 = ? 131
Correct!

What is 71 + 55 = ? 135
Wrong answer, try again? 124
Wrong answer, try again? 127
Wrong. The answer is 126

What is 37 + 9 = ? 46
Correct!

What is 85 + 45 = ? 120
Wrong answer, try again? 140
Wrong answer, try again? 130
Correct!

Your score = 55
Ok
```

Each of the three subroutines (3000, 4000, 5000) determines the operator (SIGN$) and correct answer (CORANS) for its type of problem. The subroutine starting at line 2000 does most of the work — it picks two random numbers, calls the proper subroutine and keeps track of the number of attempts (TRY) and score.

Chapter Summary

To simplify a longer program it is a good programming practice to divide it into sections called subroutines. These subroutines may be called from anywhere in a program using GOSUB which then sends program execution to a specified line. When a subroutine has completed its task, RETURN returns to the line immediately following the one which called the subroutine. Each subroutine should perform only one well-defined task. The first line of the subroutine should contain a REM statement that tells what the routine does.

The main program contains statements which call subroutines which are placed at the end of a program. To avoid mistakenly calling a subroutine its lines are numbered higher than the END statement at the end of the main program.

The ON...GOSUB statement allows a program to branch to a number of separate subroutines based on the value of a variable. When the value of the variables is 1, the program branches to the first subroutine listed, when 2 to the second subroutine, and so on.

Programs should not be written until they have been carefully planned. An algorithm should first be developed which describes the input, processing and output that the program must produce. After this the details needed to perform specific tasks can be filled in.

Top-down planning involves working on the major portions of the solution to a problem first and leaving specifics until later. The problem is first broken down into large blocks with details of the blocks filled in later. Most problems can be broken down into three broad areas: input — needed data is entered, processing — the steps required to produce the desired output, and output — new data produced by the program. The major portions of the program should be written as separate subroutines.

Debugging is the process of locating errors in a program and correcting them. The two basic types of errors are syntax errors which are caused by entering a statement improperly and logic errors which result when program output is different than what is desired. To create confidence in a program's output the program can be manually traced (hand traced) using test data. It is best to use test data that covers the range of anticipated inputs and outputs. Another useful debugging technique is to place additional PRINT statements at different program locations to check the value of variables. When the program is running properly these statements can be removed.

Program execution can be deliberately halted using STOP and resumed at the point of interruption using CONT. To print each line number as a program is executed the TRON command is used. To turn off this feature TROFF is used.

Vocabulary

CONT - Causes program execution to resume after it has been stopped. (See STOP.)

Debugging - Process of locating errors in a program and correcting them.

GOSUB - Statement that branches program execution to a subroutine starting at a specified line number.

Hand tracing - Manually tracing through a program using test data.

Input - Data entered into or used by a program.

Logic error - Error produced when program output is different than what is desired.

Main program - Contains the statements that call subroutines.

ON...GOSUB - Statement that branches to one of several subroutines depending on the value of a variable.

Output - New data produced by a program.

Processing - Steps required to take program input and produce the desired output.

RETURN - Statement located at the end of a subroutine that sends program execution back to the line immediately following where the subroutine was called.

STOP - Statement that halts program execution.

Subroutine - Section of a program that executes a specific task and is called by a GOSUB and exited by a RETURN.

Syntax error - An error caused by entering an improper statement.

Top-down planning - Working on the major portions of the solution to a problem first and leaving specifics until later.

TROFF - Turns trace mode off. (See TRON.)

TRON - Turns trace mode on which displays the sequence of line numbers a program follows as it is being executed.

Exercises

1. Write a program that asks the user to enter 3 numbers and then adds them, multiplies them, or adds the first two and divides the sum by the third. Use three subroutines, one for each process:

    ```
    RUN
    Enter 3 numbers? 27, 92, 13
    Enter S)um, M)ultiply, D)ivide? M
     27 * 92 * 13 = 32292
    Ok

    RUN
    Enter 3 numbers? 45, -12, 7
    Enter S)um, M)ultiply, D)ivide? D
    ( 45 + -12 ) / 7 = 4.714286
    Ok
    ```

2. Write a program that contains four subroutines. Each subroutine prints one of the following statements:

    > Never leave disks on top of the computer.
    > Unplug your computer during a lightning storm.
    > Open the drive door before removing a disk.
    > Opening the case will void the warranty.

    Ask the user to select an integer between 1 and 4 to display one of the messages. Have the program operate as shown with a subroutine to determine if a proper number has been entered. Allow the user to continue to display messages:

    ```
    RUN
    Enter a number (1-4)? 7
     7 is not a proper number.
    Enter a number (1-4)? 3

       Open the drive door before removing a disk.

    Display another message (y/n)? y
    Enter a number (1-4)? 2

       Unplug your computer during a lightning storm.

    Display another message (y/n)? n
    Ok
    ```

3. A large corporation receives many resumes every day. Write a program that prints a response letter depending upon the users' input. One response will tell the applicant that there is no present need for someone with his or her qualifications and the other will ask the applicant to come in for an interview:

    ```
    RUN
    Applicant Name? Mr. Jones
    Enter I)nterview or R)eject? R

    Dear Mr. Jones:

        Thank you for your resume. Presently, we
    have no need for someone with your
    qualifications. We will keep your resume on
    file for one year.

    Sincerely,
    AAA Corp.
    Ok

    RUN
    Applicant Name? Ms. Hale
    Enter I)nterview or R)eject? I

    Dear Ms. Hale:

        Thank you for your resume. We are very
    interested in meeting with you to discuss
    your qualifications further. Please call to
    arrange an interview.

    Sincerely,
    AAA Corp.
    Ok
    ```

4. An engineering firm wants to analyze the data they have gathered on the strength of 5 different types of concrete.

    a) Write a subroutine that prints the lowest value in a set of data which contains 5 positive numbers.

    b) Write a subroutine that prints the highest value in a set of data which contains 5 positive numbers.

    c) Write a subroutine that creates a horizontal bar graph using data which contains 5 positive integers. Allow the user to choose the character to be used in the output.

    d) Write a main program that asks the user to enter the strength data and then uses the subroutines written above. Allow the user to input 5 numbers. Print out the lowest and highest numbers, and a bar graph of the data:

```
RUN
Enter the 5 strengths: 21, 15, 7, 33, 14

The lowest is 7
The highest is 33
Graph character? #
1: ########################
2: #################
3: ########
4: #####################################
5: ##################
   1    5    1    1    2    2    3    3    4
             0    5    0    5    0    5    0
Ok
```

5. A builder needs a program that converts metric measurements from decimeters to meters, meters to decimeters, decimeters to centimeters, and centimeters to decimeters.

    a) Write a subroutine that converts decimeters to meters and another to convert meters to decimeters. There are 10 decimeters in a meter.

    b) Write a subroutine that converts decimeters to centimeters and another to convert centimeters to decimeters. There are 10 centimeters in a decimeter.

    c) Write a main program that prints a menu of the conversions available and allows the user to enter a measurement. Print the converted measurement using the subroutines written above:

    ```
    RUN
       1) Decimeters to meters
       2) Meters to decimeters
       3) Decimeters to centimeters
       4) Centimeters to decimeters
       5) Quit

    Enter Choice (1-5): 4
    Enter measurement? 20

     20 Centimeters = 2 Decimeters

    Enter Choice (1-5): 1
    Enter measurement? 2

     2 Decimeters = .2 Meters

    Enter Choice (1-5): 5
    Ok
    ```

6. A local pet store needs to keep track of its inventory. Write a program that reads from DATA statements the initial number of fish, puppies, kittens and canaries that the pet store has in stock. Have the program ask the user for the pet sold. Write subroutines to update and print out the current number of pets in stock. The user should not be allowed to sell more pets than available:

```
RUN
          Brown's Pet Emporium

Puppies:    5
Kittens:    3
Canaries:   2
Fish:      20

Pet sold (END to quit): PUPPY
Number sold: 1

Puppies:    4
Kittens:    3
Canaries:   2
Fish:      20

Pet sold (END to quit): BIRD
Sorry no BIRD, please reenter: CANARY
Number sold: 2

Puppies:    4
Kittens:    3
Canaries:   0
Fish:      20

Pet sold (END to quit): KITTEN
Number sold: 4
Sorry KITTEN stock is 3
Please reenter number sold (0 to cancel): 0

Puppies:    4
Kittens:    3
Canaries:   0
Fish:      20

Pet Sold (END to quit): END
Ok
```

7. A painter needs to know the surface area of a house in order to buy the correct amount of paint.

   a) Write a subroutine that calculates the area of a rectangle using the length of the two sides.

   b) Write a subroutine that calculates the total surface of a square house. (Hint: Compute the area of each side then subtract the area of the windows.)

c) Write a main program which uses the subroutines written above to calculate the area of a house given measurements entered by the user:

```
RUN
Enter dimensions in feet
House-
   Length: 20
   Width:  60

Windows-
   Length: 5
   Width: 3
   Number of windows per side: 3

Total area of house:  4,620 square feet
Ok
```

8. Write separate subroutines to perform each of the following conversions. Each subroutine should prompt the user for the value to be converted, and then print the converted value.

a) Convert a weight in pounds to kilograms. There are 2.2 pounds per kilogram.

b) Convert a temperature in degrees Fahrenheit to degrees Celsius. The formula is $C = (5/9) \times (F - 32)$.

c) Convert a temperature in degrees Celsius to degrees Fahrenheit. The formula is $F = (9/5) \times C + 32$.

d) Write a main program which allows the user to choose between each of the conversions listed above:

```
RUN
        Conversions
  1) Pounds to Kilograms
  2) Fahrenheit to Celsius
  3) Celsius to Fahrenheit
  4) Quit

Your choice (1-4)? 2
Enter Fahrenheit temperature: 32
 32 degrees Fahrenheit is 0 degrees Celsius.

Your choice (1-4)? 4
Ok
```

9. Write a program to assist in keeping a savings account balance up to date. Have three subroutines; one for deposits, one for withdrawals, and one to calculate that month's interest (1/2% per month). Round all calculated values to the nearest cent and do not allow a withdrawal to exceed the amount in the account:

```
RUN
1) Withdrawal, 2) Deposit, 3) Interest, 4) Exit
Enter selection? 2
How much would you like to deposit? 500
Your balance now stands at $500.00

1) Withdrawal, 2) Deposit, 3) Interest, 4) Exit
Enter selection? 3
The interest for this month is $2.50
Your balance now stands at $502.50

1) Withdrawal, 2) Deposit, 3) Interest, 4) Exit
Enter selection? 1
How much would you like to withdraw? 715.25
Sorry, there is not enough money in the account.
How much would you like to withdraw? 175.25
Your balance now stands at $327.25

1) Withdrawal, 2) Deposit, 3) Interest, 4) Exit
Enter selection? 4
All calculations completed. Have a good day!
Ok
```

10. Write a program to input the dimensions of a triangle from the user. Calculate and print the perimeter, and whether or not the triangle is a right triangle. Each calculation should be a separate subroutine. The output should be similar to:

```
RUN
Enter side, side, hypotenuse: 3, 4, 5
Perimeter is: 12.00
This is a right triangle.
Ok
```

Advanced Exercise   11. Lawrenceville Hardware Store needs a program to calculate its weekly payroll for its employees. The program should ask for the number of hours worked by each employee and then calculate each employee's pay based on the following considerations:

1) Gross pay equals the payrate times the number of hours worked. Time and a half (150%) is paid for hours exceeding 40 hours. For example, an employee with a payrate of $5.00 who works 50 hours earns (5.00 * 40) + (5.00 * 10 * 1.5), or $275.00.

2) Taxes are calculated as follows:

   0% taxes for first $200 earned.
   15% of gross pay for earnings exceeding $200 and less than $300.
   28% of gross pay for earnings between $300 and less than $400.
   31% of gross pay for earnings exceeding $400.

   For example, for an employee with gross pay of $550 the tax is (200 * 0) + (100 * 0.15) + (100 * 0.28) + (150 * 0.31), $89.50.

3) Social security is calculated as 7.5% of gross pay.

4) Lawrenceville Hardware has a pension plan which allows employees to have money deducted as a percentage of their gross pay. They may select to have 0%, 1%, 2% or 3% deducted. For example, an employee with gross pay of $350 who has selected 2% pension will have $7.00 deducted.

5) There is also a vacation plan which allows employees to choose 0%, 1% or 2% of gross pay to be deducted. When they go on vacation they will receive the saved money.

6) Net pay is calculated as gross pay minus taxes, social security, pension and vacation deductions.

The RUN on the next page was produced using the following DATA:

```
9000 REM ** Name, payrate, pension percent,
               vacation percent
9010 DATA Doucette, 7.65, 2, 1
9020 DATA Wang, 3.35, 0, 2
9030 DATA Rohrman, 5.00, 3, 1
9040 DATA End of Data, 0.00, 0, 0
```

```
RUN
Number of hours worked by Doucette? 46
Name                 Doucette
Pay rate             $  7.65
Gross pay            $374.85
Deductions
   Taxes             $ 35.96
   Soc. Sec.         $ 28.11
   Pension           $  7.50
   Vacation          $  3.75

NET PAY              $299.53


Number of hours worked by Wang? 27
Name                 Wang
Pay rate             $  3.35
Gross pay            $ 90.45
Deductions
   Taxes             $  0.00
   Soc. Sec.         $  6.78
   Pension           $  0.00
   Vacation          $  1.81

NET PAY              $ 81.86


Number of hours worked by Rohrman? 49
Name                 Rohrman
Pay rate             $  5.00
Gross pay            $267.50
Deductions
   Taxes             $ 10.13
   Soc. Sec.         $ 20.06
   Pension           $  8.02
   Vacation          $  2.68

NET PAY              $226.62
```

Nested Loops and Subscripted Variables

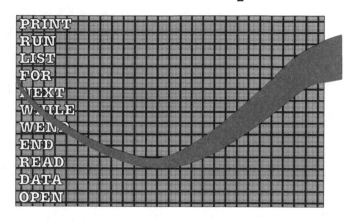

DIM

ERASE

OPTION BASE

DIM

ERASE

OPTION BASE

DIM

ERASE

OPTION BASE

Objectives

Chapter Seven

After completing this chapter you will be able to:

1. Make use of nested loops.

2. Produce arrays to store data in subscripted variables.

3. Dimension an array using DIM.

4. Produce a double-subscripted array to store data in two-dimensions, such as tables.

5. Remove an array from memory using ERASE.

6. Start numbering array elements at 1 using OPTION BASE.

*T*he FOR...NEXT and WHILE...WEND loops are important programming tools that allow the computer to repeat a series of instructions a definite or indefinite number of times. This chapter explains how these loops can be nested within each other to create multiple repetitive conditions.

There are tasks that the simple variables we have used so far cannot do. In this chapter we introduce a more complex type of variable called a subscripted variable that increases a program's ability to store and use large amounts of data.

7.1 Nested Loops

A nested loop is a loop which is located entirely within another loop. For example,

```
10 FOR NUM1 = 1 TO 10
20    FOR NUM2 = 1 TO 5
30       PRINT NUM1, NUM2
40    NEXT NUM2
50 NEXT NUM1
```

shows properly nested loops. Indenting the loops makes their structure more visible, thereby helping to prevent an error where the loops improperly overlap.

This program demonstrates the output produced by two nested loops:

```
10 REM ** Demonstrates nested loops **
20 FOR OUTER = 1 TO 3
30   FOR INNER = 1 TO 4
40     PRINT "Outer ="; OUTER, "Inner ="; INNER
50   NEXT INNER
60 NEXT OUTER
99 END
```

```
RUN
Outer = 1        Inner = 1
Outer = 1        Inner = 2
Outer = 1        Inner = 3
Outer = 1        Inner = 4
Outer = 2        Inner = 1
Outer = 2        Inner = 2
Outer = 2        Inner = 3
Outer = 2        Inner = 4
Outer = 3        Inner = 1
Outer = 3        Inner = 2
Outer = 3        Inner = 3
Outer = 3        Inner = 4
Ok
```

Note how the outside loop variable OUTER remains 1 while the inside loop variable INNER is assigned the values 1 through 4. When the inner loop completes execution, OUTER becomes 2 and INNER returns to its initial value of 1. INNER is then assigned the values 1 to 4, completes execution and OUTER becomes 3. The inner loop then executes 4 more times.

More than two loops may be nested. This program nests 3 loops to calculate all the possible combinations of quarters, dimes and nickels that add up to 50 cents:

```
10 REM ** Determines number of quarters,
          dimes, nickles that add to 50
          cents **
20 PRINT "Quarters", "Dimes", "Nickels"
30 FOR QUARTERS = 0 TO 2
40    FOR DIMES = 0 TO 5
50       FOR NICKELS = 0 TO 10
60          IF (QUARTERS * 0.25) + (DIMES *
             0.10) + (NICKELS * 0.05) = 0.50
             THEN PRINT QUARTERS, DIMES, NICKELS
70       NEXT NICKELS
80    NEXT DIMES
90 NEXT QUARTERS
99 END
```

```
RUN
Quarters            Dimes            Nickels
   0                  0                 10
   0                  1                  8
   0                  2                  6
   0                  3                  4
   0                  4                  2
   0                  5                  0
   1                  0                  5
   1                  1                  3
   1                  2                  1
   2                  0                  0
Ok
```

Carefully trace the values assigned to each of the three loops as they are executed. To determine how many times the IF statement at line 60 is evaluated we could replace it with

```
60              COUNT = COUNT + 1
```

and add the line:

```
95 PRINT "Count =" COUNT
```

```
RUN
Quarters          Dimes             Nickels
Count = 198
```

198 combinations of quarters, dimes and nickels were tested to find the 10 combinations that add up to fifty cents. Note the end values for each loop (2, 5 and 10). These were chosen because they are the maximum number of that coin which adds to 50 cents (2 quarters, 5 dimes or 10 nickels). A larger number would have been wasteful, and a smaller number would not have tested each possible combination of coins.

Both WHILE and FOR loops may be nested. This program uses a FOR...NEXT loop nested within a WHILE...WEND loop to calculate how an investment grows over 10 year intervals when invested at a specified interest rate:

```
10 REM ** Calculates interest on investment
            for 10 year periods **
20 INPUT "Enter amount invested originally"; TOTAL
30 INPUT "Enter interest rate in percent";
   INTEREST
40 WHILE MORE$ <> "n"
50   FOR YEAR = 1 TO 10
60     TOTAL = TOTAL + TOTAL * (INTEREST / 100)
70   NEXT YEAR
80   YEARS = YEARS + 10
90   PRINT "After" YEARS "years the amount = ";
100  PRINT USING "$##,###.## "; TOTAL
110  INPUT "Calculate another 10 years (y/n)"; MORE$
120  PRINT
130 WEND
140 PRINT "Calculations completed"
999 END
```

```
RUN
Enter amount invested originally? 2000
Enter interest rate in percent? 6
After 10 years the amount = $ 3,581.70
Calculate another 10 years (y/n)? y

After 20 years the amount = $ 6,414.27
Calculate another 10 years (y/n)? y

After 30 years the amount = $11,486.98
Calculate another 10 years (y/n)? n

Calculations completed
Ok
```

Note how each time the user enters a "y" at line 110 the investment is calculated for another 10 year interval. The nested FOR loop at lines 50 through 70 calculates the interest for a 10 year period. Study line 60 carefully; the new total investment is calculated by taking the current total and adding to it the total times the interest rate. This is done once for each of the 10 years. The (INTEREST / 100) is required to change the interest rate entered to its proper decimal (6% is 0.06).

Review

1. Write a program that uses nested loops to produce the following multiplication table:

```
RUN
  4 * 1 = 4        4 * 2 = 8        4 * 3 = 12
  5 * 1 = 5        5 * 2 = 10       5 * 3 = 15
  6 * 1 = 6        6 * 2 = 12       6 * 3 = 18
  7 * 1 = 7        7 * 2 = 14       7 * 3 = 21
Ok
```

2. a) Write a program that finds combinations of three numbers, the first between 5 and 10, the second between 11 and 20, and the third 21 and 30, which when multiplied together produce a product between 2970 and 2980, inclusive:

```
RUN
   7 * 17 * 25 = 2975
   9 * 11 * 30 = 2970
   9 * 15 * 22 = 2970
  10 * 11 * 27 = 2970
Ok
```

b) Add statements to the program that print the total number of combinations tested to produce the above results.

7.2 Arrays and Subscripted Variables

In certain programming applications we may want to store groups of numbers or strings without being forced to select variable names for each element of data. This problem can be solved by using an "array." An array is made up of numbered memory boxes, known as "elements," that store either numeric or string data. To use a single element of an array, the programmer must tell the computer the name of the array and the subscript number of the desired element. For example:

NUMBER (<subscript>)

The array name, in this case NUMBER, is the name by which all of its elements is known. Each individual box within an array is identified by a subscript enclosed in parentheses. For this reason, an individual element is sometimes known as a "subscripted variable." For example, we can define the array NUMBER as possessing 6 separate elements. Each element is identified by the variables NUMBER(1), NUMBER(2), NUMBER(3), NUMBER(4), NUMBER(5), and NUMBER(6), each of which can be assigned a different value. For example,

```
NUMBER(1) = 27
NUMBER(2) = 45
NUMBER(3) = -12
NUMBER(4) = 168
NUMBER(5) = 31
NUMBER(6) = 79
```

The array can be pictured as 6 boxes, each of which stores a value:

NUMBER

27	45	-12	168	31	79
1	**2**	**3**	**4**	**5**	**6**

It is important not to confuse the subscript number with the value stored by that element. For example, the third element in the array, NUMBER(3), stores the value -12 and not 3.

The subscripted variables that make up an array are used much like simple variables. For instance, there can be both numeric or string arrays. Also, subscripted variables are assigned values in the same way that simple variables are. Here we assign words to 3 elements in an array of strings:

```
WORD$(1) = "fantastic"
WORD$(2) = "totally"
WORD$(3) = "Superman"
```

We can print the contents of an element simply by listing the array name and subscript:

```
PRINT "Arrays are " WORD$(1) "!"
Arrays are fantastic!
```

A program may contain any number of arrays. This program asks the user to enter the names and ages of 4 people and then prints them in reverse order. It uses two arrays, one string array for the names and a numeric array for the ages:

```
10 REM ** Stores 4 names and ages and prints
            them in reverse order **
20 FOR COUNT = 1 TO 4
30    PRINT "Enter name" COUNT;
40    INPUT PERSON$(COUNT)
50    PRINT "Enter " PERSON$(COUNT) "'s age";
60    INPUT AGE(COUNT)
70    PRINT
80 NEXT COUNT
90 PRINT "Person's name",, "Age"
100 FOR COUNT = 4 TO 1 STEP -1
110    PRINT PERSON$(COUNT),, AGE(COUNT)
120 NEXT COUNT
999 END
```

```
RUN
Enter name 1 ? Sean
Enter Sean's age? 34

Enter name 2 ? Chris
Enter Chris's age? 23

Enter name 3 ? Alban
Enter Alban's age? 18

Enter name 4 ? Emily
Enter Emily's age? 14

Person's name              Age
Emily                      14
Alban                      18
Chris                      23
Sean                       34
Ok
```

At line 20, COUNT is initially assigned a value of 1. The first time through the loop, the user inputs at line 40 Sean into PERSON$(1), and 34 at line 60 into AGE(1). On the second pass of the loop COUNT becomes 2, and PERSON$(2) is given Chris and AGE(2) the value 23. This process continues until the four elements in PERSON$ and AGE have been given values.

At line 100 the COUNT loop counts backwards from 4 to 1. At line 110, PERSON$(4), Emily, and AGE(4), 14, are printed. On the next pass of the loop COUNT is 3 and PERSON$(3) and AGE(3) are printed. The process continues for the second and first elements of both arrays.

Review

3. Write a program that asks the user to enter 6 names and then uses a random number to select one of the names as the winner of a contest:

    ```
    RUN
    Enter name 1 ? Harry
    Enter name 2 ? Luiz
    Enter name 3 ? Mary
    Enter name 4 ? Rudolph
    Enter name 5 ? Janice
    Enter name 6 ? Wing

    Rudolph is the winner!
    Ok
    ```

4. Write a program that asks the user to enter 5 numbers between 1 and 100 and then prints the numbers in descending order:

```
RUN
Enter number 1 ? 73
Enter number 2 ? 88
Enter number 3 ? 41
Enter number 4 ? 92
Enter number 5 ? 37

Numbers in descending order:
 92
 88
 73
 41
 37
Ok
```

7.3 DIMensioning an Array

BASIC automatically allows an array to have element subscripts ranging from 0 to 10. This means an array of as many as 11 elements can be set aside in the computer's memory:

?	?	?	?	?	?	?	?	?	?	?
0	1	2	3	4	5	6	7	8	9	10

If an array requires more than 11 elements, it must be dimensioned using a DIM statement:

DIM <array name> (<size>)

The DIM statement for a string array named WORD$ which contains 101 elements is:

```
20 DIM WORD$(100)
```

Because BASIC starts numbering array elements at 0, declaring a size of 100 actually creates 101 elements. The <size> value may be a constant or a variable. For example,

```
10 NUM = 100
20 DIM WORD$(NUM)
```

It is possible to dimension multiple arrays on a single line:

```
10 NUM = 100
20 DIM WORD$(NUM), COUNT(NUM)
```

Attempting to access an element outside of the dimensioned size produces an error and halts program execution:

```
10 NUM = 100
20 DIM WORD$(NUM), COUNT(NUM)
30 COUNT(105) = 360

RUN
Subscript out of range in 30
Ok
```

A program must DIMension an array before assigning any values to it. Therefore, it is good programming style to place all DIM statements at or near the beginning of a program. It is also a good practice to define all arrays in DIM statements, even those containing less than 11 elements.

When a numeric array is first dimensioned each of its elements is assigned a value of 0. In a string array each element is initially assigned a "null" or empty character which is represented by two quotation marks (""). Knowing this can be useful because we can check if values have been assigned to array elements with statements such as:

```
60 IF COUNT(5) = 0 THEN PRINT "Not assigned"
90 IF WORD$(NUM) = "" THEN PRINT "Empty"
```

In order to better organize its business, the Lawrenceville Lawn Service has computerized its customer list. They currently have 12 customers and use the computer to determine which lawns to mow on any day of the week:

```
10 REM ** Lists customers and charge for
              specified day **
20 MAXLAWN = 12
30 DIM NAME1$(MAXLAWN), DAY$(MAXLAWN),
CHARGE(MAXLAWN)
40 FOR COUNT = 1 TO MAXLAWN
50    READ NAME1$(COUNT), DAY$(COUNT),
      CHARGE(COUNT)
60 NEXT COUNT
70 INPUT "Enter today (M, T, W, R, F, S)";
   TODAY$
80 WHILE TODAY$ <> "M" AND TODAY$ <> "T" AND
   TODAY$ <> "W" AND TODAY$ <> "R" AND TODAY$
   <> "F" AND TODAY$ <> "S"
90    PRINT "Improper day entered"
100   INPUT "Enter today (M, T, W, R, F, S)";
      TODAY$
110 WEND
120 PRINT "Name", "Charge"
130 FOR COUNT = 1 TO MAXLAWN
140    IF DAY$(COUNT) = TODAY$ THEN PRINT
       USING "\              \  $###.##";
       NAME1$(COUNT), CHARGE(COUNT)
150 NEXT COUNT
999 END
9000 REM ** Data - Name, day to mow, charge
9010 DATA Hacker, M, 15, Jones, F, 12
9020 DATA Johnston, R, 18, Smith, S, 25
9030 DATA Brewster, W, 20, Webster, R, 21
9040 DATA Carney, T, 10, Murphy, W, 7
9050 DATA Small, R, 16, West, S, 18
9060 DATA Burke, M, 15, Zitherman, T, 13
```

```
RUN
Enter today (M, T, W, R, F, S)? S
Name            Charge
Smith           $ 25.00
West            $ 18.00
Ok
```

```
RUN
Enter today (M, T, W, R, F, S)? X
Improper day entered
Enter today (M, T, W, R, F, S)? T
Name            Charge
Carney          $ 10.00
Zitherman       $ 13.00
Ok
```

MAXLAWN is the number of lawns that the service cuts. The FOR loop at lines 40 through 60 reads the customer names, days and charges from the DATA statements and assigns them to elements in the three arrays. The WHILE loop at lines 80 through 110 guarantees that only valid days can be used in searching through the arrays. Lines 130 through 150 search the DAY$ array and if the desired day is found prints the customer name and charge.

Review

5. Determine the changes that would have to be made to the program in Section 7.3 to add a thirteenth customer. Show the changed lines.

6. Write a program that picks 15 random integers between 1 and 50, inclusive and then prints the 3rd, 14th, 10th and 7th numbers chosen:

```
RUN
Number 3 = 12
Number 14 = 2
Number 10 = 44
Number 7 = 1
Ok
```

7. Write a program that picks 15 random integers between 1 and 100, inclusive and then prints them out in descending order:

```
RUN
 96        92        72        68        54
 53        53        50        49        46
 45        32        27        12         5
Ok
```

7.4 Double-Subscripted Arrays

Arrays may have more than one dimension. Double-subscripted arrays make storing and using tables of data easy. For example:

```
AGE(1,5)            BOOK$(7,3)            SEAT(4,9)
```

Double-subscripted arrays provide a convenient way for dealing with problems where the data is two-dimensional in nature, such as the location of seats in a theater.

The box analogy is again helpful. The first subscript identifies the row and the second the column in which the element is located. For example, A(2,3) is the element located in the second row, third column:

	1	2	3	4	5	6	7	8	9	10
1										
2			*							
3										
4										

A double-subscripted array must be dimensioned with a DIM statement before any of its elements are assigned values.

```
DIM CITY$(10,15)
```

dimensions the array CITY$ to contain 11 rows and 16 columns giving the array 176 elements, each of which may store a single string. (Remember, BASIC begins numbering elements at 0. For the most part, we will ignore the 0 element. Section 7.5 describes a command which numbers array elements starting at 1.)

A classroom has 5 rows of seats with 3 seats in each row. The following program randomly selects seats for a class of 14 students, leaving one seat empty:

```
10 REM ** Selects seats for 14 students **
20 DIM SEAT$(5,3)
30 RANDOMIZE TIMER
40 REM ** Assign seats
50 FOR SEAT = 1 TO 14
60    READ NAME1$
70    ROW = 1 + INT(5 * RND)
80    COLUMN = 1 + INT(3 * RND)
90    REM ** Find empty seat
100   WHILE SEAT$(ROW, COLUMN) <> ""
110     ROW = 1 + INT(5 * RND)
120     COLUMN = 1 + INT(3 * RND)
130   WEND
140   SEAT$(ROW, COLUMN) = NAME1$
150 NEXT SEAT
160 REM ** Prints seat assignments
170 FOR ROW = 1 TO 5
180    FOR COLUMN = 1 TO 3
190       IF SEAT$(ROW, COLUMN) = "" THEN PRINT
            "*Empty*", ELSE PRINT SEAT$(ROW, COLUMN),
200    NEXT COLUMN
210    PRINT
220 NEXT ROW
999 END
```

```
9000 REM ** Student names
9010 DATA Anne, Sam, Jose, Cindy, Eric
9020 DATA Lester, Kim, John, Bonnie, Kumi
9030 DATA Helen, David, Sherry, Joe
```

```
RUN
Eric           Sherry         *Empty*
Kumi           Bonnie         John
Joe            Cindy          Helen
Sam            Anne           Lester
Kim            Jose           David
Ok
```

```
RUN
David          John           Joe
Anne           Kim            Sam
Bonnie         Kumi           Jose
Lester         *Empty*        Eric
Cindy          Sherry         Helen
Ok
```

The FOR...NEXT loop at lines 50 through 150 randomly assigns students to seats by picking a random row number (line 70) and random column number (line 80). A WHILE...WEND loop at lines 100 through 130 checks to make sure the seat is empty before line 140 assigns a student to the seat.

Nested FOR...NEXT loops at lines 170 to 220 are used to print the seat assignments. The comma in line 190 causes printing to continue across the print zones, and the blank PRINT statement at line 210 moves to the beginning of the next line at the end of a row. We will continue to make use of this nested loop technique in many of our programs to produce output in proper rows and columns.

Review

8. a) Write a program which fills the elements in a double-subscripted array of 8 rows and 4 columns with random numbers between 50 and 75, inclusive, and then print the array:

```
RUN
 73      53      67      67
 59      73      55      71
 75      56      54      57
 70      60      52      63
 57      66      65      69
 62      58      69      73
 65      64      67      64
 66      68      63      57
Ok
```

b) Modify the program to calculate and print the sum of each of the rows:

```
RUN
 67        66        70        62        Sum = 265
 60        59        56        65        Sum = 240
 71        50        50        60        Sum = 231
 60        63        65        62        Sum = 250
 53        72        62        57        Sum = 244
 60        53        68        73        Sum = 254
 72        50        59        52        Sum = 233
 50        66        64        67        Sum = 247
Ok
```

9. a) Write a program that uses a double-subscripted array to store a tic-tac-toe board and randomly fill it with X's and O's:

```
RUN
O    X    X
X    O    X
X    O    O
Ok
```

b) Modify the program to include a subroutine which determines if a winner exists:

```
RUN
O    X    X
X    O    X
X    O    O
Player O wins!
Ok
```

```
RUN
O    O    X
X    X    O
O    X    X
It's a draw.
Ok
```

7.5 ERASE and OPTION BASE

Large arrays can use up a great deal of space in the computer's memory. If an array is no longer needed while a program is running, it can be removed from memory using the ERASE statement:

ERASE <array name>

Note that this does not erase the contents of the array, but actually removes the entire array itself. Assuming that an array has been DIMensioned as SEAT$(20,20), the statement

120 ERASE SEAT$

removes the SEAT$ array from memory when line 120 is executed. An attempt to later access an element in it causes an error:

130 PRINT SEAT$(15,3)
Subscript out of range in 130

The first element in an array is automatically numbered 0, for example, SEAT$(0,0) or NUMBER(0). Elements can be numbered starting at 1 using the OPTION BASE statement:

```
20 OPTION BASE 1
```

This statement must appear in the program before any reference is made to an array or a DIM statement is executed.

7.6 Permanent Storage: Disk Files

Subscripted variables enhance the programmer's ability to store and manipulate large quantities of data. But a problem exists; each time a program is run all data stored in arrays is erased, with string arrays set to empty ("") and numeric arrays set to 0. Methods for permanently storing data in disk files are presented in Chapters 11 and 12.

7.7 End of Chapter Problem

The first class section in Boca Airlines' one plane has 3 rows, 4 seats to a row. Boca Air needs a reservations program to allow them to store the names of passengers and the row and seat numbers they have been assigned to. The program should perform three functions:

allow passengers to be assigned seats.
list empty seats by row and seat number.
produce a diagram showing each passenger's name in their assigned seat.

Algorithm:

1. Print menu.
2. Get user choice.
3. Perform task:
   a) Make reservation.
   b) List empty seats.
   c) List all seats.
4. Repeat steps 2 and 3 until choice is Quit.

Input:

Row number	ROW
Seat number	SEAT
Name	SEAT$(ROW, NUMBER)

Output:

List of empty seats	SEAT$(ROW, NUMBER)
List of filled seats	SEAT$(ROW, NUMBER)

Note how the double-subscripted array SEAT$ stores all of the required data:

```
10 REM ** Airline reservation system for
            plane of 3 rows, 4 seats per row **
100 REM ** Main program
110 DIM SEAT$(3,4)
120 PRINT "  1) Make reservation"
130 PRINT "  2) List empty seats"
140 PRINT "  3) List all seats"
150 PRINT "  4) Quit"
160 INPUT "Choice (1-4):"; CHOICE
170 WHILE CHOICE <> 4
180    WHILE CHOICE < 1 OR CHOICE > 4
190      INPUT "You must enter a 1, 2, 3 or 4";
         CHOICE
200    WEND
210    ON CHOICE GOSUB 1000, 2000, 3000
220    REM ** 1000 Make reservation, 2000
                 Empty seats, 3000 List seats
230    PRINT
240    INPUT "Choice (1-4):"; CHOICE
250 WEND
999 END
1000 REM ** Make reservation
1010 INPUT "Enter row number (1-3)"; ROW
1020 INPUT "Enter seat number (1-4)"; SEAT
1030 WHILE SEAT$(ROW, SEAT) <> ""
1040    PRINT "That seat is full, pick another."
1050    INPUT "Enter row number (1-3)"; ROW
1060    INPUT "Enter seat number (1-4)"; SEAT
1070 WEND
1080 PRINT "Enter name for row" ROW "seat"
     SEAT;
1090 INPUT SEAT$(ROW, SEAT)
1100 RETURN
1990 REM
2000 REM ** List empty seats
2010 PRINT "List of empty seats"
2020 PRINT "ROW", "SEAT
2030 FOR ROW = 1 TO 3
2040    FOR SEAT = 1 TO 4
2050       IF SEAT$(ROW, SEAT) = "" THEN PRINT
           ROW, SEAT
2060    NEXT SEAT
2070 NEXT ROW
2080 PRINT
2090 RETURN
2990 REM
3000 REM ** List seat occupants
3010 PRINT "List of seat occupants
3020 FOR ROW = 1 TO 3
3030    FOR SEAT = 1 TO 4
3040       PRINT SEAT$(ROW, SEAT),
3050    NEXT SEAT
3060    PRINT
3070 NEXT ROW
3080 RETURN
```

```
RUN
  1) Make reservation
  2) List empty seats
  3) List all seats
  4) Quit
Choice (1-4)? 1
Enter row number (1-3)? 2
Enter seat number (1-4)? 3
Enter name for row 2 seat 3 ? Freitas

Choice (1-4)? 1
Enter row number (1-3)? 1
Enter seat number (1-4)? 1
Enter name for row 1 seat 1 ? Presley

Choice (1-4)? 1
Enter row number (1-3)? 2
Enter seat number (1-4)? 3
That seat is full, pick another.
Enter row number (1-3)? 3
Enter seat number (1-4)? 4
Enter name for row 3 seat 4 ? Brown

Choice (1-4)? 2
List of empty seats
ROW             SEAT
  1               2
  1               3
  1               4
  2               1
  2               2
  2               4
  3               1
  3               2
  3               3

Choice (1-4)? 3
List of seat occupants
Presley
                Freitas
                                            Brown

Choice (1-4)? 4
Ok
```

Study this program carefully because it reviews most of the programming concepts covered so far in the text. Note how the WHILE...WEND loop at lines 180 to 200 guarantees that a proper operation is chosen. Also, notice how the loop at lines 1030 to 1070 keeps the user from picking an already filled seat. The nested loops at lines 3020 through 3070 are required to print the seats in their proper rows and columns.

One problem this program has not anticipated is the input of an out of range row or seat number at lines 1010 and 1020, or 1050 and 1060. If an improper number is entered at either line the program halts execution with an error message and all entered data is lost.

When option 4, Exit, is selected at line 240, program execution halts and all data currently stored in the array is erased. In Chapters 11 and 12 you will learn how to use disk files so that data can be retained even after the computer is shut off.

Review

10. Determine the lines which must be added to the End of Chapter program to guarantee that only proper row and seat numbers are used so that an Out of range error does not occur in the reservation subroutine.

Chapter Summary

A nested loop is a loop which is located entirely within another loop. Nested loops should be indented to make their structure more visible, helping to prevent an error where the loops improperly overlap. Both FOR...TO and WHILE...WEND loops can be nested.

An array is made up of numbered memory boxes, known as "elements", that store either numeric or string data. To use a single element of an array, the computer must be told the name of the array and the subscript number of the desired element. For example, the statement

```
50 NUMBER(3) = 25
```

stores the value 25 in element 3 of an array named NUMBER. It is important not to confuse the subscript number with the value stored by that element. Strings can be stored in subscripted string variables, for example,

```
60 NAME1$(7) = "Lawrence"
```

stores the string "Lawrence" in element 7 of an array named NAME1$.

BASIC allows an array to have element subscripts ranging from 0 to 10. If an array requires more than 11 elements, the array must be dimensioned using a DIM statement. Each element of a numeric array is initially assigned a value of 0, while each element of a string array is assigned a "null" or empty character which is represented by two quotation marks ("").

Double-subscripted arrays are a convenient way to store data which is two-dimensional in nature using elements that are grouped by rows and columns. For example, SEAT$(5,3) identifies an element in the double-subscripted array SEAT$ located in row 5, column 3. A double-subscripted array must be dimensioned with a DIM statement before any of its elements are assigned. DIM SEAT$(12, 8) dimensions the array SEAT$ to contain 12 rows and 8 columns.

If an array is no longer needed while a program is running, it can be removed from memory using the ERASE statement. Rather than starting at 0, array elements can be made to start at 1 using the OPTION BASE statement.

Vocabulary

Array - A group of numbered memory boxes that store either numeric or string data.

DIM - Statement used to dimension an array, must be used if an array will contain more than 11 elements.

Double-subscripted array - Array containing rows and columns.

Element - A single memory box in an array.

ERASE - Statement that removes an array from memory.

Nested loop - A loop which is located entirely within another loop.

Null character - Empty character (ASCII code 0) which is represented by two quotation marks ("").

OPTION BASE - Statement that sets the minimum value for an array subscript to 0 or 1.

Subscripted variable - An element, or single memory box in an array.

Exercises

1. Using nested loops, have the computer print a rectangle consisting of eight lines of thirty asterisks each:

```
RUN
* * * * * * * * * * * * * * * * * * * * * * * * * * * * * *
* * * * * * * * * * * * * * * * * * * * * * * * * * * * * *
* * * * * * * * * * * * * * * * * * * * * * * * * * * * * *
* * * * * * * * * * * * * * * * * * * * * * * * * * * * * *
* * * * * * * * * * * * * * * * * * * * * * * * * * * * * *
* * * * * * * * * * * * * * * * * * * * * * * * * * * * * *
* * * * * * * * * * * * * * * * * * * * * * * * * * * * * *
* * * * * * * * * * * * * * * * * * * * * * * * * * * * * *
Ok
```

2. A Pythagorean triple is a set of three integers which are lengths of the sides of a right triangle ($C^2 = A^2 + B^2$). Have a program print all sets of three integers up to C = 20 which are Pythagorean triples. For example, A = 3, B = 4, C = 5 is a solution.

3. Write a program which picks 20 random integers between 10 and 99, inclusive. Print the odd integers on one line and even integers on the next. The output should be similar to:

```
RUN
Odd:   49 25 21 13 63 77 29 77 27 43
Even:  66 56 18 24 28 70 56 62 48 76
Ok
```

4. Write a program which allows the user to input 5 numbers and then prints them in reverse order:

```
RUN
Number 1? 234
Number 2? 178
Number 3? 68
Number 4? 12
Number 5? 399
The numbers in reverse order are:
 399
 12
 68
 178
 234
Ok
```

5. Write a program that reads the following words from DATA statements into an array:

> happy, are, we, sit, love, eat, smile, frown, joy, I, is, a
> toad, active, jungle, school, am, will, the, run, halt, cry

Randomly select 6 of the words to form a nonsense sentence. Make sure no word is used more than once in a sentence. (Hint: Once a word has been used set its element to a blank space.)

```
RUN
am is happy active toad halt
Ok

RUN
happy is will jungle halt we
Ok
```

6. Write a program that prints random integers between 1 and 99, inclusive, until it encounters a duplicate. At that point print how many numbers have been generated:

```
RUN
 97  11   2  78  62  96  55  97
Duplicate after 8 numbers
Ok

RUN
 46  71  28  13  12  96  64  87  3  45  33
71
Duplicate after 12 numbers
Ok
```

7. Stan's Grocery Store has three aisles and in each aisle there are five items. Write a program that reads 15 items into a double-subscripted array from DATA statements. Let customers enter the name of the item they want to buy and have the computer indicate the aisle and number of the item. If an item is not in stock an appropriate message should be printed. An input of DONE halts program execution:

```
RUN
What are you looking for? apples
You will find apples in aisle 1, item 4
What are you looking for? milk
You will find milk in aisle 2, item 3
What are you looking for? broccoli
I'm sorry, we don't have broccoli.
What are you looking for? DONE
Ok
```

8. Write a program that allows the user to input the names of 10 students and their class ranks. Print out the names of the students in order by their class rank.

9. Write a program to calculate the average of four grades for each of five students whose names and grades are entered from the keyboard. Print each student's name, grades and average in columns with headings. After the last student's average print a line of dashes and the class average:

```
RUN
Student 1 ? Don
Enter four grades? 42, 86, 99, 99
Student 2 ? Lester
Enter four grades? 50, 55, 45, 34
Student 3 ? Liz
Enter four grades? 100, 98, 99, 97
Student 4 ? Roberto
Enter four grades? 87, 72, 71, 86
Student 5 ? Maria
Enter four grades? 89, 91, 93, 90

Name            1     2     3     4      AVG.
Don             42    86    99    99     81.5
Lester          50    55    45    34     46.0
Liz             100   98    99    97     98.5
Roberto         87    72    71    86     79.0
Maria           89    91    93    90     90.8
                                        - - - - -
              Class Average:      79.2
Ok
```

10. Write an extended version of the game high-low. In this game, the computer picks a secret random number from 1 to 100, inclusive and gives the player an unlimited number of chances to guess it. For each wrong guess the computer tells whether to guess higher or lower and stores the guess in a subscripted variable. If the player guesses the same number twice, the computer produces the message "WAKE UP! You guessed that number before":

```
RUN
Enter a guess (1-100)? 35
Low
Enter a guess (1-100)? 75
High
Enter a guess (1-100)? 35
WAKE UP! You guessed that number before
Enter a guess (1-100)? 50
Low
Enter a guess (1-100)? 62
Correct!
Ok
```

11. Write a program that reads 10 book titles and the shelf on which they can be found from DATA statements. Allow the user to then choose between displaying the books shelf by shelf or entering a title and then displaying the shelf where that book can be found. If the book is not found, display an appropriate message:

```
RUN
  1) Display Books by Shelf
  2) Find a Specific Title
  3) Quit
Enter selection (1-3)? 1

Books by Shelf
Shelf 1:
  University Physics
  Chemistry
  . . .

Shelf 5:
  A Guide to Programming in BASIC
  A Guide to Programming in Pascal

  1) Display Books by Shelf
  2) Find a Specific Title
  3) Quit
Enter selection (1-3)? 2

Locate Specific Title
Title? A Guide to Programming in BASIC
This book can be found on shelf 5.

  1) Display Books by Shelf
  2) Find a Specific Title
  3) Quit
Enter selection (1-3)? 3
Program complete.
```

12. Write a program that rolls two dice 1000 times and prints the number of times each different point total (2, 3, 4, 5 ..., 12) appeared. The output should resemble the following:

```
RUN
Points             Times Appearing
  2                  23
  3                  50
  4                  87
  5                  106
  6                  147
  7                  157
  8                  150
  9                  104
 10                  86
 11                  65
 12                  25
Ok
```

13. A dental office wants you to program the computer to keep track of the dentist's busy schedule. Use proper program design and subroutines.

   a) Write a program to allow a patient to choose the day and time he or she wants to see the dentist. There are 5 days and 6 time slots for each day. If the desired slot is empty, the patient enters his or her name. If it is full, the program asks the patient to choose another slot:

   ```
   RUN
       Dental Appointments
   What day (M, T, W, R, F)? R
   Time slot (1-6)? 5
   What is your name? Dana
   Dana, you are scheduled for Thursday, time
   slot 5

   Another appointment (y/n)? y
   What day (M, T, W, R, F)? M
   Time slot (1-6)? 3
   What is your name? Chris
   Chris, you are scheduled for Monday, time
   slot 3

   Another appointment (y/n)? y
   What day (M, T, W, R, F)? R
   Time slot (1-6)? 5
   That time slot is filled, please pick an-
   other.
   What day (M, T, W, R, F)? T
   Time slot (1-6)? 1
   What is your name? Carlos
   Carlos, you are scheduled for Tuesday, time
   slot 1

   Another appointment (y/n)? n
   Ok
   ```

   b) Add a subroutine to allow the office to print the dentist's schedule for any particular day.

Advanced Exercises

The following exercises require the development of detailed algorithms. The programs should not be written until all details of the algorithms have been worked out.

14. Penny Pitch is a popular game in amusement parks. Pennies are tossed onto a board on which numbers have been printed. By adding up the numbers in the squares on which the pennies fall, a score is accumulated. Write a program which simulates such a game in which ten pennies are to be randomly pitched by the computer onto the board shown on the next page:

Have the computer print the board with an X indicating where each penny has landed and then the score. Note that more than one penny can land on one square. If so, that score is only counted once. Below is a sample run:

```
RUN
1   X   1   1   X   1
1   2   2   2   2   1
X   2   3   3   2   X
1   X   3   X   2   1
1   2   2   2   X   1
X   1   1   X   1   X

Score = 14
Ok
```

15. Use the computer to play a modified game of Othello. Have it randomly fill an 8 x 8 array with X's and O's and print the array with row and column numbers. Examples are shown below. The X's are for player 1, the O's for player 2. Have the program ask the players alternately for the row and column of the opponent's piece that should be flipped (changed from an X to an O or vice versa). All of the opponent's pieces along the horizontal or vertical line passing through the flipped piece are then flipped. For example, if player 1 flipped the O at (1,8) board A would be changed to board B:

	A										B							
	1	2	3	4	5	6	7	8			1	2	3	4	5	6	7	8
1	X	X	O	O	X	O	X	O		1	X	X	X	X	X	X	X	X
2	O	O	O	X	X	O	X	X		2	O	O	O	X	X	O	X	X
3	X	O	X	X	O	X	O	O		3	X	O	X	X	O	X	O	X
4	O	O	X	O	X	O	X	O		4	O	O	X	O	X	O	X	X
5	O	O	X	X	X	O	X	O		5	O	O	X	X	X	O	X	X
6	O	O	X	O	O	X	X	O		6	O	O	X	O	O	X	X	X
7	O	O	X	X	O	X	O	X		7	O	O	X	X	O	X	O	X
8	X	X	O	X	X	O	X	X		8	X	X	O	X	X	O	X	X

After ten turns for each, the player with the most pieces left on the board wins.

16. Write a program that produces a computerized mailing list. The program should be able to record up to twenty names, addresses and phone numbers. It prompts the user for one of four options: Insert data, Delete data, Print list or Exit. The program should be written so that new data is inserted into the first available empty element, including an element that has been previously deleted:

```
            MAILING LIST

    1 - Insert a name
    2 - Delete a name
    3 - Display list
    4 - Exit
    Choose an option (1-4)? 1

    INSERT
    Name? Rick Deckert
    Address? L.A. Towers Apt. 9609
    City? Los Angeles
    State? CA
    Telephone? 555-1752

    Choose an option (1-4)? 1
    INSERT
    Name? Tony Montana
    Address? 300 Orange Way
    City? Ft. Lauderdale
    State? FL
    Telephone? 555-3822

    Choose an option (1-4)? 4
    EXIT - Program Complete
    Ok
```

17. Rewrite Advanced Exercise #22 from Chapter 5, the Bookstore problem, using arrays. The program should produce the same output and perform the same tasks as described in that chapter. After completing this exercise you should see the power that arrays have to simplify complex problems.

Chapter 8

String Functions and Data Types

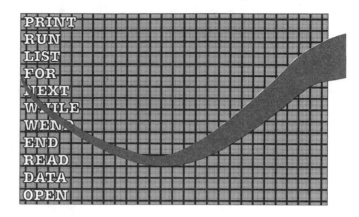

LEN ( )

MID$ ( )

LEFT$ ( )

RIGHT$ ( )

VAL ( )

Objectives

Chapter Eight

After completing this chapter you will be able to:

1. Understand how the binary system works and how it is employed by computers to store data.

2. Understand and make use of the ASCII code.

3. Use functions to convert strings into ASCII values and vice versa.

4. Make use of the data types: string, integer and floating point number.

5. Manipulate strings using the LEN(), MID$(), LEFT$() and RIGHT$() functions.

6. Convert a string which stores digits into its numeric value using the VAL() function.

Modern computers have resulted from the union of the binary number system with the principles of electricity. The binary number system uses only two digits, 0 and 1, and can be represented by the two states of an electric circuit, off or on. Digital computers are possible because they operate by reducing all data to a binary code. This chapter explains how data is stored using the binary system, and describes the different data types available.

8.1 Binary Numbers

The most familiar number system, the decimal system, uses ten digits, 0, 1, 2, 3, 4, 5, 6, 7, 8, 9 and is therefore called base ten. In contrast, the binary system, which uses only the digits 0 and 1, is base two.

In the base ten system, columns are used to represent powers of ten with the first column to the left of the decimal point representing 10^0, the second 10^1, the third 10^2, and so on. For example, in the number 458, the 4 represents 4×10^2, 5 represents 5×10^1, and 8 represents 8×10^0. The number itself represents the sum $4 \times 10^2 + 5 \times 10^1 + 8 \times 10^0$, 400 + 50 + 8.

The binary system works identically except the columns represent powers of two instead of ten. For example, in the binary number 101, the 1 on the right represents 1×2^0, the 0 represents 0×2^1, and the 1 on the left represents 1×2^2. The number itself represents the sum $1 \times 2^2 + 0 \times 2^1 + 1 \times 2^0$, which is equal to 5 in the base ten system. Several binary numbers are shown below:

Base Two		Base Ten
1	$= 1 \times 2^0$	= 1
10	$= 1 \times 2^1 + 0 \times 2^0$	= 2
11	$= 1 \times 2^1 + 1 \times 2^0$	= 3
100	$= 1 \times 2^2 + 0 \times 2^1 + 1 \times 2^0$	= 4
1011	$= 1 \times 2^3 + 0 \times 2^2 + 1 \times 2^1 + 1 \times 2^0$	= 11
11001	$= 1 \times 2^4 + 1 \times 2^3 + 0 \times 2^2 + 0 \times 2^1 + 1 \times 2^0$	= 25

To convert a number from base ten to base two, we must find the powers of two which add up to the number. Since 13 = 8 + 4 + 1, the base two representation for 13 is 1101 (1×8 + 1×4 + 0×2 + 1×1). Some other conversions are shown on the next page:

Base Ten   **Base Two**

$$6 \quad = \qquad\qquad\qquad\qquad 4 \quad +2 \quad +0 \quad = \quad 110$$
$$= \qquad\qquad\qquad 1\times2^2 \quad +1\times2^1 \quad +0\times2^0$$

$$29 \quad = \qquad 16 \quad +8 \quad +4 \quad +0 \quad +1 \quad = \quad 11101$$
$$= \qquad 1\times2^4 \quad +1\times2^3 \quad +1\times2^2 \quad +0\times2^1 \quad +1\times2^0$$

$$52 \quad = 32 \quad +16 \quad +0 \quad +4 \quad +0 \quad +0 \quad = \quad 110100$$
$$= 1\times2^5 \quad +1\times2^4 \quad +0\times2^3 \quad +1\times2^2 \quad +0\times2^1 \quad +0\times2^0$$

8.2 Computer Memory and Processing

The computer is composed of solid-state electronic memory which stores information and a central processing unit (CPU) which performs calculations, makes decisions and moves information. All information inside the computer is stored as electrical charges, and represented using binary numbers.

Because electricity has two basic states, ON and OFF, it is ideal for expressing binary numbers. When a circuit (called a "flip-flop") is ON it stands for a "1", and when OFF stands for a "0." By designing computers to contain millions of simple flip-flop circuits, huge quantities of information can be stored.

A single binary digit (0 or 1) is called a "bit", and eight of these bits constitute a "byte." Single characters require one byte and integers two bytes of memory for storage. The memory stores both instructions for the CPU and data as binary digits.

The power of a computer is vastly increased when it is capable of storing letters and special characters as well as numbers. In order to do this, a code has been established to translate letters and other characters into numbers which can then be stored in binary form. This code has been standardized by the computer industry as the American Standard Code for Information Interchange, or ASCII. In the ASCII code, each letter of the alphabet, both upper case and lower case, each symbol, and each control function used by the computer is represented by a number. For example, the name JIM is translated by the computer into the ASCII numbers 74, 73, 77. In turn these numbers are then stored by the computer in binary form:

Character	Decimal	Binary
J	74	01001010
I	73	01001001
M	77	01001101

In order for the computer to store a name such as JIM, or any piece of non-numeric information, it must be converted character by character into ASCII codes, and then stored in memory as binary numbers. The computer performs these tasks automatically. The table on the next page shows the ASCII character codes available on the IBM PC computer (and compatibles):

ASCII value	Character	ASCII value	Character	ASCII value	Character	ASCII value	Character	ASCII value	Character
0	(null)	52	4	104	h	156	£	208	⊥
1	☺	53	5	105	i	157	¥	209	⊤
2	☻	54	6	106	j	158	Pt	210	⊤
3	♥	55	7	107	k	159	ƒ	211	⊔
4	♦	56	8	108	l	160	á	212	⊢
5	♣	57	9	109	m	161	í	213	⊤
6	♠	58	:	110	n	162	ó	214	⊤
7	(beep)	59	;	111	o	163	ú	215	╫
8	◘	60	<	112	p	164	ñ	216	╪
9	(tab)	61	=	113	q	165	Ñ	217	⌐
10	(line feed)	62	>	114	r	166	ª	218	⌐
11	(home)	63	?	115	s	167	º	219	■
12	(form feed)	64	@	116	t	168	¿	220	▬
13	(carriage return)	65	A	117	u	169	⌐	221	▐
14	♫	66	B	118	v	170	¬	222	▐
15	☼	67	C	119	w	171	½	223	▬
16	►	68	D	120	x	172	¼	224	α
17	◄	69	E	121	y	173	¡	225	β
18	↕	70	F	122	z	174	«	226	Γ
19	‼	71	G	123	{	175	»	227	π
20	¶	72	H	124	¦	176	▓	228	Σ
21	§	73	I	125	}	177	▓	229	σ
22	▬	74	J	126	~	178	▓	230	µ
23	↨	75	K	127	⌂	179	│	231	τ
24	↑	76	L	128	Ç	180	┤	232	Φ
25	↓	77	M	129	ü	181	╡	233	Θ
26	→	78	N	130	é	182	╢	234	Ω
27	←	79	O	131	â	183	╖	235	δ
28	(cursor right)	80	P	132	ä	184	╕	236	∞
29	(cursor left)	81	Q	133	à	185	╣	237	Ø
30	(cursor up)	82	R	134	å	186	║	238	∈
31	(cursor down)	83	S	135	ç	187	╗	239	∩
32	(space)	84	T	136	ê	188	╝	240	≡
33	!	85	U	137	ë	189	╜	241	±
34	''	86	V	138	è	190	╛	242	≥
35	#	87	W	139	ï	191	┐	243	≤
36	$	88	X	140	î	192	└	244	⌠
37	%	89	Y	141	ì	193	┴	245	⌡
38	&	90	Z	142	Ä	194	┬	246	÷
39	'	91	[	143	Å	195	├	247	≈
40	(	92	\	144	É	196	─	248	°
41	)	93	]	145	æ	197	┼	249	•
42	*	94	∧	146	Æ	198	╞	250	·
43	+	95	—	147	ô	199	╟	251	√
44	,	96	`	148	ö	200	╚	252	ⁿ
45	-	97	a	149	ò	201	╔	253	²
46	.	98	b	150	û	202	╩	254	■
47	/	99	c	151	ù	203	╦	255	(blank 'FF')
48	0	100	d	152	ÿ	204	╠		
49	1	101	e	153	Ö	205	═		
50	2	102	f	154	Ü	206	╬		
51	3	103	g	155	¢	207	╧		

Review

1. Convert the following decimal (base 10) numbers to their binary (base 2) equivalents:

   a) 4   c) 7   e) 8
   b) 9   d) 35   f) 256

2. Convert the following binary numbers to their decimal equivalents:

   a) 100111   c) 111001   e) 010011
   b) 101010   d) 001010   f) 010101

3. Using the ASCII table, give the code numbers for the following characters in both decimal and binary:

   a) "A"   c) "a"   e) "5"
   b) "!"   d) "Z"   f) " " (a space)

8.3 ASCII Code and Character Conversions

The ASCII code was described as a method by which the computer converts information in the form of strings into numbers. Functions exist to convert characters strings into ASCII values and vice versa:

Function Format	Operation
X = ASC(P$)	Converts the first character in P$ to its ASCII code number.
P$ = CHR$(X)	Assigns the character with the ASCII code number X to P$, which now contains only one character.
P$ = STRING$(X, Y)	Generates a string of length X composed of characters having the ASCII code number Y.

STRING$ may also be used with the actual character instead of the ASCII code. For example STRING$(5,"*") creates the string "*****".

This program demonstrates the use of ASCII conversion functions:

```
10 REM ** Demonstrates ASCII conversions **
20 MORE$ = "Y"
30 WHILE (ASC(MORE$) = 89) OR (ASC(MORE$) = 121)
40    INPUT "Enter a character"; CHAR$
50    ASCII = ASC(CHAR$)
60    PRINT "The ASCII value of '"; CHAR$;
      "' is "; ASCII
70    NEWSTR$ = STRING$(17, ASCII)
80    PRINT "'"; CHR$(ASCII); "' repeated 17
      times is ";
90    PRINT NEWSTR$
100   PRINT
110   INPUT "Run this again"; MORE$
120 WEND
999 END
```

```
RUN
Enter a character? V
The ASCII value of 'V' is 86
'V' repeated 17 times is VVVVVVVVVVVVVVVVV

Run this again? y
Enter a character? *
The ASCII value of '*' is 42
'*' repeated 17 times is *****************

Run this again? n
Ok
```

Note how line 30 uses the ASCII codes for "y" (89) and "Y" (121) rather than the letters to determine the condition for repeating the WHILE loop.

Strings can be joined using the plus sign (+). This is called "concatenation." For example,

```
10 FIRST$ = "Jonathan "
20 LAST$ = "Swift"
30 PRINT FIRST$ + LAST$
99 END

RUN
Jonathan Swift
Ok
```

This program allows a user to enter a word character by character, adding 3 to each character's ASCII code. The coded word formed by the new characters is then output. Entering an asterisk (*) halts the input. Notice how line 50 forms a string by joining characters with the "+" sign:

```
10 REM ** Converts message into code **
20 INPUT "Enter a letter (* to end)"; LETTER$
30 WHILE LETTER$ <> "*"
40    CODE = ASC(LETTER$) + 3
50    CODE$ = CODE$ + CHR$(CODE)
60    INPUT "Enter a letter (* to end)"; LETTER$
70 WEND
80 PRINT "The coded word is " CODE$
99 END
```

```
RUN
Enter a letter (* to end)? b
Enter a letter (* to end)? r
Enter a letter (* to end)? o
Enter a letter (* to end)? w
Enter a letter (* to end)? n
Enter a letter (* to end)? *
The coded word is eurzq
Ok
```

Review

4.   Write a program that translates the coded messages produced by the program in Section 8.3 back into English.

8.4 Data Types

When information is entered into the computer, it can take one of three forms: characters, integers, or floating point numbers. An integer is a number without decimal places, while a floating point number has either a decimal point and decimal places or an implied decimal point. For example, the number 29 could be either integer or floating point, but 29.73 is definitely floating point. Floating point numbers are sometimes called "real" numbers.

Floating point numbers can be either single precision or double precision. A single precision floating point number is stored in the computer with seven significant figures, and up to seven are printed, but only six are accurate. A double precision floating point number is accurate to seventeen significant figures but rounded to sixteen when printed.

Storage of an integer requires 16 bits (2 bytes), a floating point number either 32 or 64 bits (4 or 8 bytes), depending on whether it is single or double precision, and an ASCII character 8 bits. Because of storage requirements it is important to distinguish between the different types. When files are presented in Chapters 11 and 12, the significance of this will become apparent.

The four data types employ different symbols to inform the computer which is being used. String variables use the familiar dollar sign ($) for their names (e.g., NAME1$). Integers, which are restricted to the range -32768 to 32767, are denoted by a percent sign (%). For example, NUM% and AGE% are variable names for integers. While integers have a limited range, they are processed fastest by the computer. Double precision floating point variables are denoted by a number sign (e.g., GRADE#). While they are more accurate, calculations involving double precision numbers are the slowest. Single precision floating point variables are denoted by an exclamation mark (e.g., COUNT!). Variable names without a declaration symbol (#, !, $, %) are considered single precision floating point variables.

The precision of constants as well as variables can be specified and determines the precision of the calculations in which they are used. For example, single precision division

```
PRINT 2 / 3
```

produces

```
.6666667
```

while double precision division

```
PRINT 2# / 3#
```

produces:

.6666666666666667

Note that 2 / 3 is the same as 2! / 3!.

Review

5. Write a program that takes a character as input and prints the character that follows it:

```
RUN
Enter a character? A
The character following 'A' is: B
Ok
```

6. Write a program that takes a capital letter as input and prints the remaining alphabet:

```
RUN
Enter a capital letter? R
STUVWXYZ
Ok

RUN
Enter a capital letter? Z
Ok
```

8.5 String Length: LEN()

When dealing with string data, it is often necessary to determine the number of characters contained in a string. The LEN() function is used to accomplish this task and takes the form

```
NUM = LEN(WORD$)
```

where NUM is assigned the number of characters in the string variable WORD$. If WORD$ has not yet been assigned a value, the LEN() is 0.

The following program demonstrates how the LEN() function could be used to center report headings:

```
10 REM ** Centers report headings **
20 FOR COUNT = 1 TO 3
30    READ HEAD$
40    LENGTH = LEN(HEAD$)
50    CENTER = INT((80 - LENGTH) / 2)
60    PRINT TAB(CENTER); HEAD$
70 NEXT COUNT
99 END
1000 REM ** Titles to center
1010 DATA Lawrenceville Press Inc.
1020 DATA First Quarter
1030 DATA Sales Report
```

```
RUN
              Lawrenceville Press Inc.
                   First Quarter
                   Sales Report
Ok
```

Notice how the variables LENGTH and CENTER are used. LENGTH is assigned the length of HEAD$. In order to center the heading the length of the string is subtracted from the total width of the screen, 80. This value is divided by 2 to get the number of spaces to be tabbed in line 60.

8.6 String Modification: MID$(), LEFT$(), RIGHT$()

It is possible to isolate one part of a string using the MID$(), LEFT$() and RIGHT$() functions. The LEFT$() and RIGHT$() functions are similar and take the form:

```
LEFT$(<string>, <length>)
RIGHT$(<string>, <length>)
```

For example:

```
L$ = LEFT$(B$, N)
R$ = RIGHT$(B$, N)
```

In the first example, L$ is assigned a "substring" of B$ starting from the leftmost character up to and including the Nth character, while the second example assigns R$ a substring of B$ consisting of the rightmost N characters. For example, if

```
B$ = "Computer"
```
and
```
N = 3
```

then:

```
L$ = "Com"
R$ = "ter"
```

More flexible than either LEFT$() or RIGHT$() is the MID$() function. MID$() takes the form:

```
MID$(<string>, <start>, <length>)
```

In the statement

```
M$ = MID$(A$, N, L)
```

M$ is assigned a substring of A$ beginning with the Nth character and running for a length of L characters. For example, given that

```
A$ = "Computer"
M$ = MID$(A$, 4, 3)
```

then:

```
M$ = "put"
```

This program reads a sentence from a DATA statement and then prints the sentence over and over subtracting a word each time. When no more words are left, it reads a second sentence and adds a word each time it is printed:

```
10 REM ** Prints sentences subtracting and
            then adding words **
20 READ SENTENCE$
30 FOR CHARNUM = LEN(SENTENCE$) TO 1 STEP -1
40   IF MID$(SENTENCE$, CHARNUM, 1) = " "
        THEN PRINT LEFT$(SENTENCE$, CHARNUM)
50 NEXT CHARNUM
60 READ SENTENCE$
70 FOR CHARNUM = LEN(SENTENCE$) TO 1 STEP -1
80   IF MID$(SENTENCE$, CHARNUM, 1) = " "
        THEN PRINT RIGHT$(SENTENCE$,
        LEN(SENTENCE$) - CHARNUM)
90 NEXT CHARNUM
999 END
1000 REM ** Sentence data
1010 DATA "I seem to keep forgetting one word"
1020 DATA "But I think it's coming back to me
            now"
```

```
RUN
I seem to keep forgetting one word
I seem to keep forgetting one
I seem to keep forgetting
I seem to keep
I seem to
I seem
I
now
me now
to me now
back to me now
coming back to me now
it's coming back to me now
think it's coming back to me now
I think it's coming back to me now
But I think it's coming back to me now
Ok
```

At line 30 LEN(SENTENCE$) determines the number of characters in the sentence read by line 20 and assigns that number to the loop variable CHARNUM. Each time the loop is executed CHARNUM decreases by 1. If the MID$ function at line 40 finds a blank space at position CHARNUM, the sentence is printed from the leftmost character up to and including the space. Lines 60 through 90 repeat a similar routine to print a new sentence from the rightmost character.

Review

7. The output of the following program is Jill's message to Jack. What is the message? Check by running the program:

```
10 REM ** Produces secret message **
20 FOR MESSAGE = 1 TO 6
30    READ WORD1$, WORD2$, WORD3$
40    PRINT LEFT$(WORD1$,1); MID$(WORD2$,2,2);
      RIGHT$(WORD3$,1)
50 NEXT MESSAGE
99 END
1000 REM ** Message data
1010 DATA JDO, XILP, LUL
1020 DATA SSS, HAYE, RRS
1030 DATA HYF, OELR, EVP
1040 DATA WER, LILO, VEL
1050 DATA CIS, TOMH, EIE
1060 DATA SRS, WOOI, SHN
```

8. Write a program which accepts a word and then prints its first and last letters:

```
RUN
Enter a word? toads
The first and last letters: ts
Ok
```

9. a) Write a program which inputs a person's first and last name into a single string variable and then prints the person's initials:

```
RUN
Enter first and last name? Heidi Crane
Initials are: H. C.
Ok
```

b) Modify the program to create a monogram if given the person's full name (monograms list the first, last and middle initials):

```
RUN
Enter full name? Heidi Theresa Crane
Monogram is: H C T
Ok
```

8.7 Input Protection: VAL()

It is often useful to convert a string which stores numbers (digits) into its numeric value. This is done using the VAL() function:

VAL (<string>)

The <string> may be either a string variable or a string of characters within quotation marks:

```
N = VAL(A$)
B = VAL("23")
```

VAL() converts all characters 0-9 into numeric values. The first non-numeric character found causes the conversion to halt. A string that begins with a non-numeric character is converted to 0:

```
PRINT VAL("1234")
 1234

PRINT VAL("2") + VAL("3")
 5

PRINT VAL("007 JAMES BOND")
 7

PRINT VAL("two")
 0
```

A program attempting to INPUT a numeric value halts with an error if the user types a letter or symbol. VAL() can be used to prevent this by using a string to input the data. After the data is entered, the string can be changed into its numeric value using VAL(). The following example shows how this technique can be used:

```
50 INPUT "Enter a number"; NUMBER$
60 NUMBER = VAL(NUMBER$)
```

It is good programming style to prevent errors by using "preventive programming" techniques like this whenever possible. A program which anticipates and avoids errors in this way is called "user-friendly."

Review

10. Write a program that analyzes a user's input and determines whether the input is numeric or alphanumeric:

```
RUN
Enter data? 14254
The input is numeric
Ok


RUN
Enter data? 1K42P054
The input is alphanumeric
Ok
```

8.8 End of Chapter Problem

We wish to write a program to play a simple game of "Hangman." The program selects a word at random from a list stored in DATA statements, and the player is prompted to enter a letter. If the letter is in the word, the player is shown its position. At any point in the game entering a dollar sign allows the player to guess the complete word. The program should keep track of the number of guesses taken.

Algorithm:	1. Randomly select a word.
	2. Have the player pick a letter.
	3. If the letter is in the word display it.
	4. Increment the number of guesses.
	5. Player may guess the word by entering $. If the guess is correct the player wins, and the number of guesses is printed.
	6. Repeat steps 2 through 5 until the word is guessed.

| Input: | Letter player guesses | LETR$ |
| | Word player guesses | GUESS$ |

| Output: | Word to guess | WORD$ |
| | Count of user guesses | GUESS |

```
10 REM ** Plays word guessing game with user **
100 REM ** Main body
110 RANDOMIZE TIMER
120 GOSUB 1000 : REM ** Select word
130 GOSUB 2000 : REM ** Guess word
140 IF GUESS$ = WORD$ THEN PRINT "You Win!"
    ELSE PRINT "You lose"
150 PRINT "The word was " WORD$
160 PRINT "You took" GUESS "guesses."
999 END
1000 REM ** Select random word
1010 FOR COUNT = 1 TO INT(1 + 15 * RND)
1020    READ WORD$
1030 NEXT COUNT
1040 RETURN
1900 REM
2000 REM ** Guess the word
2010 GUESS = 0
2020 LENGTH = LEN(WORD$)
2030 PRINT "The word has" LENGTH "letters"
2040 GUESS$ = STRING$(LENGTH, "-")
2050 INPUT "Enter a letter ($ to guess
     word)"; LETR$
2060 WHILE (LETR$ <> "$") AND (GUESS$ <>
     WORD$)
2070    GUESS = GUESS + 1
2080    FOR LETR = 1 TO LENGTH
2090       IF LETR$ = MID$(WORD$,LETR,1) THEN
          MID$(GUESS$,LETR,1) = LETR$
2100    NEXT LETR
2110    PRINT GUESS$
2120    IF GUESS$ <> WORD$ THEN INPUT "Enter a
       letter ($ to guess word)"; LETR$
2130 WEND
2140 IF LETR$ = "$" THEN INPUT "Enter your
     guess"; GUESS$
2999 RETURN
```

```
9000 REM ** Words to guess
9010 DATA computer, diskette, byte
9020 DATA binary, string, variable
9030 DATA subroutine, function, numeric
9040 DATA letter, program, loops
9050 DATA syntax, errors, testing
```

```
RUN
The word has 10 letters
Enter a letter ($ to guess word)? r
--r------
Enter a letter ($ to guess word)? c
--r------
Enter a letter ($ to guess word)? u
-u-r-u----
Enter a letter ($ to guess word)? s
su-r-u----
Enter a letter ($ to guess word)? $
Enter your guess? subroutine
You Win!
The word was subroutine
You took 4 guesses
Ok
```

```
RUN
The word has 6 letters
Enter a letter ($ to guess word)? o
------
Enter a letter ($ to guess word)? r
----r
Enter a letter ($ to guess word)? s
----r
Enter a letter ($ to guess word)? e
-e--er
Enter a letter ($ to guess word)? t
-etter
Enter a letter ($ to guess word)? l
letter
You Win!
The word was letter
You took 6 guesses.
Ok
```

The loop at lines 1010 to 1030 randomly selects one of the 15 words from the DATA statements. Line 2020 assigns LENGTH the number of characters in WORD$ and line 2040 produces a string of LENGTH dashes and assigns it to GUESS$. Study the loop formed by lines 2060 through 2130 carefully. Note how line 2090 uses MID$ to check each letter in WORD$ to determine whether it has been guessed. If it has, the letter is assigned to its appropriate position in GUESS$. The loop ends when the guessed word is correct, or the user has typed a "$". If a "$" is entered the user is given a chance to guess the word. The program then returns to line 140 to determine if the user has won or lost, and prints out the correct word and number of guesses taken.

Chapter Summary

The binary (base 2) system uses only the digits 0 and 1. To convert a number from base ten to base two, the powers of two which add up to the number must be found. For example, $13 = 8 + 4 + 1$, the base 2 representation is 1101 ($1\times8 + 1\times4 + 0\times2 + 1\times1$). The computer stores data and instructions using the binary system. A single binary digit is called a "bit", and eight of these bits constitutes a "byte."

The computer stores letters and special characters using the ASCII code where each letter of the alphabet, each symbol, and each control function used by the computer is represented by a number. Functions exist to convert strings into ASCII values and vice versa. ASC(P$) converts the first character in P$ to its ASCII code number, CHR$(X) returns the character with the ASCII code number X and STRING$(X, Y) generates a string of length X composed of characters having the ASCII code number Y.

Information entered into the computer can take one of three forms: strings, integers or floating point numbers. An integer is a number without decimal places and a floating point number has either a decimal point and decimal places or an implied decimal point. Floating point numbers can be specified to be either single precision (accurate to seven significant figures) or double precision (accurate to seventeen significant figures).

Storage of an integer requires 16 bits, a floating point number either 32 (single precision) or 64 bits (double) and an ASCII character 8 bits. The four data types employ different symbols in variable names: string variables the dollar sign ($), integers (restricted to the range -32768 to 32767) by a percent sign (%), double precision floating point variables by a number sign (#) and single precision floating point variables by an exclamation mark (!). Variable names without a declaration symbol are considered single precision floating point variables.

The LEN() function returns the number of characters in a string. The function LEFT$(B$, N) returns a substring of B$ starting from the leftmost character up to and including the Nth character while RIGHT$(B$, N) returns a substring of B$ consisting of the rightmost N characters. MID$(A$, N, L) returns a substring of A$ beginning with the Nth character and running for a length of L characters. VAL(A$) returns the numeric value of the first set of numeric character in A$. For example, if A$ = "37 Houston Street", VAL(A$) equals the numeric value 37.

Vocabulary

ASC(P$) - Function that converts first character in P$ to its ASCII code number.
ASCII code - Code in which each letter of the alphabet, each symbol and each control function used by the computer is represented by a number.
Binary system - Number system which uses only the digits 0 and 1 (base 2).

Bit - Single binary digit (0 or 1).

Byte - Eight bits (eight binary digits).

CHR$(X) - Function that returns the character with the ASCII code number X.

Double precision - A floating point number accurate to seventeen significant figures but rounded to sixteen when printed.

Floating point number - A number which has either a decimal point and decimal places or an implied decimal point (real number).

Integer - Number without decimal places in the range -32768 to 32767.

LEFT$(P$, N) - Function which returns a substring of P$ starting from the leftmost character up to and including the Nth character.

LEN(P$) - Function which returns the number of characters contained in P$.

MID$(P$, N, L) - Function which returns a substring of P$ beginning with the Nth character and running for a length of L characters.

RIGHT$(P$, N) - Function which returns a substring of P$ consisting of the rightmost N characters.

Single precision - Floating point number with seven significant figures.

STRING$(X, Y) - Function that generates a string of length X composed of characters having the ASCII code number Y.

VAL(P$) - Function that returns a numeric value of the first set of numeric characters (digits) in P$.

Exercises

1. Write a program which accepts a string and then prints the ASCII code
    of each of its characters:

    ```
    RUN
    Enter a string? Sally

    Character      ASCII code
       S              83
       a              97
       l             108
       l             108
       y             121
    Ok
    ```

2. Input three letters, add their ASCII numbers, find the INT of one third
    of their sum and print the character corresponding to the result. Is there
    any meaning to this process?

3. Using properly selected ASCII numbers read from a DATA statement,
    print the sentence "ASCII did this!".

4. Using ASCII codes 45 and 124 and the PRINT TAB statement, print the
    following figure:

    ```
    RUN
     - - - - - - -
    |             |
    |             |
    |             |
     - - - - - - -
    Ok
    ```

    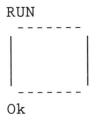

5. Write a program which allows the user to input a word and prints the
    ASCII number of the letter which appears most often in the word:

    ```
    RUN
    Enter a word? FREDDY
    Most common letter is D
    which is ASCII code 68.
    Ok
    ```

6. Have the user input a string of digits. Use string functions to obtain two numbers N1 and N2, N1 being the number represented by the first three digits in the string and N2 the number represented by the last three digits. Print the sum of N1 and N2:

```
RUN
Enter a number? 19562038
N1 = 195
N2 =  38
N1 + N2 = 233
Ok
```

7. Produce a string which consists of the first seven letters of the alphabet. Using the string construct the triangle shown below:

```
RUN
A
AB
ABC
ABCD
ABCDE
ABCDEF
ABCDEFG
Ok
```

8. As a young boy Franklin Roosevelt signed his letters to his mother backwards: TLEVESOOR NILKNARF. Write a program that accepts a person's name and prints it backwards:

```
RUN
Enter a name? Patti Hengy
ygneH ittaP
Ok
```

9. Write a program which generates fifteen random integers from 65 to 90, inclusive, to serve as ASCII code numbers. Convert these fifteen integers to letters and print the results.

10. a) Using random numbers and the ASCII code numbers from 32 to 126, inclusive, have the computer generate 100 characters, allowing repetitions. Tabulate how many of the characters are letters, numbers or special characters and print the results:

```
RUN
There are: 47 letters
           16 numbers
           37 special characters
Ok
```

b) Modify the program to keep track of both upper- and lowercase letters:

```
RUN
There are: 23 lowercase letters
           24 uppercase letters
           18 numbers
           35 special characters
Ok
```

11. You are a spy who must use the computer to produce a secret code.

a) Write a program which inputs a short message and prints the message in a coded form. To produce the coded words, convert each letter in the original message to its corresponding ASCII code number, add two to the numbers and convert back to characters to produce the message. Keep all spaces between the words in their original places and realize that the letters Y and Z are to be converted to A and B. Note: Use only capital letters in your message:

```
RUN
Enter phrase: HELLO THERE
Coded phrase: JGNNQ VJGTG
```

b) Write a program that decodes the messages produced by the program in part (a):

```
RUN
Decoder Program
Enter coded phrase: JGNNQ VJGTG
Translated phrase:  HELLO THERE
```

12. a) Using string and ASCII functions, write a program that inputs a string and then prints the string in all lowercase letters. Be careful not to change letters which are already lowercase or special characters:

```
RUN
Enter a string: Hello There!
hello there!
Ok
```

b) Write a program that inputs a string and then prints the string in all uppercase letters:

```
RUN
Enter a string: Hello There!
HELLO THERE!
Ok
```

c) Write a program that inputs a string and then prints only the first letter of each word in uppercase. All other letters should be lowercase:

```
RUN
Enter a string: HeLlO ThErE!
Hello There!
Ok
```

13. Write a program which prints a triangle made up of parts of the word "TRIANGLE" exactly as shown below. The program should ask for the height of the triangle.

```
RUN
Enter triangle height? 10
T
 RI
  IAN
   ANGL
    NGLET
     GLETRI
      LETRIAN
       ETRIANGL
        TRIANGLET
         RIANGLETRI
Ok
```

14. You have decided to start your own corporation. In the tradition of DEC, GTE, RCA, IBM and other corporate conglomerates, you want your corporate name to be composed of initials, each standing for a word (e.g., International Business Machines becomes IBM). Write a program which accepts a string of up to ten words and then prints a block of letters composed of the first letters of each word. For example, given "Lawrenceville Press Inc." the program should print "LPI".

15. a) Write a program that converts an integer to its binary form:

```
RUN
Decimal to Binary Conversion
Input integer? 13
 13 decimal is: 1101
Ok
```

b) Write a program that converts a binary number of up to 8 digits to its decimal form. (Hint: Read the binary number as a string.):

```
RUN
Binary to Decimal Conversion
Input binary number? 1101
1101 binary is 13 decimal.
Ok
```

Advanced Exercises

Each of the following exercises requires the development of a detailed algorithm. The program should not be written until all details of the algorithm have been worked out.

16. Using string functions, write a program to play a word guessing game. Ask the player to guess a secret word. Search through each guess to see if it contains any correct letters. If any letters are correct, have the computer print them. If the entire word is guessed, type "You guessed it!!".

```
RUN
Guess a word? hangman
'a' is in the word.
'a' is in the word.
Guess a word? dataphone
'a' is in the word.
'a' is in the word.
'e' is in the word.
Guess a word? terminal
'e' is in the word.
'r' is in the word.
'a' is in the word.
'l' is in the word.
Guess a word? scrabble
You guessed it!!
Ok
```

17. Literary critics often argue over the identity of the author of some ancient manuscript. To resolve such disputes, it is helpful to show similarities between the anonymous text and a text by a known author. Write a program which checks a text and tabulates the occurrences of each article ("a", "an", and "the"), each adverb (check for "ly"), and each mark of punctuation (".", ",", "!", "?", ";", ":").

The following DATA would produce the output shown below:

```
9000 DATA "Dear Mr. Fields,"
9010 DATA "We happily announce that you have won"
9020 DATA "the grand prize in our Publisher's"
9030 DATA "Warehouse Sweepstakes! What have I won?,"
9040 DATA "you may ask. You've won the following:"
9050 DATA "1) a 1958 Edsel,"
9060 DATA "2) a year's supply of puppy chow,"
9070 DATA "3) a cuddly pair of Siamese cats,"
9080 DATA "and finally,"
9090 DATA "4) a trip for 2 to the South Pole!"
9100 DATA "Sincerely,"
9110 DATA "M. West"

RUN
There are:  3 periods
            7 commas
            2 exclamation marks
            1 question marks
            0 semicolons
            1 colons
            4 'a's
            0 'an's
            1 'the's
            5 adverbs
Ok
```

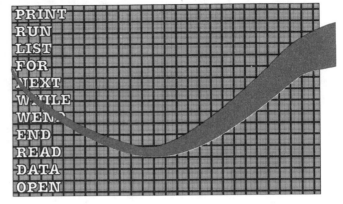

Chapter 9

Color Graphics and Sound

Objectives

Chapter Nine

After completing this chapter you will be able to:

1. Use SCREEN to switch between the three different screen modes; text, medium-resolution graphics and high-resolution graphics.

2. Switch between 40 column and 80 column text modes using WIDTH.

3. Remove the function key shortcuts from the bottom of the screen with KEY OFF and return them to the screen using KEY ON.

4. Select colors using COLOR and place the cursor at any screen location using LOCATE.

5. Draw and erase points using PSET and PRESET.

6. Draw lines using LINE.

7. Pause program execution using INPUT.

8. Draw boxes and filled boxes using options to LINE.

9. Determine the color of a specified point using the POINT() function.

10. Draw circles, arcs and ellipses using CIRCLE.

11. Fill a figure with color using PAINT.

12. Add sound to a program with BEEP and SOUND.

13. Produce songs using PLAY.

*O*ften a picture or graphic is the best way to get a message across. Using a pie chart to represent sales percentages or a bar diagram to show a company's revenues are just two examples of how a picture is "worth a thousand words." This chapter deals with the BASIC statements needed to create graphic displays on the IBM PC and compatibles, and how these commands may be implemented in programs.

In order to create graphics on the IBM PC, a monitor which is capable of displaying graphics must be properly installed on your machine.

9.1 Screen Modes and WIDTH

There are three different screen modes in BASIC; text, medium-resolution graphics and high-resolution graphics. A mode is merely the way the computer displays information on the screen. The first method is called text mode because it allows only character data (letters, numbers, special characters, etc.) to be displayed on the screen in a variety of text and background colors. The second, medium-resolution graphics mode provides an area for graphing which is 320 horizontal positions by 200 vertical positions. Finally, the high-resolution graphics mode provides for pictures of even finer detail by further subdividing the screen into an area of 640 horizontal positions by 200 vertical positions.

Text display has two different modes itself; 40 column and 80 column. These modes control the number of characters which may be displayed on a single line, 40 or 80. Eighty column mode is the standard, but it is possible to switch between them using the WIDTH statement

```
WIDTH <columns>
```

where <columns> is the number of columns (letters) across the screen.

```
WIDTH 40
```

sets the display to 40 column mode which uses larger than normal characters.

```
WIDTH 80
```

returns the display to the standard 80 column display. After graphics operations are complete, it is a good programming practice to return the screen to 80 column mode using WIDTH 80.

9.2 The SCREEN Command

In order to create graphic displays on the screen, the computer must first be put into the correct mode. This is accomplished using the SCREEN statement, which takes the form

```
SCREEN <mode>, <burst>
```

where <mode> represents which of the three graphics modes to use and <burst> tells the computer whether to display output in black & white or color. Burst operates differently in different modes. The following table shows the relationship between mode and burst in the three different graphics modes:

MODE	MEANING	BURST
0	text	0 = black & white 1 = color
1	medium-resolution	0 = color 1 = black & white
2	high-resolution	no effect

For example, the statement

```
SCREEN 0, 0
```

puts the computer into text mode with a black & white display, while

```
SCREEN 1, 0
```

selects medium-resolution graphics mode with the color turned on. The statement

```
SCREEN 2
```

puts the computer into high-resolution mode. Notice that burst was not used in this example because high-resolution mode produces pictures in only black and white. Since color is not available in high-resolution mode, the burst value has been omitted.

Remember that related commands may be joined in a single statement by separating them with colons (:). This is especially useful with graphics commands. For example,

```
240 SCREEN 0, 0 : WIDTH 80
```

returns the computer to black and white text display in 80 column mode, which is the standard. This is especially important after using medium resolution graphics, which leaves the screen in 40 column mode.

9.3 Available COLORs

The COLOR statement selects the color characteristics of the display after a SCREEN command has been issued. There are a total of 16 colors available on the computer. However, the number of colors a programmer may access is limited by which mode the computer is in. The available colors are:

```
0 – Black          8 – Gray
1 – Blue           9 – Light Blue
2 – Green         10 – Light Green
3 – Cyan          11 – Light Cyan
4 – Red           12 – Light Red
5 – Magenta       13 – Light Magenta
6 – Brown         14 – Yellow
7 – White         15 – Bright White
```

The Alt key shortcut for COLOR is Alt-C.

9.4 COLOR in Text Mode

When using color text mode (SCREEN 0, 1), the COLOR statement takes the form

```
COLOR <foreground>, <background>, <border>
```

The foreground, or color of the text, may have a value of 0 to 15. For example, having the foreground color set to 5 produces magenta characters on the screen. The characters can be made to blink on and off by adding 16 to the foreground value (producing a number between 16 and 31). Using the previous example, we could produce blinking magenta characters by making the foreground value 21 (5 + 16). The background can only be a color with a value of 0 to 7. Finally the border, or edge of the screen, can be any color, so it can take the value of 0 to 15. The statements

```
10 SCREEN 0, 1
20 COLOR 0, 4, 8
30 PRINT "This is color"
```

produce black characters on a red background with a gray border. Note that border colors can be slightly off when using a VGA or MCGA monitor. To remove a border when using these displays, set it to the same color as the background, e.g., COLOR 7,0,0.

It is possible to change one of the COLOR values during the program without changing the others. Any value which is omitted from the COLOR statement will retain its current value. For example

```
90 COLOR , 8
```

leaves the foreground (character) and border colors at their current values and changes the background only to gray. It is important to remember to use the appropriate number of commas when changing only one or two of the values of the COLOR statement.

The CLS statement should be used following the COLOR statement. This not only clears the screen of unwanted text but also changes the screen color entirely to the background color.

The following program illustrates the different colors available in the text mode:

```
10 REM ** Using SCREEN and COLOR in text mode **
20 SCREEN 0, 1 : REM ** Color text mode
30 COLOR 0, 5, 1
40 CLS
50 PRINT
60 PRINT "You can write in: BLACK"
70 FOR C = 1 TO 15
80    COLOR C
90    READ HUE$
100   PRINT TAB(19); HUE$
110 NEXT C
999 END
1000 DATA BLUE, GREEN, CYAN, RED
1010 DATA MAGENTA, BROWN, WHITE
1020 DATA GRAY, LIGHT BLUE
1030 DATA LIGHT GREEN, LIGHT CYAN
1040 DATA LIGHT RED, LIGHT MAGENTA
1050 DATA YELLOW, BRIGHT WHITE
```

```
You can write in: BLACK
                  BLUE
                  GREEN
                  CYAN
                  RED

                  BROWN
                  WHITE
                  GRAY
                  LIGHT BLUE
                  LIGHT GREEN
                  LIGHT CYAN
                  LIGHT RED
                  LIGHT MAGENTA
                  YELLOW
                  BRIGHT WHITE
Ok
```

The words will be in color on your screen

Line 20 puts the computer into text mode with the color option on. Line 30 sets the background color to magenta, with black characters and a blue border. When the CLS is executed, the entire background becomes magenta with a blue border. This does not automatically occur when the COLOR statement is executed. If line 40 were omitted, the background and border would change only as new lines were printed. Line 80 sets the foreground (character) color to the value of C; the background and border values are not included in the statement and therefore remain unchanged. This causes HUE$ to be printed in its appropriate color at line 100. Notice how color #5 (magenta) is "invisible" — text printed in the same color as the background cannot be seen.

To return the screen to text mode after running this program, type:

```
SCREEN 0, 0 : WIDTH 80
```

9.5 Placing Text: LOCATE

The text screen displays 25 lines of 40 or 80 characters each. LOCATE allows text to be displayed starting at any of these positions. The statement

```
LOCATE <row>, <column>
```

places the cursor at the position on the screen identified by specified row and column. Any text then printed starts at that location. For example,

```
10 LOCATE 12, 37
20 PRINT "Hello!"
```

displays "Hello!" near the middle of the 80 column text screen. The "H" is placed at row 12, column 37.

Review

1. Write a program to display the following output

    ```
    OLD GLORY IS MADE UP OF
    RED
    WHITE
    AND BLUE STRIPES.
    ```

    using gray characters with a green background. Have the words for each color (red, white and blue) print in that color.

2. a) Write a program which displays the words GREEN, CYAN, BROWN and YELLOW in their proper colors. One word should be in each of the four corners of the 80 column text screen.

    b) Modify the program written for part (a) above and have it work for the 40 column screen.

    c) Modify the program written for part (b) to have the words CYAN and YELLOW appear in blinking letters.

9.6 COLOR in Graphics Mode

Of the two graphics modes, the COLOR statement can be used only in medium-resolution mode. This is because the high-resolution mode creates pictures in black and white only. The format for the COLOR statement in medium-resolution graphics mode is:

```
COLOR <background>, <palette>
```

The background can have the value of 0 to 15, thus taking on any color available to the computer. Medium-resolution graphics mode contains a <palette> option which can be either 0 or 1. Each of the two palettes allows the programmer to select one of three foreground colors which may be used to create graphic displays:

	PALETTE 0		**PALETTE 1**
Color #	Color Name	Color #	Color Name
0	<background>	0	<background>
1	Green	1	Cyan
2	Red	2	Magenta
3	Brown	3	White

In addition to the three foreground colors, it is possible to choose the background color (0 in both palettes) which makes the foreground and background the same color, as selected in the COLOR statement. The statements

```
10 SCREEN 1, 0
20 COLOR 12, 1
```

put the computer into medium-resolution color graphics mode and select a background color of light red (pink). The use of palette 1 means that the available plotting colors are cyan (1), magenta (2) and white (3), as well as the background color of light red (0). The statements

```
10 SCREEN 1, 0
20 COLOR 14, 0
```

put the computer into medium-resolution graphics mode and select a background color of yellow. Using palette 0 means that the colors green (1), red (2) and brown (3), as well as the background color of yellow (0) are available for display. Because these statements are closely related they are often grouped on the same line. For example,

```
10 SCREEN 1, 0 : COLOR 14, 0
```

Review

3. Describe what each of the following sets of statements accomplish:

```
a) 10 SCREEN 0, 1          b) 10 SCREEN 1, 0
   20 COLOR 12, 6, 8          20 COLOR 12, 1
   30 COLOR 5, , 6            30 COLOR 5
   40 COLOR 25, 7            40 COLOR , 0
   50 COLOR , 3, 3           50 COLOR 5, 1
   60 COLOR , , 1
```

9.7 PSET and PRESET

After the SCREEN and COLOR have been selected, special graphics statements are used to produce pictures on the screen. The simplest graphing statement is PSET which plots a single point on the screen at a position indicated by the programmer. The computer must be in one of the two graphics modes (SCREEN 1 or SCREEN 2) for PSET to work. The general form of the PSET statement is:

```
PSET (X, Y), <color>
```

The (X,Y) values refer to the horizontal (X) and the vertical (Y) coordinates which are to be used to plot the point. If the medium-resolution screen is being used, X can have a value from 0 to 319, and in high-resolution mode X can vary from 0 to 639. In either mode, however, the Y value can range from 0 to 199:

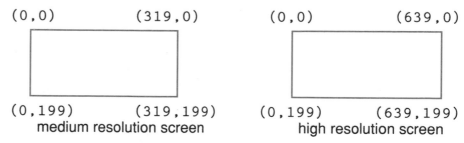

(0,0)   (319,0)   (0,0)   (639,0)

(0,199)   (319,199)   (0,199)   (639,199)
medium resolution screen   high resolution screen

In medium-resolution graphics mode, the <color> value in the PSET refers to the color of the point to be plotted, which is based upon the palette chosen in the most recent COLOR statement. For example,

```
10 SCREEN 1, 0
20 COLOR 9, 0
30 PSET (250, 125), 2
```

plots a red (color 2 from palette 0) point at coordinates (250,125) on the medium-resolution screen. Remember that only four colors are available for plotting as determined by the palette selected in the COLOR statement.

PSET does not need the <color> value in high-resolution mode, since it automatically takes on the color white with a background color of black. If the <color> value is omitted in medium-resolution mode, a value of 3 is automatically assumed.

To erase a plotted point, the PRESET statement is used, which selects the background color to do its plotting. The PRESET statement takes the form:

```
PRESET (X,Y)
```

This program flashes a point at (160,100) on and off 50 times. This is accomplished by setting the point on in line 50 and off in line 70:

```
10 REM ** Flashes point at (160,100) **
20 SCREEN 1, 0
30 COLOR 12, 1
40 CLS
50 FOR COUNT = 1 TO 50
60    PSET (160,100), 3
70    FOR PAUSE = 1 TO 500 : NEXT PAUSE :
      REM ** Delay
80    PRESET (160,100)
90    FOR PAUSE = 1 TO 500 : NEXT PAUSE :
      REM ** Delay
100 NEXT COUNT
110 SCREEN 0, 0 : WIDTH 80
999 END
```

Lines 20 through 40 put the computer into medium-resolution graphics mode with a background color of light red using palette 1. Line 50 plots a white point at location (160,100) and line 80 erases it. Take special note of lines 70 and 90. These FOR loops act as a pause to delay the program. Without them the point would flash so quickly that it could not be seen. Changing the 500 would allow for a shorter or longer delay. Line 110 returns the display to text mode, in 80 column width.

As seen in the last program the point produced by PSET is very small. This program draws a vertical line from (100,10) to (100,150) by plotting a number of adjacent points. It then erases the line by setting each of the points back to the background color:

```
10 REM ** Draws a line using points **
20 SCREEN 1, 0 : COLOR 2, 0
30 CLS
40 REM ** Plot the line
50 FOR Y = 10 TO 150
60   PSET (100, Y), 2 : REM ** Plot a point
70 NEXT Y
80 FOR PAUSE = 1 TO 750 : NEXT PAUSE
90 REM ** Now erase the line
100 FOR Y = 10 TO 150
110   PRESET (100, Y) : REM ** Erase a point
120 NEXT Y
130 FOR PAUSE = 1 TO 500 : NEXT PAUSE
140 SCREEN 0, 0 : WIDTH 80
999 END
```

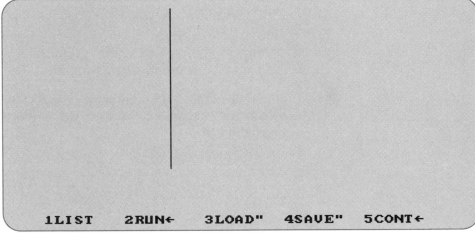

Line 20 sets the computer to medium-resolution graphics mode with the background color green and the palette 0. Lines 50 through 70 make up the loop used to draw the line. At line 60, the points used to form the line are plotted in color 2 (red). Line 80 creates a brief pause. Lines 100 through 120 erase the line point by point using PRESET, and line 130 creates another pause.

Note line 140 which sets the screen back into text mode with the color off and restores the width to 80 characters. This is a good practice for any medium resolution graphics program.

Review

4. Write a program using PSET to draw 500 randomly placed "stars" on a black background. Use all three available colors. Print "Starry Starry Night" on the 24th line.

9.8 KEY OFF and KEY ON

You may have noticed that the list of function key shortcuts stays on the bottom of the screen even in graphics mode. There are times when this is undesirable, especially when creating large graphics. The statement

```
KEY OFF
```

removes this list from the screen. The area formerly occupied by the keys can now be used for graphics or text. The list remains hidden until the statement

```
KEY ON
```

is issued. Along with returning the screen to 80 column text mode, it is a good idea to turn the key list back on at the end of a program.

9.9 The LINE Statement

In the program above PSET was used to draw a line by plotting 140 adjacent points with a FOR...NEXT loop. A more efficient way of drawing a line is to use the LINE statement. In its simplest form, the LINE statement is:

```
LINE (X1, Y1) - (X2, Y2), <color>
```

The LINE statement uses the same coordinate system as the PSET statement and plots a single line from the point (X1,Y1) to the point (X2,Y2). The <color> value is chosen from the current palette. The statements

```
100 SCREEN 1, 0 : COLOR 0, 1
110 LINE (0,0) - (319,199), 2
```

draw a line from the upper-left corner of the screen (0,0) to the lower-right corner (319,199). The line is drawn using color 2 from palette 1, magenta.

Another format of the LINE statement omits the first set of coordinates

```
LINE - (X2, Y2), <color>
```

and draws a line from the last point referenced (by the last LINE, PSET, etc.) to the point (X2,Y2). The <color> works the same way as in the first example. The statements

```
100 SCREEN 1, 0 : COLOR 0, 0
110 PSET (319,0), 1
120 LINE - (0,199), 1
```

create a line from the last point drawn, (319,0) in upper-right corner of the screen, to (0,199) using color 2 from palette 0, green. The line starts at point (319,0) because that was the last point plotted, by the PSET at line 110.

9.10 Pausing Graphic Output

It is a good programming practice to return the graphics screen to 80 column text mode when a program is finished. However, this causes the output produced by the program to be erased, often before it can be viewed by the user.

A good way to pause the program until the user has viewed the graphic is to include an INPUT statement before the SCREEN 0, 0 command. This pauses the program, allowing the user to view the output of the program until the Enter key is pressed. The question mark prompt generated by the INPUT statement can be placed anywhere on the screen by using LOCATE first. For example,

```
280 LOCATE 24, 1
290 INPUT PAUSE$
```

places the prompt in the lower left corner of the screen, and waits for the user to press Enter. (LOCATE 25,1 may be used when KEY OFF has been executed.)

9.11 Drawing Boxes

Besides drawing lines, the LINE statement can be adapted to draw boxes by including a B (for block) after the color. To construct a box, the LINE statement takes on the form:

```
LINE (X1, Y1) - (X2, Y2), <color>, B
```

This statement draws a box starting from the upper-left corner (X1,Y1) to the lower-right corner (X2,Y2):

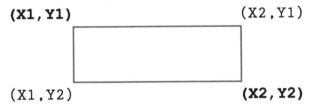

The LINE statement can also be used to created solid boxes using the BF (box fill) option. It takes the form:

```
LINE (X1, Y1) - (X2, Y2), <color>, BF
```

This creates a filled box with upper-left corner at (X1,Y1) and lower-right at (X2,Y2) using the specified color.

This program draws a house using the various features of the LINE statement:

```
10 REM ** Draws a house using LINE statements
          with Box and Box Fill options **
20 SCREEN 1, 0 : COLOR 0, 0 : KEY OFF : CLS
30 REM ** Draw the roof in red
40 LINE (10,60) - (155,0), 2
50 LINE - (300,60), 2
```

```
60  REM ** Draw the body of the house
70  LINE (10,60) - (300,190), 2, B
80  REM ** Draw the door in brown
90  LINE (130,120) - (180,190), 3, BF
100 REM ** Draw the windows in green
110 LINE (60,80) - (90,100), 1, BF
120 LINE (220,80) - (250,100), 1, BF
130 INPUT PAUSE$
140 SCREEN 0, 0 : WIDTH 80 : KEY ON
999 END
```

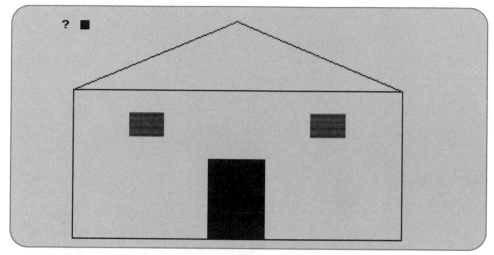

Line 20 puts the computer into medium-resolution graphics mode, sets the background to black and chooses palette 0, and turns the function key line off. Line 40 draws a red line from (10,60) to (155,0) which will be used as the left side of the roof. Line 50 continues the red line drawn by line 40 to form the right side of the roof. In line 70 the block (B) option is used to form the body of the house. The block-fill (BF) option is used in line 90 to draw the door in brown, and in lines 110 and 120 to draw the windows in green.

Review

5. Write a program to draw 6 filled rectangles, each 60 x 30 on the screen. Draw two rectangles in each of the three available colors. Use any color you wish as the background.

9.12 Checking the Color of POINTs

The POINT() function returns the value of the color currently displayed at a specified point on the screen. The statement

```
N = POINT(X, Y)
```

assigns N a value from 0 to 3 (in medium-resolution mode). A value of 0 indicates that the color of the selected point is the same as the background color. A value of 1, 2 or 3 corresponds to a color from the current palette, as selected by the most recent COLOR statement. If -1 is returned by POINT(), the coordinates given are not on the screen. Remember that in medium-resolution mode, the X value must be between 0 and 319, while the Y value must lie between 0 and 199.

In high-resolution mode, POINT() returns either 0 for a black point or 1 for a white point. -1 is returned if the specified point is not on the screen. In high-resolution mode, the X value must be between 0 and 639, while the Y value must lie between 0 and 199.

This program illustrates the POINT() function in medium resolution mode:

```
10 REM ** Demonstrates POINT() function **
20 SCREEN 1, 0 : COLOR 8, 0 : KEY OFF : CLS
30 PSET (100,120), 1
40 LINE (140,80) - (185,80), 2
50 LINE (150,125) - (185,145), 3, BF
60 FOR PNT = 1 TO 5
70    READ X, Y : REM ** Coordinates
80    C = POINT(X, Y)
90    PRINT "Point at ("; X; ","; Y; ") is "; C
100 NEXT PNT
110 INPUT PAUSE$
120 SCREEN 0, 0 : WIDTH 80 : KEY ON
999 END
1000 DATA 100,120, 160,80, 160,135
1010 DATA 100,100, 500,500
```

```
Point at ( 100 , 120 ) is  1
Point at ( 160 , 80 ) is  2
Point at ( 160 , 135 ) is  3
Point at ( 100 , 100 ) is  0
Point at ( 500 , 500 ) is -1
? █
```

Line 20 selects the medium-resolution graphics screen with a gray background and palette 0. Lines 30 through 50 plot a point in green, a line in red and a filled box in brown. The loop at lines 60 through 100 reads an (X,Y) coordinate and determines the color of that position using the POINT() function. The point (500,500) returns -1 because it is off the medium-resolution screen. Line 110 pauses the program until the user presses the Enter key and line 120 restores the normal text screen. The question mark on the screen was caused by the INPUT statement at line 110.

9.13 Drawing CIRCLEs

The CIRCLE statement is used to draw a circle or ellipse on the screen. The general form of the CIRCLE statement is:

```
CIRCLE (X, Y), <radius>, <color>
```

The coordinates (X,Y) specify the center of the circle and the <radius> specifies the distance from the center of the circle to its perimeter. In medium-resolution mode only, the <color> value is used to select a color from the current palette defined by the COLOR statement.

Using the CIRCLE statement, this program produces the five ring Olympic logo:

```
10 REM ** Draws the Olympic symbol using 5
          CIRCLE statements **
20 SCREEN 1, 0 : COLOR 8, 0 : KEY OFF : CLS
30 FOR RADIUS = 20 TO 22
40    CIRCLE (100,80), RADIUS, 2
50    CIRCLE (149,80), RADIUS, 2
60    CIRCLE (198,80), RADIUS, 2
70    CIRCLE (124,100), RADIUS, 2
80    CIRCLE (174,100), RADIUS, 2
90 NEXT RADIUS
100 INPUT PAUSE$
110 SCREEN 0, 0 : WIDTH 80 : KEY ON
999 END
```

Line 20 sets the computer to medium-resolution graphics mode with a background color of gray using palette 0. Lines 30 through 90 create a loop which draws each of the 5 rings three times, with radii of 20, 21 and 22, respectively. This allows the program to draw thicker circles by drawing concentric circles with increasingly larger radii. Lines 40 through 80 actually draw the circles which form the Olympic rings. Notice how the radius of each circle is represented by the loop variable RADIUS.

9.14 Creating Arcs

The CIRCLE statement can also be used to create a portion of a circle called an arc by specifying the starting and ending angles in radians:

```
CIRCLE (X,Y), <radius>, <color>, <start>, <end>
```

Note that <start> and <end> must be expressed in radians, rather that the more familiar degrees. To convert from degrees to radians, multiply the number of degrees by π (Pi) + 180. For example:

45 degrees = 45 × (Pi ÷ 180) = Pi/4 radians (approximately 0.7854)

The start and end angles specify where the arc is to begin and end as follows:

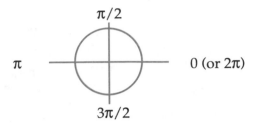

Both 0 and 2π represent the same position. The arc is drawn counter-clockwise from the start angle to the end angle.

Any value between 0 and 2π may be used. If either the <start> or <end> angle is negative, the arc is connected to the center point (X,Y) with a line. The angle is then treated as if it were positive.

This program uses the CIRCLE statement to draw a variety of arcs:

```
10 REM ** Draws various arcs **
20 SCREEN 1, 0 : COLOR 0, 1 : KEY OFF : CLS
30 PI = 3.14159
40 PRINT "Some Simple Arcs"
50 CIRCLE (24,40), 20, 2, PI / 2, PI
60 CIRCLE (84,40), 20, 2, PI / 2, 0
70 CIRCLE (175,40), 25, 1, 0, PI
80 CIRCLE (225,40), 25, 1, PI, 2 * PI
90 LOCATE 11, 1
100 PRINT "Arcs with negative angles:"
110 CIRCLE (122,120), 22, 3, -5 * PI / 4,
     -3 * PI / 4
120 CIRCLE (175,135), 38, 2, -3 * PI / 8,
     -5 * PI / 8
130 INPUT PAUSE$
140 SCREEN 0, 0 : WIDTH 80 : KEY ON
999 END
```

![Screen display showing "Some Simple Arcs" with four arcs across the top and "Arcs with negative angles:" with a question mark prompt, a Pac-Man-like shape and a pie-slice triangle shape at the bottom]

Line 40 displays a title on the screen. Note that PRINT may be used even in graphics mode. Lines 50 through 80 draw arcs with positive angles. Note the arc produced by line 60 which is drawn counter-clockwise from the top at Pi/2 to the right at 0. Lines 110 and 120 create arcs with negative angles, causing a line to be drawn from the center of the arc to the start and end points.

9.15 Drawing Ellipses

The CIRCLE statement can be further expanded to draw ellipses by specifying the ratio of the X-radius to the Y-radius:

    CIRCLE (X, Y), <radius>, <color>, <start>, <end>, <ratio>

If the <ratio> is less than 1, the <radius> is the X-radius. That is, the value given for the <radius> represents the horizontal distance from the center of the ellipse (X,Y) to its perimeter. The Y-radius will then be equal to <ratio> * <radius>.

If the <ratio> is greater than one, the <radius> refers to the Y-radius, the vertical distance from the ellipse's center to its perimeter. The X-radius will then be equal to the <radius> / <ratio>. For example, the statement

    CIRCLE (100, 85), 60, 1, , , 0.3

produces:

This program draws a face using the CIRCLE statement and its ellipse option:

```
10 REM ** Draws a face using CIRCLEs **
20 SCREEN 1, 0 : COLOR 0, 1 : KEY OFF : CLS
30 PI = 3.14159
40 REM ** Draw the outline of the face
50 CIRCLE (150,95), 130, 1, , , 0.7
60 REM ** Draw the nose
70 CIRCLE (150,80), 35, 3, , , , 7
80 REM ** Draw the eyes
90 CIRCLE (99,60), 15, 3
100 CIRCLE (199,60), 15, 3
110 CIRCLE (99,60), 2, 2
120 CIRCLE (199,60), 2, 2
130 REM ** Draw the mouth
140 CIRCLE (150,130), 50, 3, -PI, -2 * PI,
    0.4
150 LOCATE 25, 1
160 INPUT PAUSE$
170 SCREEN 0,0 : WIDTH 80 : KEY ON
999 END
```

Line 50 uses the ellipse option of the CIRCLE statement to draw an oval face, and line 70 draws the nose. Lines 90 through 120 draw concentric circles to form the eyes. Line 140 uses both the arc and ellipse options to create the mouth. Because the angles are negative, a line is drawn from the center to the start and end points.

Review

6. Write a program to draw the pattern of concentric ellipses below. There are 30 ellipses total, with 10 of each color.

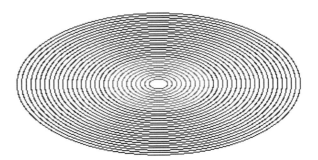

9.16 PAINT

The PAINT statement is used to fill a figure on the screen with color. The general form of PAINT is:

```
PAINT (X, Y), <color>, <edge>
```

The coordinates must be any point located within the figure to be painted. The figure is filled with the selected <color> from the current palette. The color of the figure's outline must be specified in <edge>. For example, the statement to fill a circle centered at (60,150) with the color green which has a red perimeter is:

```
PAINT (60, 150), 1, 2
```

If the point is not inside the figure, or the figure is not closed (does not have a continuous edge), the paint will "spill out" and color the entire screen. This is also the case if the edge value is not specified correctly.

This program draws a painter's palette which has four paint blotches on it using the PAINT statement:

```
10 REM ** Draws palette using PAINT **
20 SCREEN 1, 0 : COLOR 0, 0 : KEY OFF : CLS
30 PI = 3.14159
40 LOCATE 1, 15
50 PRINT "Palette #0"
60 REM ** Draw palette
70 CIRCLE (150, 90), 150, 3, 5 * PI / 4,
   3 * PI / 4, 0.5
80 LINE (44, 36) - (44,144), 3
90 REM **  Draw paint blotches
100 CIRCLE (80, 120), 25, 2, , , 0.5 : REM **
    Thumb hole
110 CIRCLE (123, 50), 25, 2, , , 1.5 : REM **
    Color 0
120 PAINT (123, 50), 0, 2
130 LOCATE 7, 15 : PRINT " 0 "
140 CIRCLE (171, 60), 25, 2, , , 1.5 : REM **
    Color 1
150 PAINT (171, 60), 1, 2
160 LOCATE 8, 21 : PRINT " 1 "
170 CIRCLE (220, 70), 25, 2, , , 1.5 : REM **
    Color 2
180 PAINT (220, 70), 2, 2
190 LOCATE 9, 27 : PRINT " 2 "
200 CIRCLE (268, 80), 25, 2, , , 1.5 : REM **
    Color 3
210 PAINT (268, 80), 3, 2
220 LOCATE 10, 33 : PRINT " 3 "
230 LOCATE 24, 1
240 INPUT PAUSE$
250 SCREEN 0, 0 : WIDTH 80 : KEY ON
999 END
```

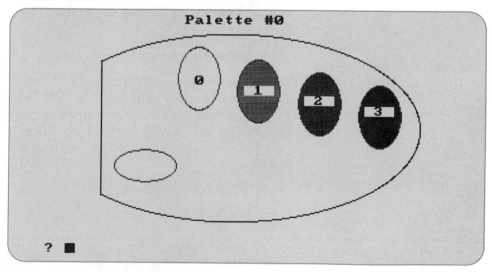

Lines 40 and 50 print a title centered above the picture. Lines 70 and 80 draw the palette using an arc and a line. Line 100 uses CIRCLE to draw the thumb-hole in the palette. Lines 110 through 220 draw the paint blotches, using three lines for each blotch. The first draws an outline of the blotch using CIRCLE. The second fills that outline with the appropriate color using PAINT. Finally, LOCATE and PRINT are used to display the color value inside the blotch. Note that changing the COLOR statement in line 20 produces an appropriate display for palette 1.

Review

7. Using the PAINT statement, rewrite the program from Section 9.15 to fill in the face with color.

ADDING SOUND TO PROGRAMS

9.17 BEEP

The BEEP statement causes the computer to produce a short, beeping sound (a tone of 800 Hz for 1/4 second) which can attract the user's attention. For example, that statements

```
100 INPUT "Enter a grade (A-F)"; GR$
110 IF GR$ < "A" OR GR$ > "F" THEN BEEP :
    PRINT "Wrong!"
```

cause the computer to beep and print "Wrong!" if an invalid grade is entered.

9.18 Making SOUND

Some programs can be made more interesting if sound is used as part of the output. The BEEP statement works well, but it is limited to only one note of fixed duration. If a variety of sounds are desired, the SOUND statement is more applicable. The general form of the SOUND statement is:

SOUND <frequency>, <duration>

where the frequency is expressed in Hertz (cycles per second, Hz). The allowable frequency range is 37 to 32767 Hz. It should be noted that the human ear can only hear sounds up to approximately 20,000 Hz. Duration refers to how long the sound is emitted and is measured in "clock ticks." There are 18.2 clock ticks per second. For example, the statement

SOUND 523, 18.2

plays middle C for 1 second.

Substituting 0 for the duration in the sound statement terminates the note created by any previous SOUND statement. The following chart shows several notes and their corresponding frequencies in Hertz:

Note	Frequency	Note	Frequency
C	130.81	C	523.25
D	146.83	D	587.33
E	164.81	E	659.26
F	174.61	F	698.46
G	196.00	G	783.99
A	220.00	A	880.00
B	246.94	B	987.77
C	261.63	C	1046.50
D	293.66	D	1174.70
E	329.63	E	1318.50
F	349.23	F	1396.90
G	392.00	G	1568.00
A	440.00	A	1760.00
B	493.88	B	1975.50

This program utilizes the SOUND statement to produce the sound of a fire engine siren whose pitch (frequency) first rises then falls:

```
10 REM ** Produces fire engine siren **
20 LOW = 440
30 HIGH = 1568
40 PRINT "Here comes a fire engine..."
50 REM ** Increasing pitch
60 FOR I = 1 TO 5
70    FOR FREQ = LOW TO HIGH STEP 17
80       SOUND FREQ, 0.4
90    NEXT FREQ
100 REM ** Decreasing pitch
110    FOR FREQ = HIGH TO LOW STEP -9
120       SOUND FREQ, 0.4
130    NEXT FREQ
140 NEXT I
999 END
```

Lines 20 and 30 set the starting (LOW) and ending (HIGH) pitches to 440 Hz (A) and 1568 Hz (G). The loop at line 60 sounds the siren 5 times. Lines 70 through 90 cause the pitch of the siren to rise. Notice how the loop variable is substituted for <frequency> in line 80. Each note sounds for approximately one 45th of a second. The loop at lines 110 through 130 creates the falling pitch.

9.19 PLAYing Songs

BASIC provides an easy way to create songs using the PLAY statement

PLAY <string>

where the string consists of notes and durations. Notes can be A through G with notations for sharps (♯ or +) and flats (-). For example,

```
PLAY "B-"
```

plays the note B-flat. The length of each note is specified using the letter L followed by a number from 1 to 64, where 1 represents a whole note, 2 is a half note, 3 is a triplet, and so on:

```
PLAY "L2 A#"
```

plays the an A-sharp for the length of a half note. If no length is given, all notes are assumed to be quarter notes. Notes may be listed together, or stored in strings. For example:

```
10 SONG$ = "L6 ABACABAC"
20 PLAY SONG$
```

Pauses or rests are specified using P followed by a number from 1 to 64. The tempo may be changed using T followed by a number from 32 to 255 which specifies the number of beats per minute. The default tempo is 120 beats per minute. The statement

```
10 PLAY "T90 AA BB P4 CC DD"
```

sets the tempo to 90 beats per minute, plays 4 quarter notes, rests for a quarter, and plays 4 more quarter notes.

The octave in which the notes are taken from may also be specified using O and a number. Seven octaves are available, numbered from 0 to 6. Each octave runs from note C to B. Octave 2 starts with middle C, and the default octave is 4. The statement

```
10 PLAY "L2 O0 C O1 C O2 C O3 C O4 C O5 C O6 C"
```

plays a half note C in each of the seven octaves.

The following program plays the song Happy Birthday:

```
10 PART1$ = "T140 L4 GG L3 AG O5C O4B P3"
20 PART1A$ = "L4 GG L3 AG O5DC P3"
30 PART2$ = "L4 O4 GG O5 L2G O4 L3 ECBA P3"
40 PART1B$ = "L4 FF L3 ECDC"
50 PLAY PART1$
60 PLAY PART1A$
70 PLAY PART2$
80 PLAY PART1B$
999 END
```

PART1$ defined in line 10 sets the tempo to 140 beats per minute, and then plays two quarter-note G's for "Hap-py". The length is then set to one third of a whole note (or "triplet") and plays the notes AG for "Birth-day". The octave is raised to number 5, and a C played for "to", and then reset to octave 4 and a B played for "you". Finally, it pauses for a triplet. The other parts are similar.

9.20 End of Chapter Problem

This chapter ends by solving a problem which requires a carefully thought out algorithm. Once the algorithm has been developed, we can then determine what input and output are needed and assign appropriate variable names. Finally, the program can be coded.

A bookstore needs a program that keeps track of the number of books they carry by subject. The store would like the program to be able to list all the available subjects as well as display the stock in each subject as a bar graph.

Algorithm:

1. Read in information on the books (subject, stock).
2. Print menu.
3. Get user choice (subject, bar graph or exit).
4. Perform the selected activity until choice is Exit:
   a) Subject – List all available subjects.
   b) Bar Graph – Draw a graph showing the number in stock for each subject.
   c) Exit – Leave the program.

Input:

Number of Subjects	NUMSUBJ
Subject name	SUBJECT$
Number in stock	STOCK
User menu selection	CHOICE

Output:

Subject	SUBJECT$
Bar Graph	

```
10 REM ** Displays bookstore statistics **
20 REM ** Main program
30 READ NUMSUBJ : REM ** Number of subjects
40 DIM SUBJECT$(NUMSUBJ), STOCK(NUMSUBJ)
50 FOR BOOKS = 1 TO NUMSUBJ
60   READ SUBJECT$(BOOKS), STOCK(BOOKS)
70 NEXT BOOKS
80 SCREEN 0, 1 : COLOR 14, 1, 1 : KEY OFF :
   CLS
90 WHILE CHOICE <> 3
100   CLS
110   LOCATE 6, 12
120   COLOR 18 : PRINT "Bookstore Statistics"
130   PRINT : PRINT
140   COLOR 4 : PRINT TAB(15); "1 ";
150   COLOR 14 : PRINT "Subjects List"
160   COLOR 4 : PRINT TAB(15); "2 ";
170   COLOR 14 : PRINT "Bar Graph"
180   COLOR 4 : PRINT TAB(15); "3 ";
190   COLOR 14 : PRINT "Exit"
200   PRINT
210   INPUT "Enter selection (1-3): ", CHOICE
```

```
220   WHILE (CHOICE < 1) OR (CHOICE > 3)
230     BEEP
240     INPUT "Enter selection (1-3): ",
        CHOICE
250   WEND
260   IF CHOICE <> 3 THEN ON CHOICE GOSUB
      1000, 2000
270 WEND
280 SCREEN 0, 0 : KEY ON : CLS
999 END
1000 REM  ** List available subjects
1010 CLS
1020 LOCATE 4, 1
1030 COLOR 5 : PRINT "     List of Subjects"
1040 PRINT
1050 COLOR 3
1060 FOR SUBJECT = 1 TO NUMSUBJ
1070   PRINT TAB(9); SUBJECT$(SUBJECT)
1080 NEXT SUBJECT
1090 PRINT : PRINT
1100 LOCATE 25, 1
1110 COLOR 14
1120 INPUT "Press Enter to continue ", PAUSE$
1130 RETURN
1990 REM
2000 REM ** Draw bar graph of stock
2010 SCREEN 1, 0 : COLOR 1, 1 :
     REM ** Color graphics mode
2020 WIDE = 12            : REM ** Width of bar
2030 START = 20           : REM ** Starting
     position of bar
2040 BARCOLOR = 1         : REM ** Color of bar
2050 FOR BAR = 1 TO NUMSUBJ
2060   REM ** Draw bar
2070   LINE (START, 180) - (START + WIDE,
       180 - STOCK(BAR)), BARCOLOR, BF
2080   REM ** Print subject name
2090   LOCATE 2 + BAR, 25 : PRINT
       SUBJECT$(BAR)
2100   REM ** Draw marker beside subject
2110   CIRCLE (180, 11 + (BAR * 8)), 3,
       BARCOLOR
2120   BARCOLOR = BARCOLOR + 1 : REM **
       Change color
2130   IF BARCOLOR > 3 THEN BARCOLOR = 1
2140   START = START + (WIDE * 2)
2150 NEXT BAR
2160 REM ** Wait for user to press Enter
2170 LOCATE 25, 22
2180 INPUT "Enter to continue ", PAUSE$
2190 REM ** Set color text mode
2200 SCREEN 0, 1 : WIDTH 80 : COLOR 14, 1, 1
2210 RETURN
```

```
9000 REM ** Inventory Data **
9010 REM ** Number of subjects
9020 DATA 5
9030 REM ** Subject name, Amount in stock
9040 DATA Novel, 55
9050 DATA Biography, 112
9060 DATA Poetry, 139
9070 DATA Science, 170
9080 DATA Philosophy, 76
```

Lines 10 through 999 make up the main program which handles displaying the menu and entering user choices. Line 30 reads the number of subjects from a DATA statement. Line 40 dimensions the arrays to store the subject names and numbers of items in stock. The loop at lines 50 through 70 reads the current inventory from DATA. The display is set to color text mode in line 80, with yellow letters on a blue background. The loop at lines 90 through 270 repeats until the user chooses the Exit option. The menu is printed with red numbers followed by yellow letters. Note the title at line 120. Setting the color to 18 prints the letters in flashing green (2 + 16). The subject list starts at line 1000, and uses different colors to display the title and subject names. The LOCATE at line 1100 places the user prompt at the very bottom of the screen.

The bar graph subroutine starts at line 2000. The screen is set to color graphics mode with palette 1 at line 2010. Each bar is 12 positions wide, and will begin at position 20. These numbers can be changed at lines 2020 and 2030. Lines 2050 through 2150 create a loop which executes once for each subject. Line 2070 draws a filled box to represent the bar. Note lines 2090 and 2110. The first prints the name of the subject to the right of the bars. The second draws a small circle in the same color as the bar to the left of the subject name. This acts as a legend for the graph. Because there are only three colors available, lines 2120 and 2130 change the color for the next bar and set it back to 1 if necessary. Line 2140 sets the starting position of the next bar based on the current bar width. Lines 2170 through 2200 prompt the user to press Enter, and then reset the screen to color text mode.

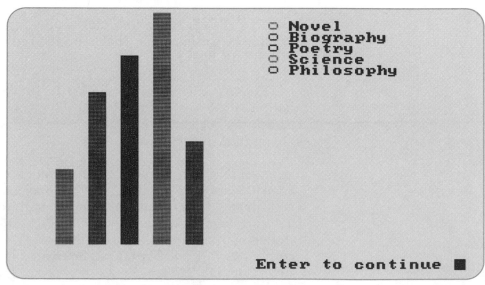

Chapter Summary

A mode is the way in which the computer displays information on the screen. In BASIC there are three modes: text mode which displays only character data, medium-resolution graphics mode which provides a graphing area of 320 horizontal positions by 200 vertical, and high-resolution graphics mode which provides a graphing area of 640 horizontal positions by 200 vertical.

Text display can be switched between either 40 column or 80 column mode using the WIDTH statement. After graphics operations are complete, it is best to return the screen to 80 column mode using WIDTH 80.

To switch between the three graphics modes the SCREEN <mode>, <burst> statement is used where <mode> represents which of the three graphics modes is to be used and <burst> determines whether to display output in black & white or color. In high-resolution mode (mode 2) <burst> is omitted since only black and white graphics can be displayed.

After the SCREEN statement is executed the COLOR statement is needed to determine what color is used to produce a display. In text mode the COLOR statement takes the form COLOR <foreground>, <background>, <border>. The foreground, or color of the text, may have a value of 0 to 15, the background a value of 0 to 7, and the border a value of 0 to 15. If the CLS statement is executed following the COLOR statement the screen is cleared of unwanted text and the screen color changed entirely to the background color with border.

LOCATE <row>, <column> can be used to place the cursor at any screen location. Any text then printed starts at this location.

The format of the COLOR statement in medium-resolution graphics mode is COLOR <background>, <palette> where the background can have the value of 0 to 15. The palette can be either 0 or 1 and each palette allows one of three foreground colors to be used.

PSET (X, Y), <color> plots a point on the graphics screen at the specified coordinates and in the specified color. To erase a plotted point PRESET (X,Y) is used.

KEY OFF removes the list of function key shortcuts on the bottom of the screen while KEY ON displays the list. Erasing a graphics screen can be delayed by placing an INPUT statement at the appropriate location in a program.

LINE (X1, Y1) - (X2, Y2), <color> draws a line between the coordinates (X1, Y1) and (X2, Y2) in the selected color. Omitting the first coordinates draws a line from the last point referenced to the point (X2, Y2). Adding a B at the end of the LINE statement causes a box to be drawn starting from the upper-left corner (X1, Y1) to the lower-right corner (X2, Y2). Solid boxes can be created in a selected color using the BF option: LINE (X1, Y1) - (X2, Y2), <color>, BF

The POINT(X, Y) function returns the value of the color currently displayed at a specified point on the screen.

CIRCLE (X, Y), <radius>, <color> can draw a circle, arc or ellipse on the screen. The coordinates (X, Y) specify the center of the circle and the <radius> specifies the distance from the center of the circle to its perimeter. In medium-resolution the <color> value selects a color from the current palette. CIRCLE can be used to create an arc by specifying the starting and ending angles in radians: CIRCLE (X, Y), <radius>, <color>, <start>, <end>. To convert from degrees to radians multiply the number of degrees by $\pi/180$. CIRCLE can be expanded to draw ellipses by specifying the ratio of the X-radius to the Y-radius: CIRCLE (X, Y), <radius>, <color>, <start>, <end>, <ratio>

PAINT (X, Y), <color>, <edge> is used to fill in a figure with color. The coordinates are any point located within the figure and <edge> specifies the color of the figure's outline.

BEEP produces a short, beeping sound. SOUND <frequency>, <duration> produces a sound of the specified frequency and duration. Duration is measured in clock ticks (18.2 clock ticks per second).

PLAY "L2 F#" plays the note F sharp for a length of half note. Pauses or rests are specified using P followed by a number from 1 to 64. Tempo may be changed using T followed by a number from 32 to 255 which specifies number of beats per minute. O followed by a number from 0 to 6 specifies the octave.

Vocabulary

BEEP - Statement used to produce a short beeping sound.
Burst - Parameter to SCREEN that determines whether graphics are displayed in black and white or color.
CIRCLE - Statement used to draw a circle, arc or ellipse.
COLOR - Statement that selects the color of a graphics display.
High-resolution graphics mode - Provides a black and white graphing area of 640 horizontal positions by 200 vertical positions.
KEY OFF - Removes the list of function key shortcuts from the bottom of the screen.
KEY ON - Returns the list of function key shortcuts to the bottom of the screen.
LINE - Statement that draws a line between selected coordinates in a chosen color. Also used to create boxes and filled boxes.
LOCATE - Statement that places the cursor at a specified row and column.
Medium-resolution graphics mode - Provides a graphing area which is 320 horizontal positions by 200 vertical positions.
Mode - The way the computer displays information on the screen.
PAINT - Statement used to fill in a figure on the screen with color.
Palette - Used in medium-resolution graphics, it can have a value of 0 or 1 which then allows one of three foreground colors to be selected.
PLAY - Statement that produces a variety of notes which allows songs to be programmed.

POINT() - Function that returns the value of the color displayed at a specified point on the screen.

PRESET - Statement that erases a point on the screen at specified coordinates.

PSET - Statement that draws a point on the screen at specified coordinates in a selected color.

SCREEN - Statement which selects the desired graphics display.

SOUND - Statement that produces a sound of a specified frequency and duration.

Text mode - Displays character data on the screen in a variety of text and background colors.

WIDTH - Statement which switches between 40 column and 80 column text mode.

Exercises

1. Have the computer draw a solid red rectangle with its upper left corner at (38, 18), a length of 70 columns, and a height of 30 rows.

2   Using medium resolution graphics, draw a solid cyan square with side length of 20 in the center of the screen.

3. Have the computer draw a green letter L about two inches high in the upper left corner of the screen:

4. Using medium resolution graphics, draw a cyan vertical line and a white horizontal line which intersect at (140, 80):

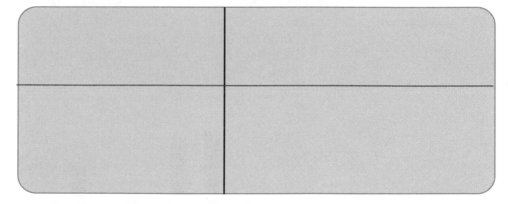

5. Modify Exercise 4 so that there is a magenta ellipse of radius 60 and of ratio 2 whose center is at the intersection of the lines.

6. Have the computer display a brown right triangle with the coordinates at (250, 20), (250, 110), (130, 110).

7. An easy method for drawing a star is to draw two equilateral triangles of the same size, one pointing up and the other superimposed pointing down. Using this method, draw a green star.

8. Place a flashing red notice on the text screen which advertises Uncle Bill's Whamburgers for $.79. The screen should have a gray background and a green border:

    ```
    Today only!
    Uncle Bill's
    WHAMBURGERS!
    Only $0.79
    ```

9. In high resolution mode draw the letter A with the top at (350, 30) and the lowest point on the left side at (200, 160):

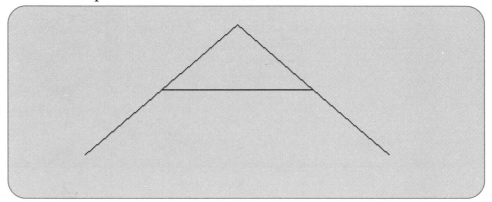

10. In high resolution mode draw the letter Z utilizing the entire screen.

11. Have the computer generate 200 random integers between 1 and 10, inclusive. Using medium resolution graphics, plot a properly labeled bar graph showing the number of occurrences of each random number:

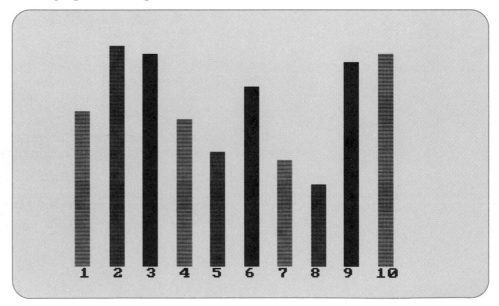

12. Produce the following Hatman in red with a green hat and a brown eye. The Hatman should be surrounded by the color white:

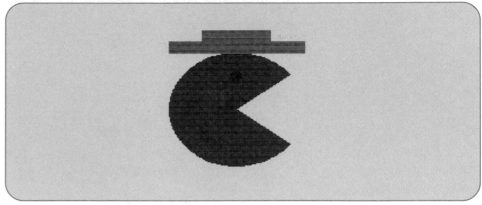

13. The following table shows production output per day for each employee of Papa's Pizza Parlor:

Employee	Pizza Production
Smith	18, 12, 9, 10, 16, 22, 14
Munyan	12, 21, 19, 16, 28, 20, 22
Ricardo	18, 20, 14, 19, 11, 16, 23
Fazioli	23, 27, 18, 16, 21, 14, 24

Plot a bar graph showing the average output per week for each of Papa's employees:

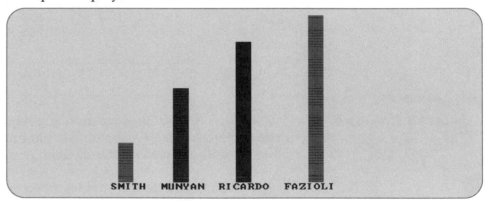

14. Using only a single CIRCLE statement and a single FOR...NEXT loop, have the computer produce the following sphere:

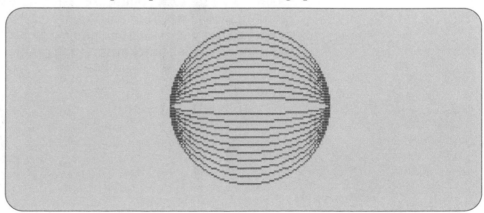

15. Using medium resolution graphics, have the computer produce the following figure:

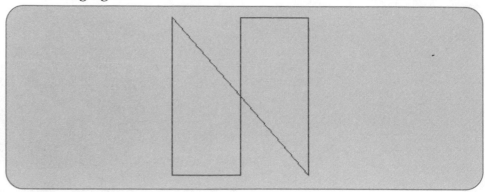

16. Using a single loop and one CIRCLE statement, produce the following wagon wheel in red:

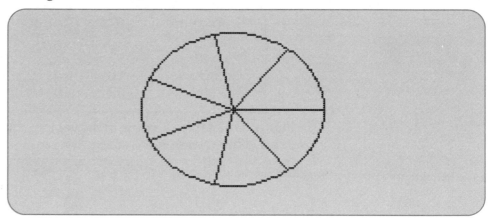

Advanced Exercises

Each of the following exercises requires the development of a detailed algorithm. The program should not be written until all details of the algorithm have been worked out.

17. Using medium resolution graphics, have the computer generate a 90 x 90 circular dart board using the colors 1 through 3, where brown (color 3, palette 0) occupies the center, red the middle band and green the outer band. Have the computer take ten random shots at points on the board. Use the POINT() function to tabulate the computer's score. If the point of impact is within the brown area, the computer scores 3 points; if within the red, 2 points and green, 1 point. Show where each dart hits by plotting a small black cross at the point of impact.

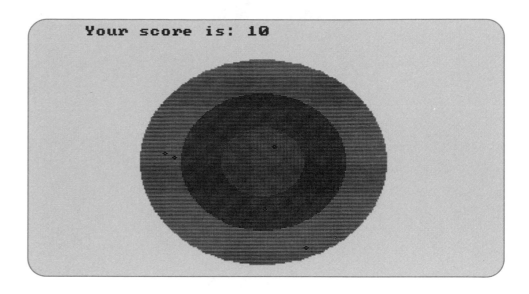

18. Many board games are being converted into computer format. Write a "Name That Tune" program that allows 5 songs of 8 notes each to be stored along with their respective lengths and octaves in DATA statements. The game should randomly choose a song and allow two players to each pick the number of notes in which they could guess the song. The player who inputs the least number of notes (greater than zero) will be told to guess the song after the clue has been PLAYed. If the first player guesses wrong, the second player is given a chance to hear the number of notes he or she chose. If both guess wrong, the game continues by playing the song in its entirety for the first player and then the second. Points are awarded based on the following scale:

> First player correct on chance 1 – 10 points
> Second player correct on chance 1 – 5 points
> Either player correct on chance 2 – 2 points

The game continues until all five songs have been played. Make sure not to play the same song more than once.

Chapter 10

Mathematical Functions

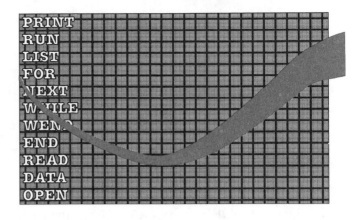

SQR()

SGN()

ABS()

SIN(), COS(), TAN()

ATN()

LOG()

EXP()

DEF FN

Objectives

Chapter Ten

After completing this chapter you will be able to:

1. Use functions to perform mathematical calculations.

2. Use the SQR(), SGN() and ABS() functions.

3. Use the trigonometric functions SIN(), COS(), TAN() and ATN().

4. Find arcsine and arccosine through equations which make use of the ATN() function.

5. Find natural logarithms and logs to base 10 using the LOG() function.

6. Find values of the exponential function, e^x, using the EXP() function.

7. Create user-defined functions with DEF FN.

8. Create string functions using DEF FN.

9. Create user-defined functions with more than one argument.

*T*he ability to interpret and work with mathematical expressions has made the computer an indispensable tool for the mathematician and scientist. Since this chapter introduces the various mathematical functions that the computer can perform, it should be read by those who possess a sufficient mathematical background. It is not within the scope of this book to teach mathematics but instead to illustrate how the computer can be used to solve mathematical problems.

10.1 Functions

A function is a name used in BASIC to perform some specified task. This task can be mathematical, as described in this chapter, or some other type. A good example of a function which you have learned is the TAB() function, which moves the cursor a specified number of places on the screen:

```
PRINT TAB(15); "Hello"
```

In this example, the cursor is moved to the 15th column on the screen before "Hello" is printed.

In the expression TAB(15), TAB is the function name and 15 the "argument." Note that the argument of a function must be enclosed in parentheses, and may be a variable, constant or expression. When executing a function, the computer first evaluates the argument and then performs the function itself. For example, we can write:

```
PRINT TAB(5 * 3); "Hello"
PRINT TAB(ROW); "There"
```

Some functions have a limitation on the value of the argument. Attempting to use an argument outside of those limits results in an `Illegal function call` error. When a function is executed, it is said to be "called." The result of a function is "returned" by the function.

This chapter presents some of the more common mathematical functions available in BASIC, and shows how you may write your own. To differentiate between function and variable names, we will show all functions with parentheses, such as TAB() or SQR().

10.2 SQR(), SGN() and ABS()

Because the following functions perform specific operations, they are presented individually and then demonstrated together in a program.

SQR():

The SQR() function calculates the positive square root of a number. For example,

```
X = SQR(NUM)
```

assigns X the square root of NUM. The square root of a number is defined as that value which, when multiplied by itself, gives the number.

With the SQR() function, the argument may be any mathematical expression with a non-negative value. For example, SQR(3 * NUM + 5) is perfectly acceptable provided that the expression 3 * NUM + 5 produces a non-negative value.

SGN():

In some situations it may be necessary to know if a variable is positive or negative. The SGN() function has only three possible values: 1, 0, and -1 which indicate this. For example,

```
X = SGN(NUM)
```

assigns X the value 1 if NUM > 0, 0 if NUM = 0, or -1 if NUM < 0.

ABS():

The ABS() function returns the absolute value of a number, which is always positive. In the example

```
X = ABS(NUM)
```

X = NUM if NUM > 0, or X = -NUM if NUM < 0.

This program asks the user to input a number for which the square root is desired. The SGN() function is used to avoid the error message printed when the user mistakenly asks for the square root of a negative number. The ABS() function is used to print the square root of the absolute value of the number if a negative number has been entered:

```
10 REM ** Demonstrates the SQR(), ABS() and
            SGN() functions **
20 INPUT "Enter a number"; NUM
30 IF SGN(NUM) = -1 THEN PRINT "You entered
   a negative number."
40 NUM = ABS(NUM)
50 PRINT "The square root of" NUM "=";
   SQR(NUM)
99 END
```

```
RUN
Enter a number? 67
The square root of 67 = 8.185353
Ok
```

```
RUN
Enter a number? -80
You entered a negative number.
The square root 80 = 8.944272
Ok
```

Line 30 uses the SGN() function to determine if a negative number has been entered, and if so prints a message. Line 40 takes the absolute value of the entered number so that its square root may be calculated without causing an error. The SQR() function is used at line 50 to calculate the square root.

Review

1. What is X when X = ABS(–12 + 6 * SGN(–9 + 9 / 3) + 1.8) – 18.2?

2. Write a program which determines if an input number is positive or negative using the SGN() function:

    ```
    RUN
    Enter a number? 37.84
     37.84 is positive.
    Ok

    RUN
    Enter a number? -36
    -36 is negative.
    Ok
    ```

10.3 Trigonometric Functions: SIN(), COS(), TAN()

BASIC includes several trigonometric functions. The functions SIN(), COS() and TAN() produce the value of the sine, cosine and tangent of their argument, which is an angle measured in radians. To convert an angle from degrees to radians it is multiplied by π (pi, 3.14159) divided by 180, since 180 degrees equals π radians.

The following program illustrates how the values of the sine, cosine and tangent can be found for an angle input in degrees:

```
10 REM ** Calculates trigonometric values for
            an input angle **
20 PI = 3.14159
30 INPUT "Enter an angle in degrees"; ANGLE
40 RADANG = ANGLE * (PI / 180)
50 PRINT USING "##.# degrees   = #.####
   radians"; ANGLE, RADANG
60 PRINT USING "sine (###.#)    = #.####";
   ANGLE, SIN(RADANG)
70 PRINT USING "cosine (###.#)  = #.####";
   ANGLE, COS(RADANG)
80 PRINT USING "tangent (###.#) = #.####";
   ANGLE, TAN(RADANG)
99 END
```

```
RUN
Enter an angle in degrees? 30
30.0 degrees   = 0.524 radians
sine (30.0)    = 0.500
cosine (30.0)  = 0.866
tangent (30.0) = 0.577
Ok
```

```
RUN
Enter an angle in degrees? 45
45.0 degrees   = 0.785 radians
sine (45.0)    = 0.707
cosine (45.0)  = 0.707
tangent (45.0) = 1.000
Ok
```

10.4 Arctangent: ATN()

The only inverse trigonometric function supplied in BASIC is the principle arctangent function ATN(). ATN(X) returns the angle whose tangent is X. The value produced by the ATN() function is in radians. To convert an angle from radians to degrees it is multiplied by 180 divided by π. The ATN() function, just like the principal arctangent function in mathematics, gives values only between $-\pi/2$ and $\pi/2$ radians. There is no limitation on the value that the argument may assume.

This program finds the angle whose tangent is entered and prints the result in degrees:

```
10 REM ** Converts tangent of an angle to
          degrees **
20 PI = 3.14159
30 INPUT "Enter the tangent"; TANGENT
40 RADANG = ATN(TANGENT)
50 DEGREES = RADANG * (180 / PI)
60 PRINT USING "Angle with tangent #.#### is
   ##.# degrees"; TANGENT, DEGREES
99 END
```

```
RUN
Enter the tangent? 1.0
Angle with tangent 1.000 is 45.0 degrees
Ok
```

```
RUN
Enter the tangent? 0.0
Angle with tangent 0.000 is  0.0 degrees
Ok
```

```
RUN
Enter the tangent? 0.577
Angle with tangent 0.577 is 30.0 degrees
Ok
```

Note the PRINT USING at line 60 which rounds the degrees when printed.

10.5 Arcsine and Arccosine

To find the principal arcsine of a number, it is necessary to use the trigonometric identity:

$$\text{ARCSINE}(X) = \text{ARCTAN}(X / \text{SQR}(1 - X^2))$$

Therefore, to find the principal angle whose sine is X, the expression ATN(X / SQR(1 – X^2)) is used. This angle is measured in radians and must be between $-\pi/2$ and $\pi/2$. The value of X, however, must be between –1 and 1, not inclusive.

To find the arccosine of X the expression ATN(SQR(1 – X^2) / X) is used. This gives the angle which is between $-\pi/2$ and $\pi/2$ (whose cosine is X). In this expression, X must be between –1 and 1, inclusive, but not equal to 0.

This program calculates the angle in degrees when given its sine or cosine in radians:

```
10 REM ** Calculates angle when given its
          sine or cosine **
20 PI = 3.14159
30 INPUT "Value of sine"; SINE
40 DEGREES = (180 / PI) * ATN(SINE / SQR(1 -
   SINE^2))
50 PRINT USING "Angle with sine #.#### is ##.#
   degrees"; SINE, DEGREES
60 INPUT "Value of cosine"; COSINE
70 DEGREES = (180 / PI) * ATN(SQR(1 -
   COSINE^2) / COSINE)
80 PRINT USING "Angle with cosine #.#### is
   ##.# degrees"; COSINE, DEGREES
99 END
```

```
RUN
Value of sine? 0.5
Angle with sine 0.500 is 30.0 degrees
Value of cosine? 0.5
Angle with cosine 0.500 is 60.0 degrees
Ok
```

```
RUN
Value of sine? 0.707
Angle with sine 0.707 is 45.0 degrees
Value of cosine? 0.707
Angle with cosine 0.707 is 45.0 degrees
Ok
```

10.6 *Logarithm and Exponential Function: LOG(), EXP()*

The LOG() function can be used to find natural logarithms, that is, logarithms to the base *e*. To find the natural logarithm of NUM, LOG(NUM) is used. Do not confuse the natural logarithm (ln) with the common logarithm. The common logarithm, logarithm base 10 ($\log_{10}$), can be found from the natural logarithm by using the formula:

$$\log_{10}(NUM) = LOG(NUM) / LOG(10)$$

The argument to the LOG function must always be positive.

The EXP() function is used to find values of the exponential function, e^x, where *e* = 2.71828. This number is the same as the base of the natural logarithm function. EXP's argument cannot be greater than 88, because this causes an Overflow error.

This program finds the natural (base *e*) and common (base 10) logarithms of a number as well as the value of e^x:

```
10 REM ** Finds the natural and common
           logarithms and e raised to a power
           for an entered number **
20 INPUT "Enter a number"; NUMBER
30 PRINT "Natural logarithm of"; NUMBER; "=";
   LOG(NUMBER)
40 PRINT "Common logarithm of"; NUMBER; "=";
   LOG(NUMBER) / LOG(10)
50 IF NUMBER < 88 THEN PRINT "e raised to";
   NUMBER; "="; EXP(NUMBER) ELSE PRINT
   "e^Number cannot be calculated"
99 END
```

```
RUN
Enter a number? 1
Natural logarithm of 1 = 0
Common logarithm of 1 = 0
e raised to 1 = 2.718282
Ok
```

```
RUN
Enter a number? 0.01
Natural logarithm of .01 =-4.60517
Common logarithm of .01 =-2
e raised to .01 = 1.01005
Ok
```

```
RUN
Enter a number? 10000
Natural logarithm of 10000 = 9.210341
Common logarithm of 10000 = 4
e^Number cannot be calculated
Ok
```

Review

3. Write a program to test the trigonometric identity Tan(x) = Sin(x) ÷ Cos(x) for an input angle in degrees:

```
RUN
Enter angle in degrees? 45.6
Sin/Cos = 1.02117
Tan =      1.02117
Ok
```

4. Write a program that produces the following table:

Num	Natural log	Log base 10
1	0	0
10	2.302585	1
100	4.60517	2
1000	6.907755	3
10000	9.210341	4
100000	11.51293	5

```
Ok
```

10.7 Creating Functions: DEF FN

A number of the built-in mathematical functions have been introduced in this chapter. In addition, the programmer can create new functions by using the DEF FN statement. The major advantage of DEF FN lies in the fact that the expression for the function need only be written once, even though the function can be evaluated at more than one location within the program. The form of the DEF FN statement is:

```
DEF FN<function name> (<argument names>) = <expression>
```

The <function name> may be any legal numeric variable name (e.g., FNSUM, FNAVG, FNGPA). The <argument name> must always appear within parentheses and may be any legal numeric variable. In the following example,

```
10 DEF FNP(X) = X^2 - 2 * X - 1
```

FNP is the function name, X is the argument name, and $X^2 - 2 * X - 1$ is the expression used to compute the function's value. For instance, FNP(5) is 14 because $5^2 - 2 * 5 - 1 = 14$. Because they are created by the programmer, such functions are called "user-defined." All user-defined function names begin with the letters FN. A user-define function must be defined before it may be used. Therefore it is a good programming practice to place all DEF FN statements at the beginning of a program.

Within a program reference to a function is made using the function name. The argument may be a variable, constant or expression. For example, in evaluating function P declared above, it is possible to use the variable A as the argument:

```
20 A = 5
30 PRINT FNP(A)
```

```
RUN
 14
Ok
```

The following program evaluates the user-defined polynomial function FNPOLY() several times:

```
10 REM ** Evaluates user-defined polynomial
          function **
20 DEF FNPOLY(X) = X^2 - 2 * X - 1
30 PRINT " X", "FNPOLY(X)"
40 FOR COUNT = 1 TO 5
50   PRINT COUNT, FNPOLY(COUNT)
60 NEXT COUNT
70 INPUT "Enter a number"; NUMBER
80 PRINT "FNPOLY("; NUMBER; ") is ";
   FNPOLY(NUMBER)
99 END
```

```
RUN
 X                FNPOLY(X)
 1                 -2
 2                 -1
 3                  2
 4                  7
 5                 14
Enter a number? -10
FNPOLY(-10 ) is   119
Ok
```

When the function is evaluated at line 50, the argument is COUNT. When FNPOLY is evaluated at line 80, the argument is NUMBER. Remember, the name of the argument may be the same as or different from the variable name used in the DEF statement. Note also that if the DEF FN statement were not used, the formula on line 20 would have to appear twice (lines 50 and 80).

Another advantage of using the DEF statement is that it can be easily modified to define a different function. This is illustrated by re-running the above program with line 20 changed to:

```
20 DEF FNPOLY(X) = X^3 - 5 * X^2 + 1
```

```
RUN
 X                FNPOLY(X)
 1                 -3
 2                -11
 3                -17
 4                -15
 5                  1
Enter a number -10
FNPOLY(-10 ) is -1499
Ok
```

Review

5. Write a program that produces the following output. Two user-defined functions should be used: one to convert degrees to radians and another to convert radians to degrees:

```
RUN
Enter angle in degrees? 30
 30.0 degrees is 0.524 radians

Enter angle in radians? 0.524
 0.524 radians is 30.0 degrees
Ok
```

6. What output is produced by the following program? Check by running the program:

```
10 DEF FNX(N) = 3 * N - 6
20 FOR COUNT = -4 TO 6 STEP 2
30    IF SGN(FNX(COUNT)) = 1 THEN PRINT
      "FNX("; COUNT; ") is positive"
40    IF SGN(FNX(COUNT)) = 0 THEN PRINT
      "FNX("; COUNT; ") is zero"
50    IF SGN(FNX(COUNT)) = -1 THEN PRINT
      "FNX("; COUNT; ") is negative"
60 NEXT COUNT
99 END
```

10.8 User-Defined String Functions

String functions may also be created using DEF FN. This technique is handy for simplifying certain string operations such as joining (concatenating) several strings.

This program illustrates how a user-defined string function can be implemented:

```
10 REM ** Uses a function to combine strings **
20 DEF FNADD$(C$) = C$ + " is bright and " +
   C$ + " is my favorite color"
30 FOR COUNT = 1 TO 4
40    READ COLR$
50    PRINT FNADD$(COLR$)
60 NEXT COUNT
99 END
1000 REM ** Data colors
1010 DATA red, blue, pink, green
```

```
RUN
red is bright and red is my favorite color
blue is bright and blue is my favorite color
pink is bright and pink is my favorite color
green is bright and green is my favorite color
Ok
```

Four different colors are read at line 40. Line 50 prints the results of the user-defined string function FNADD$ for each color. (The variable name COLR$ was used because COLOR is a reserved word, making COLOR$ an illegal variable.)

It is important to remember that a function represents a value or an expression, and therefore must always be part of another statement. In line 50, the function call is part of a PRINT statement. Attempting to use the function alone,

```
50    FNADD$(COLR$)
```

results in a Syntax error.

10.9 Multiple and Zero Arguments

User defined functions may have more than one argument. For example, the statement

```
20 DEF FNRAND(L, H) = L + INT((H - L + 1) * RND)
```

defines the function FNRAND() which returns a random integer between L and H, inclusive. The statement

```
30 DEF FNC$(X$, Y$, Z$) = X$ + "," + Y$ + "," + Z$
```

defines a function which combines three string variables, and inserts commas between each.

This program shows how FNRAND() may be used to simulate the rolling of two dice:

```
10 REM ** Uses FNRAND to roll 2 dice **
20 DEF FNRAND(L, H) = L + INT((H - L + 1) * RND)
30 FOR ROLL = 1 to 5
40    PRINT FNRAND(1,6) + FNRAND(1,6)
50 NEXT ROLL
99 END
```

```
RUN
 5
11
 6
 6
 7
```

A function does not require arguments. An example of this is the built-in function RND which returns a random number. We can write a function without any arguments to roll one die:

```
20 DEF FNROLL1 = 1 + INT(6 * RND)
```

Each time FNROLL1 is called it returns a number between 1 and 6, inclusive.

Here is a rewrite of the previous program using the FNROLL1 function to roll two dice:

```
10 REM ** Uses FNROLL1 to roll 2 dice **
20 DEF FNROLL1 = 1 + INT(6 * RND)
30 FOR ROLL = 1 to 5
40   PRINT FNROLL1 + FNROLL1
50 NEXT ROLL
99 END
```

```
RUN
 5
 11
 6
 6
 7
```

Note that because RANDOMIZE TIMER was not used, this program prints the same values as the previous one.

Both FNRAND and FNROLL1 made use of the built-in function RND. All built-in functions are available for use in DEF FN statements. Additionally, all previously defined user-defined functions are also available. For example, we can create a new function which rolls two dice by calling FNROLL1:

```
20 DEF FNROLL1 = 1 + INT(6 * RND)
30 DEF FNROLL2 = FNROLL1 + FNROLL1
```

Review

7. Write a program using a user-defined string function which returns the initials of a person whose first, middle and last names are used as arguments.

8. Using a user-defined function, write a program which calculates the area of a rectangle given its length and width.

10.10 End of Chapter Problem

One of the most valuable mathematical problems a computer is capable of solving is finding the area under a curve, a process which is usually difficult to do and requires integral calculus if done mathematically.

For most curves a trapezoid represents a good approximation of the area under the curve. Consider the graph of the function $y = 1 / x$:

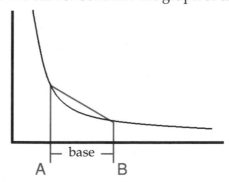

base

A   B

Note how closely a trapezoid fits the area between the limits A and B. The area of this trapezoid can be calculated using the formula

Area = 0.5 × (heightA + heightB) × base

where heightA and heightB are the altitudes of the trapezoid at points A and B, and base is the length of the base.

A single trapezoid is a good approximation for a function as simple as y = 1 / x, but for more complicated functions, for example y = 1 / (x^3) it is a poor approximation. Breaking the area into a large number of trapezoids and then summing the areas of the separate trapezoids usually increases the accuracy of the calculated area.

Algorithm:
1. Input the limits between which the area is desired.
2. Input the number of trapezoids to use.
3. Calculate the size of the base.
4. For each trapezoid:
   Calculate the area
   Add the area to the sum
5. Print the sum of all trapezoid areas.

Input:

Function to evaluate	FNY()
Upper limit	UPTRAP
Lower limit	LOWTRAP

Output:

Area under graph	AREA

```
10 REM ** Calculates area under graph between
entered limits **
20 DEF FNY(X) = 1 / X
30 INPUT "Enter starting point"; XLOW
40 INPUT "Enter ending point"; XHIGH
50 INPUT "Enter number of trapezoids"; NUMBER
60 BASE = (XHIGH - XLOW) / NUMBER
70 FOR X = XLOW TO (XHIGH - BASE) STEP BASE
80   AREATRAP = 0.5 * (FNY(X) +
     FNY(X + BASE)) * BASE
90   AREA = AREA + AREATRAP
100 NEXT X
110 PRINT "Area = "; AREA
999 END
```

```
RUN
Enter starting point? 1
Enter ending point? 2
Enter number of trapezoids? 100
Area = .6931537
Ok
```

Line 60 calculates the base, which is the same for each trapezoid, by calculating the length along the x-axis above which the area will be found (XHIGH – XLOW) and dividing it by the number of trapezoids NUMBER. The loop formed by lines 70 to 100 is executed NUMBER times, with the loop variable equal to the value of X where the trapezoid is located. Line 80 calculates the area of a single trapezoid by evaluating the function at the two altitudes and using the area equation. At line 90 the areas of the separate trapezoids are summed.

Changing line 20 to read

```
20 DEF F(X) = 1 / (X^2)
```

and running the program twice, first using five trapezoids and then 1000 trapezoids makes clear a large number of trapezoids must often be used to produce a good approximation. The correct answer is very close to 0.5:

```
RUN
Enter starting point? 1
Enter ending point? 2
Enter number of trapezoids? 5
Area = .4499189
Ok
```

```
RUN
Enter starting point? 1
Enter ending point? 2
Enter number of trapezoids? 1000
Area = .4997382
Ok
```

This example also shows the power of user-defined functions. To have this program calculate the area under a totally different curve, all that need be changed is line 20.

Review

9. Modify the End of Chapter problem to use double-precision variables. What differences are there in the calculated values?

10. Modify the End of Chapter problem by creating a second user-defined function that calculates the area for a single trapezoid.

Chapter Summary

A function is a name used in BASIC to perform a specified task. The argument is the value passed to a function. For example, for the function TAB(20), TAB is the function name and 20 the argument. When executing a function, the computer first evaluates the argument and then performs the function.

The SQR() function calculates the positive square root of a number. Its argument may be any mathematical expression with a non-negative value. The SGN() function returns the sign of a number as one of three possible values: 1, 0, or -1. The ABS() function returns the absolute value of a number.

The SIN(), COS() and TAN() functions respectively return the sine, cosine and tangent of an angle measured in radians. To convert an angle from degrees to radians it is multiplied by π (3.14159) divided by 180.

The only inverse trigonometric function supplied by BASIC is the principle arctangent ATN(X) which returns the angle in radians whose tangent is X. To convert an angle from radians to degrees it is multiplied by 180 divided by π. The arcsine and arccosine can be found using the equations given in the chapter.

The LOG() function finds the natural logarithm (base e) of its argument. To find the common logarithm (base 10) of a number NUM the equation LOG(NUM)/LOG(10) is used. Values of the exponential function e^x, where $e = 2.71828$, are found using the EXP() function.

A new function can be created within a program using the DEF FN statement which takes the form DEF FN<function name> (<argument names>) = <expression>. The <function name> may be any legal numeric variable name and the <argument name> may be any numeric variable. For example, in the statement

```
10 DEF FNEVAL(X) = 2 * X^2 - 5 * X + 15
```

FNEVAL is the function name, X is the argument name and 2 * X^2 - 5 * X + 15 is the expression used to compute the function's value. The value of FNEVAL(3) = 18 because 2 * 3^2 - 5 * 3 + 15 = 18.

String functions may be created using DEF FN; for example, FNHAPPY$(SMILE$) = SMILE$ + " life is a bowl of cherries." It is important to remember that a function represents a value or an expression, and therefore must always be part of another statement.

User-defined functions may contain more than one argument. For example,

```
20 DEF FNKNOW$(NAME1$, NAME2$) = NAME1$ +
   " knows " + NAME2$
```

creates a user-defined string function with two string arguments.

It is also possible to create a function with no argument, for example,

```
30 DEF FNRAND = 10 + INT(11 * RND)
```

which produces a random number between 10 and 20, inclusive, each time it is called.

Vocabulary

ABS () - Function that returns the absolute value of a number.

Argument - The value passed to a function.

ATN () - Function that returns the angle in radians whose tangent is the argument.

COS () - Function that returns the cosine of an angle measured in radians.

DEF FN - Statement used to create a user-defined function.

EXP () - Function that finds the value of e^x.

Function - Name used in BASIC to perform a specified task.

LOG () - Function that finds the natural log (base e) of its argument.

SGN () - Function that returns the sign of a number as one of three possible values: 1, 0, or -1.

SIN () - Function that returns the sine of an angle measured in radians.

SQR () - Function that returns the positive square root of a number.

TAN () - Function that returns the tangent of an angle measured in radians.

User-defined function - Function created by the programmer using DEF FN.

Exercises

1. Write a program which calculates the square roots for an input number. Be sure to account for a negative input. An input of 0 terminates the program:

   ```
   RUN
   Enter a number (0 to end)? 4
   Square roots = + 2 or -2

   Enter a number (0 to end)? -1
   The square root of a negative number cannot
   be found.

   Enter a number (0 to end)? 0
   Ok
   ```

2. Write a program which prints the integers from 121 to 144, inclusive, and their respective square roots. Label each column of output.

3. Write a program that prints a table of the COS(X) and SIN(X+90) where X varies from 0 to 360 degrees in increments of 10 degrees.

4. Input a number N and if the number is zero, print 0. Otherwise, print ABS(N)/N. What does the program do?

5. Input a number N and print the product of SGN(N) and N. What does this program do?

6. Input a number, square it and print the square root of the result. What should the program produce?

7. Print a table consisting of 2 columns with headings showing each angle in radians and degrees. The angles in radians are to be 0, .25, .5, .75, ..., 3.0. Remember that 180 = pi radians.

8. Input an angle in degrees and convert it to a fraction of a revolution (1 revolution = 360°) and to radians.

9. Input an angle in degrees. Of the three functions sine, cosine and tangent, print the value of the one which has the greatest value:

```
RUN
Enter angle? 0
Cosine = 1
Ok
```

10. For angles from 0° to 180° (at intervals of 10°) print the angle in degrees, the sine, the cosine, and the sum of their squares in columns with headings. What patterns emerge?

11. Input two numbers A and B. Print the quantity FNP(B) - FNP(A), given that $FNP(X) = 9X^3 - 7X^2 + 4X - 1$.

12. Input a number N. Print the values of FNJ(N) and FNJ(FNJ(N)), where $FNJ(X) = 20 * SQR(ABS(X)) - 10 * SGN(X) + 5 * INT(X)$.

13. Print a table (with headings) of X, the natural logarithm of X and the exponential function of X for X = 1 to 20.

14. Print a table of X, the logarithm of X to the base 10, and 10 raised to the power X for X = 1 to 20.

15. Using three user-defined functions, have the computer evaluate the following for integers from -10 to 10:

$$X^2 + 3X + 2$$
$$LOG(X^2 + 1) - X$$
$$ATN(SIN(X))$$

16. Write a program to convert from polar to rectangular coordinates (i.e., from (r,Θ) to (X,Y)).

17. If two functions, f and g, are inverse to each other, the following relations hold: $f(g(x)) = x$ and $g(f(x)) = x$.

    a)   Tabulate the values of X, EXP(X) and LOG(EXP(X)) for X = -5 to 10.
    b)   Print a table for X = 1 to 151 of X, LOG(X), EXP(LOG(X)), using STEP 10.
    c)   Do EXP and LOG appear to be inverse to each other?

18. Produce your own sequence of random numbers without using the RND function. To do this, let X vary from 1 to 100 in steps of 1. Obtain SIN(X) and multiply this by 1000, calling the absolute value of the product Y. Divide INT(Y) by 16, and let the remainder R serve as your random number.

19. A six year old invests $0.50 in a savings account which earns 8% interest compounded annually. Starting with the 11th year, he withdraws 5 cents at the beginning of each year. The formula for interest compounded annually is $P = P_0 e^{it}$, where t is the elapsed time in years, P_0 is the initial deposit, P is the balance at time t, and i is the interest rate. In this case the formula would be $P = P_0 e^{0.08t}$. What is the balance of the account after 50 years?

20. Use the SIN() and TAB() functions to generate the following graph:

```
RUN
SHAZAM!
     SHAZAM!
       SHAZAM!
          SHAZAM!
            SHAZAM!
              SHAZAM!
                SHAZAM!
                  SHAZAM!
                   SHAZAM!
                    SHAZAM!
                    SHAZAM!
                     SHAZAM!
                      SHAZAM!
                      SHAZAM!
                       SHAZAM!
                       SHAZAM!
                       SHAZAM!
                      SHAZAM!
                      SHAZAM!
                     SHAZAM!
                    SHAZAM!
                    SHAZAM!
                   SHAZAM!
                  SHAZAM!
                SHAZAM!
              SHAZAM!
            SHAZAM!
          SHAZAM!
       SHAZAM!
     SHAZAM!
```

Advanced Exercise   The following exercise requires the development of a detailed algorithm. The program should not be written until all details of the algorithm have been worked out.

21. Write a program that will solve a triangle (compute the unknown sides and angles) for the following situations:

    a) given two sides and the included angle
    b) given two angles and any side
    c) given three sides

```
RUN
Select: 1) two sides and included angle
        2) two angles and any side
        3) three sides
Enter selection (1-3)? 1

Sides 1 and 2? 3, 3
Included angle? 60

Side            Angle
3               60
3               60
3               60
Ok


RUN
Select: 1) two sides and included angle
        2) two angles and any side
        3) three sides
Enter selection (1-3)? 2

Angles 1 and 2? 60, 60
Side? 3
Is that the included side <Y/N>? Y

Side            Angle
3               60
3               60
3               60
Ok


RUN
Select: 1) two sides and included angle
        2) two angles and any side
        3) three sides
Enter selection (1-3)? 3

Three sides? 3, 4, 5
Side            Angle
3               37
4               53
5               90
Ok
```

Sequential Files

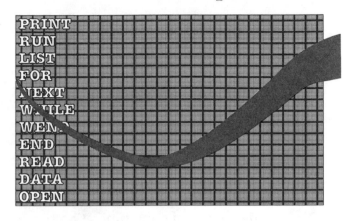

OPEN

CLOSE

WRITE #

INPUT #

KILL, NAME

EOF ( )

PRINT #

LINE INPUT #

Objectives

Chapter Eleven

After completing this chapter you will be able to:

1. Store data in a sequential file on disk.

2. Establish a line of communication between a program and file using OPEN.

3. Terminate communication between a program and file using CLOSE.

4. Transfer data from a program into a sequential file using WRITE #.

5. Transfer data from a sequential file to a program using INPUT #.

6. Append data to the end of a sequential file.

7. Update a sequential file by altering its data while transferring the data to a new file.

8. Use NAME to rename a file and KILL to erase a previously created file.

9. Determine the location of the end of a file using EOF().

10. Determine if a string contains a specified character using INSTR().

11. Enter data containing commas into a sequential file using PRINT #.

12. Read files created with PRINT # using LINE INPUT #.

*S*o far we have discussed only two methods for saving the data used by a computer program, variables and DATA statements. Variables can be assigned constant values (e.g., A = 5), or the values can be placed in DATA statements that are read when the program is run. There are two drawbacks to these methods. First, if it becomes necessary to update the data, program lines have to be retyped, thus altering the program and increasing the chance of error. Second, since the data is an integral part of a program, it cannot be shared by other programs. The solution to these problems is to store the data in a "file." A file is a collection of related data items stored on a disk. Since files are separate from programs, they can be updated without changing any part of a program. Also, a single data file can be accessed by many programs, allowing more flexible use of the data. Files and programs should not be confused: A program is a set of instructions that tells the computer what to do; a file is a separate set of data used by a program or programs.

A computer file is analogous to a filing cabinet which stores information that can be recalled and cross referenced. As such, the computer file provides the means for storing large quantities of data indefinitely.

The computer utilizes two different types of files: "sequential" and "random-access." The sequential file is best adapted to situations requiring data to be recalled in the same order as it was originally stored in the file. Proceeding line-by-line from the beginning of the file, the computer reads the file sequentially until all the desired information has been retrieved, or the end of file has been reached. If information is to be retrieved from a random location in the file (for example, a single entry in a mailing list), random-access files are better suited. Since these are more complex, random-access files are discussed separately in the next chapter.

It is suggested that before proceeding to learn the use of files, that you first read Appendix A in order to become familiar with the special aspects of the Disk Operating System (DOS), such as file naming conventions and disk commands.

11.1 OPEN

The OPEN statement establishes a line of communication between a program and a file and prepares the file for use. The general format for the OPEN statement is:

OPEN "<mode>", #<file number>, "<file name>"

Note that the mode and the file name must be enclosed in quotation marks, and that the file number is preceded by a pound sign (#). The OPEN statement options are described below.

The <mode> tells the computer how to access the data on the disk. The four modes of access are:

O : <u>Sequential Output</u>. The computer outputs data from the program to the file, starting at the beginning of the file. If the file does not already exist, it is automatically created. If a file with the same name already exists, the new data is written over any previously existing data stored in the file.

I : <u>Sequential Input</u>. The computer inputs data from the file starting at the beginning of the file. If the file does not already exist, a "File not found" error is generated.

A : <u>Append</u> (sequential output at end of file). The data is appended to the end of a previously created file. Previously stored data is added to, not lost. If the file does not already exist, a new one is created.

R : <u>Random Input and Output</u>. This option is discussed in Chapter 12.

Attempting to use a mode other than those listed here displays a "Bad file mode" error.

Each open file must be given a <file number> by which it is referred to in later statements. It is possible to have up to three open files at a time. Attempting to use a file number other than 1, 2 or 3 displays a "Bad file number" error.

The <file name> is a unique label used by the computer to identify each file or program stored on a diskette. It is important to remember that no two files may have the same name. The rules for file names are the same for programs given in Chapter 2 — up to eight letters and digits followed by a period and three more letters or digits. For example,

30 OPEN "I", #2, "PAYROLL.DAT"

opens a file named PAYROLL.DAT for sequential input ("I") giving it the number 2. It is a good convention to use the extension .DAT as part of each data file name to identify it as a data file. A disk drive identifier may be used in the OPEN statement to access a file on another disk, for example:

30 OPEN "O", #1, "B:NEWFILE.DAT"

The keyboard shortcut for OPEN is Alt-O.

11.2 CLOSE

Any previously OPENed file must be CLOSEd. This is necessary to terminate the communication between the program and file that was established by the OPEN statement. A file is closed by specifying its number in a CLOSE statement. For example,

```
90 CLOSE #2
```

closes the file previously opened as file number 2. If a file number is omitted in the CLOSE statement, all previously OPENed files are closed. Closing a file insures that all its information is properly stored. Make sure not to remove a diskette from a drive on which files are open, since there is no way to guarantee whether all of the data has been written to the file until it is closed. Removing a disk prematurely may result in loss of data.

11.3 WRITE

While the OPEN statement establishes a line of communication between the program and file, the WRITE # statement is used to transfer data from a program into a file:

```
WRITE #<file number>, <variable>, <variable> . . .
```

Data stored by the variables listed in the WRITE # statement are transferred to the file associated with the specified <file number>. The WRITE # statement automatically places quotation marks around string data and commas between both numeric and string data when the data is written to the file. The commas and quotation marks act as markers so that the computer can tell the different items of data apart when later reading them from the file. For example, if A$="Hello" and B = 124, the statement

```
WRITE #1, A$, B
```

would write the data

```
"Hello", 124
```

to the file OPENed as #1.

This program creates a sequential file named TIMECARD.DAT. The file will store the names of four employees, their hourly wages and the number of hours they have worked. The data is input from the keyboard by the user:

```
10 REM ** Creates TIMECARD.DAT **
20 PRINT "Enter data for 4 employees"
30 OPEN "O", #1, "TIMECARD.DAT"
40 FOR EMP = 1 TO 4
50   INPUT "Name"; EMPLOYEE$
60   INPUT "Wage"; WAGE
70   INPUT "Hours worked"; HOURS
80   WRITE #1, EMPLOYEE$, WAGE, HOURS
90   PRINT
100 NEXT EMP
110 CLOSE #1
120 PRINT "File closed"
999 END
```

```
RUN
Enter data for 4 employees
Name? Roger Waters
Wage? 4.45
Hours worked? 39

Name? Beth Brown
Wage? 8.05
Hours worked? 28

Name? Bill Bruford
Wage? 3.55
Hours worked? 14

Name? Lisa Ciechon
Wage? 7.25
Hours worked? 30

File closed
Ok
```

Line 30 opens an "O"utput file named TIMECARD.DAT as file number 1. Lines 40 through 100 form a loop which prompts the user to input 4 sets of data and then writes them to TIMECARD.DAT. Line 80 is important. This statement writes the data stored in the variables to the TIMECARD.DAT file. TIMECARD.DAT is used because it was specified as file number 1 in the OPEN statement. Line 110 closes the file, and line 120 prints a message. It is a good practice to include such a message to inform the user of the actions of the program. Note that this message is displayed on the screen only — it is not written to the file because it is not a WRITE # statement.

After this program is run, the contents of TIMECARD.DAT are:

```
"Roger Waters", 4.45, 39
"Beth Brown", 8.05, 28
"Bill Bruford", 3.55, 14
"Lisa Ciechon", 7.25, 30
```

Each complete entry in a file is called a "record," and TIMECARD.DAT now stores 4 records.

Review

1. Write a program that creates a sequential file named MONTHS.DAT containing the months of the year starting with "January."

2. Write a program that creates a sequential file named DWARF.DAT containing the name and number for each of the seven dwarfs:

NUMBER	NAME	NUMBER	NAME
1	DOPEY	5	HAPPY
2	SLEEPY	6	BASHFUL
3	SNEEZY	7	DOC
4	GRUMPY		

11.4 INPUT

The INPUT # statement is used to transfer information from a sequential file to a program. Its format is similar to the WRITE # statement:

INPUT #<file number>, <variable>, <variable> . . .

The order in which the variables are listed in the INPUT # statement must be the same as the order in the WRITE # statement that originally transferred the data to the file. For example, a program that reads data from TIMECARD.DAT created by the program in Section 11.3 must have a string followed by two numbers. The variable *names* do not have to be the same, only the *types*. After the file has been closed the same file number need not be used to access it at a later time. For example, a program accessing TIMECARD.DAT might use file number 2 instead of file number 1.

This program opens the TIMECARD.DAT file created in Section 11.3, inputs data from the file, and then prints the name and hours worked of each of the four employees:

```
10 REM ** Reads TIMECARD.DAT **
20 OPEN "I", #1, "TIMECARD.DAT"
30 PRINT "    Timecard Data"
40 PRINT "Name", "Hours Worked"
50 FOR EMP = 1 TO 4
60    INPUT #1, EMPNAME$, RATE, HOURS
70    PRINT EMPNAME$, HOURS
80 NEXT EMP
90 CLOSE #1
100 PRINT "File closed"
999 END
```

```
RUN
      Timecard Data
Name                Hours Worked
Roger Waters        39
Beth Brown          28
Bill Bruford        14
Lisa Ciechon        30
File closed
Ok
```

Line 20 opens the file TIMECARD.DAT for "I"nput using file number 1. Lines 50 through 80 create a loop which reads and prints 4 records. Line 60 inputs data from file #1 (TIMECARD.DAT) and line 70 prints the information on the screen. Note that even though WAGE is not printed, it must be read in line 70. This is necessary to keep the data being read from the file in proper sequence. After four records have been read the file is closed at line 90.

Review

3. a) Write a program that prints the names of the first six months of the year found in the file MONTHS.DAT created in Review 1.

b) Modify the program written in part (a) to print only the names of the last three months found in MONTHS.DAT.

4. Write a program that reads the names and numbers of the seven dwarfs from the DWARF.DAT file created in Review 2, and prints them out in a table similar to:

```
Number          Name
------          ----
  1             DOPEY
  2             SLEEPY
  3             SNEEZY
  4             GRUMPY
  5             HAPPY
  6             BASHFUL
  7             DOC
```

11.5 Appending Data to Sequential Files

Specifying the "A"ppend mode in the OPEN statement tells the computer to append data to the end of an existing file. When an OPEN statement is executed in Output mode the computer opens the file and prepares to write to it starting at the beginning of the file. Thus, any new data added to the file will write over existing data. To avoid this loss of data, the Append mode instructs the computer to write any new data starting at the current *end* of the file rather than the beginning.

This program updates the TIMECARD.DAT file created in Section 11.3 so that it includes information for two new employees:

```
10  REM ** Appends TIMECARD.DAT **
20  OPEN "A", #1, "TIMECARD.DAT"
30  PRINT "Enter data for 2 new employees"
40  FOR EMP = 1 TO 2
50    INPUT "Name"; EMPLOYEE$
60    INPUT "Wage"; WAGE
70    INPUT "Hours worked"; HOURS
80    WRITE #1, EMPLOYEE$, WAGE, HOURS
90    PRINT
100 NEXT EMP
110 CLOSE #1
120 PRINT "File closed"
999 END
```

```
RUN
Enter data for 2 new employees
Name? Jill White
Wage? 6.85
Hours worked? 27
```

```
Name? William Hobbs
Wage? 4.90
Hours worked? 40

File closed
Ok
```

Line 20 opens TIMECARD.DAT in Append mode as file number 1. This tells the computer to write any additional data starting at the current end of the file. Lines 40 through 100 create a loop which gets employee data from the user and writes it to the file. The file is then closed at line 110, and the contents of TIMECARD.DAT are now:

```
"Roger Waters", 4.45, 39
"Beth Brown", 8.05, 28
"Bill Bruford", 3.55, 14
"Lisa Ciechon", 7.25, 30
"Jill White", 6.85, 27
"William Hobbs", 4.9, 40
```

11.6 Updating Sequential Files

There is no single command that will remove or alter data in a sequential file. To change such a file, the corrected data must be transferred to a new file along with the remaining original data. After the corrected data has been stored in the new file, the old file can be deleted.

For example, suppose that we wish to change the pay rate for employee Bill Bruford in the TIMECARD.DAT file. To do so we would read each employee's record in the file. If the employee is not Bill Bruford, the information is written to a new file unchanged. If the employee is Bill Bruford, then his information is written to the new file with a new pay rate:

Original File		New File
`"Roger Waters", 4.45, 39`	copied →	`"Roger Waters", 4.45, 39`
`"Beth Brown", 8.05, 28`	copied →	`"Beth Brown", 8.05, 28`
`"Bill Bruford", 3.55, 14`	new rate →	`"Bill Bruford", `**5.15**`, 14`
`"Lisa Ciechon", 7.25, 30`	copied →	`"Lisa Ciechon", 7.25, 30`
`"Jill White", 6.85, 27`	copied →	`"Jill White", 6.85, 27`
`"William Hobbs", 4.9, 40`	copied →	`"William Hobbs", 4.9, 40`

Deleting a record is a similar process. To delete Lisa Ciechon we read each employee's record in the file. If the employee is not Lisa, the data is written to a new file unchanged. If the employee is Lisa, then nothing is written:

Original File		New File
`"Roger Waters", 4.45, 39`	copied →	`"Roger Waters", 4.45, 39`
`"Beth Brown", 8.05, 28`	copied →	`"Beth Brown", 8.05, 28`
`"Bill Bruford", 3.55, 14`	copied →	`"Bill Bruford", 3.55, 14`
`"Lisa Ciechon", 7.25, 30`	not copied	
`"Jill White", 6.85, 27`	copied →	`"Jill White", 6.85, 27`
`"William Hobbs", 4.9, 40`	copied →	`"William Hobbs", 4.9, 40`

11.7 KILL and NAME

The techniques described above make use of a new file to store the updated information. After updating a file in this way we would like to delete the old file (because it is no longer valid) and rename the new file to the original name. This can be accomplished with the KILL and NAME statements.

The KILL statement erases a previously created file from the disk:

    KILL "<file name>"

The file name can specify either a program or a data file. For example,

    KILL "TIMECARD.DAT"

erases the file named TIMECARD.DAT. Take special care when using KILL because once erased, a file cannot be recovered.

The name of an existing file may be changed using the NAME statement:

    NAME "<old name>" AS "<new name>"

The file can be either a program or a data file. For example,

    NAME "EXER7.BAS" AS "EXER7A.BAS"

renames the program from EXER7.BAS to EXER7A.BAS.

Both of these statements may be used in either immediate mode or placed in a program, and a disk drive identifier (e.g., B:) may be specified as needed. Remember to include the proper extension with the file name, e.g., .BAS, .DAT, etc. If the file listed in the statement does not exist, BASIC displays the message "File not found." NAME and KILL should only be used on files which are CLOSEd.

This program removes an employee's information from the TIMECARD.DAT file. All of the data is read sequentially from TIMECARD.DAT and the information that is to be retained is placed in a new file named TIMECARD.TMP:

```
10 REM ** Deletes a TIMECARD employee **
20 INPUT "Delete which employee"; DELNAME$
30 OPEN "I", #1, "TIMECARD.DAT"
40 OPEN "O", #2, "TIMECARD.TMP"
50 FOR EMP = 1 TO 6
60   INPUT #1, EMPLOYEE$, WAGE, HOURS
70   IF EMPLOYEE$ <> DELNAME$ THEN
     WRITE #2, EMPLOYEE$, WAGE, HOURS
80 NEXT EMP
90 CLOSE #1, #2
100 KILL "TIMECARD.DAT"
110 NAME "TIMECARD.TMP" AS "TIMECARD.DAT"
120 PRINT DELNAME$; " has been removed."
999 END
```

```
RUN
Delete which employee? Lisa Ciechon
Lisa Ciechon has been removed.
Ok
```

Line 20 gets the name of the person to delete from the user. Line 30 opens the TIMECARD.DAT file for Input as file number 1. Line 40 creates a new file named TIMECARD.TMP for Output as file number 2. We use the extension .TMP to indicate that this is a temporary file, which is a good programming practice. Lines 50 through 80 create a loop which reads each employee record and checks the name in the file against the name of the person to delete. If the names do not match, the employee's data is written to the temporary file (TIMECARD.TMP). At the end of the loop, both files are closed. Line 100 erases the original TIMECARD.DAT and line 110 changes the name of the temporary file to TIMECARD.DAT. Line 120 prints a message informing the user that the operation is complete.

This program works well in this limited example, but the technique it uses is not always practical. The FOR...NEXT loop prevents the program from attempting to read past the end of the data file. However, this method could only be used because the length of TIMECARD.DAT was known, which is not always the case. Attempting to read past the end of a file generates an "Input past end" error, and the program is halted. If this occurs, files will be left open and important data may be lost. A technique to read a file of unknown length is given in the next section.

Review

5. Write a program which accesses the data in MONTHS.DAT created in Review 1 and updates it so that it stores only months containing a letter R.

6. Sneezy and Bashful would like to retire. Write a program which updates DWARF.DAT created in Review 2 by removing them from the file.

11.8 The EOF() Function

When the computer closes a file it places a character called an end of file (EOF) marker after the last record in the file. The EOF() function allows the programmer to determine whether the EOF marker has been reached. Its form is:

EOF (<file number>)

The function is true when the end of the specified file has been reached, otherwise it is false. When combined with a WHILE...WEND loop, EOF() allows us to process files of unknown length. For example, the following loop continues to execute until the end of file number 1 is reached:

```
100 WHILE NOT EOF(1)
      . . .
160   INPUT #1, <variables>
      . . .
190 WEND
```

This program is a revision of the one in Section 11.4 which allows TIMECARD.DAT to be of any length:

```
10 REM ** Reads TIMECARD.DAT **
20 PRINT "      Timecard Data"
30 OPEN "I", #1, "TIMECARD.DAT"
40 PRINT "Name", "Hours Worked"
50 WHILE NOT EOF(1)
60   INPUT #1, EMPNAME$, RATE, HOURS
70   PRINT EMPNAME$, HOURS
80 WEND
90 CLOSE #1
100 PRINT "File closed"
999 END
```

```
RUN
     Timecard Data
Name                Hours Worked
Roger Waters          39
Beth Brown            28
Bill Bruford          14
Jill White            27
William Hobbs         40
File closed
Ok
```

This is a major improvement over the original program. Because the EOF() function and a WHILE...WEND loop are utilized, this program works for a file of any length (including 0, an empty file). This technique is recommended for reading most sequential files since it avoids the error which occurs when an attempt is made to read beyond the end of a file.

Review

7. Rewrite the answers for Review problems 3 and 4 to work for a file of any length, using WHILE...WEND loop with the EOF() function.

8. a) Rewrite the program from Section 11.7 to work for a file of unknown length.
   b) Modify the program to print a message if the employee to be deleted is not found in the file.

11.9 User Entered File Names: INSTR()

The OPEN statement accepts a string variable for the file name. This allows the user to enter the name of the file, allowing a program to work for many different files. For example,

```
50 INPUT "Enter file name"; FILE$
60 OPEN "I", #1, FILE$
```

The program then attempts to open a file with the name entered at line 50. If the file name is illegal, BASIC prints the message "Bad file number". (This can be confusing because the file *number* is correct, but the file *name* is not valid.) If the file name entered does not exist, a "File not found" error is generated.

The program can automatically add the file name extension ".DAT" if the user does not type one. The INSTR() function returns a 0 if a character is not found in the specified string (or the position of the character if it is). We can use INSTR() to search for a period (which starts the file name extension) and to add an extension if one is not present:

```
50 INPUT "Enter file name"; FILE$
60 IF INSTR(FILE$, ".") = 0 THEN FILE$ =
   FILE$ + ".DAT"
70 OPEN "I", #1, FILE$
```

Line 60 checks the user-entered file name for a period. If no period is found, the extension .DAT is added to the end of the file name. For example, if the user types "MYFILE" as the file name, the IF statement would determine that no extension was entered, and would add .DAT to the end of FILE$. Line 70 would then attempt to open the file named "MYFILE.DAT".

11.10 PRINT

When creating a file, the WRITE # statement automatically places commas between each piece of data. The INPUT # statement then uses these commas as data separators. Therefore, these statements cannot be used when the data in a file contains embedded commas. This is only a problem when dealing with strings. For example, the string "Jack, Bill, and Trisha went to a party." cannot be placed in a file by the WRITE # statement because it contains commas.

Rather than using commas to separate data the PRINT # statement places a carriage return (Enter) character after each item of data to separate it from the next. Since commas are not used as separators, the PRINT # statement may be used for strings which contain commas. PRINT # has the form:

PRINT #<file number>, <string variable>

This program creates a file containing a form letter used by a company. The file name is entered by the user:

```
10 REM ** Create form letters **
20 INPUT "Name of letter"; FILENAME$
30 IF INSTR(FILENAME$, ".") = 0 THEN
   FILENAME$ = FILENAME$ + ".DAT"
40 OPEN "O", #1, FILENAME$
50 PRINT
```

```
60 PRINT "Enter lines. Type END to quit..."
70 LINE INPUT ">"; TEXT$
80 WHILE TEXT$ <> "END"
90    PRINT #1, TEXT$
100   LINE INPUT ">"; TEXT$
110 WEND
120 CLOSE #1
130 PRINT
140 PRINT FILENAME$ " is closed"
999 END
```

```
RUN
Name of letter? REJECT

Enter lines. Type END to quit...
>        Thank you for your manuscript, "Belling
>the Mouse." It was very good, but we already
>have over two hundred works with that title.
>We are sorry, but your material does not meet
>our current needs.
>
>Sincerely,
>Happy Book Publishers
>END

REJECT.DAT is closed
Ok
```

Line 20 reads the name of the file from the user. Line 30 checks for an extension and adds one if necessary. Line 40 opens that file for Output as file number 1. Line 70 inputs the first line of the letter from the keyboard. Lines 80 through 110 form a loop which is repeated for each line in the letter — the current line is written to the file and the user is prompted for another. The LINE INPUT statement, first discussed in Chapter 3, allows the user to input a string which contains commas. Notice that a ">" prompt is printed at the beginning of each line to prompt the user. This prompt is not written to the file. When the user types "END" the loop ends, and the file is closed at line 120. Note that the filename printed by line 140 includes the .DAT extension added by line 30.

11.11 LINE INPUT

A file created by PRINT # statements cannot be read by the INPUT # statement because INPUT # requires commas as data separators. Instead, the LINE INPUT # statement must be used which recognizes carriage returns as separators rather than commas. Its form is:

LINE INPUT #<file number>, <string variable>

This is similar to the LINE INPUT statement covered in Chapter 3 which reads strings containing commas from the keyboard.

It is important not to confuse the use of LINE INPUT # and PRINT # with INPUT # and WRITE #. A file created with WRITE # can be read using LINE INPUT #, but a file created using PRINT # cannot be read using INPUT #. Use LINE INPUT # and PRINT # only when dealing with files containing strings with embedded commas.

This program prints a form letter created by the program in Section 11.9. The user indicates how many copies and enters the name of the recipient for each copy:

```
10  REM ** Prints form letters **
20  INPUT "Print which letter"; LETTER$
30  IF INSTR(LETTER$, ".") = 0 THEN LETTER$ =
    LETTER$ + ".DAT"
40  INPUT "How many recipients"; NUMBER
50  FOR LETTER = 1 TO NUMBER
60    REM ** Get recipient name
70    PRINT "Recipient #" LETTER;
80    INPUT RECIPIENT$
90    REM ** Print letter
100   PRINT
110   OPEN "I", #1, LETTER$
120   PRINT "Dear " RECIPIENT$ ":"
130   WHILE NOT EOF(1)
140     LINE INPUT #1, L$
150     PRINT L$
160   WEND
170   CLOSE #1
180   PRINT
190 NEXT LETTER
200 PRINT "Printing complete"
999 END
```

```
RUN
Print which letter? REJECT.DAT
How many recipients? 2
Recipient #1? Mr. Steinbeck

Dear Mr. Steinbeck:
     Thank you for your manuscript, "Belling
the Mouse." It was very good, but we already
have over two hundred works with that title.
We are sorry, but your material does not meet
our current needs.

Sincerely,
Happy Book Publishers

Recipient #2? Ms. Christie

Dear Ms. Christie:
     Thank you for your manuscript, "Belling
the Mouse." It was very good, but we already
have over two hundred works with that title.
We are sorry, but your material does not meet
our current needs.
```

```
    Sincerely,
    Happy Book Publishers

    Printing complete
    Ok
```

Lines 20 and 30 get the file name from the user and add an extension if needed. Line 40 asks the user to input the number of copies of the letter to be printed. Lines 50 through 190 form a loop which executes once for each letter — the recipient's name is input, and then printed in a greeting along with the text of the letter. Note that the letter file is opened at line 110. Because the OPEN statement is inside the loop, reading starts at the first character in the file for each copy of the letter. Lines 130 through 160 print the contents of the letter file, and the file is closed at line 170.

11.12 End of Chapter Problem

This chapter ends by solving a problem which requires a carefully thought out algorithm. Once the algorithm has been developed, we can then determine what input and output are needed and assign appropriate variable names.

A baseball team needs a program to keep track of the player's batting averages. The information about the players should be kept in a sequential access file. Besides the creation of the file, BATAVG.DAT, the user should be able to add new players to the file, update their averages, and print out a chart of the players with their respective averages from the data in the file.

Algorithm:

1. Choose which option the user wishes to perform (create, append, update, print or exit).
2. Perform the required routine(s):

   a) Create File: Find out number of players. Enter the player information.
   b) Append File: Find out number of new players. Enter the player information.
   c) Update File: Find out whose record to update. Search for the correct player. Update the player's information.
   d) Print File: Print player's information.
   e) Exit: Leave the program.

Input:

Player Name	PNAME$
At Bats	ATBATS
Hits	HITS
Number of Players	NUMPLAYERS
Name to Search For	NAMETOFIND$
New At Bats	ADDATBATS
New Hits	ADDHITS

Output:

Player Name	PNAME$
At Bats	ATBATS
Hits	HITS
Batting Avg	AVG

```
10 REM ** Keeps track of players' batting
         averages **
100 REM ** Main program
110 WHILE CHOICE <> 5
120    CLS
130    PRINT "1: Create File"
140    PRINT "2: Append File"
150    PRINT "3: Update File"
160    PRINT "4: Print File"
170    PRINT "5: Exit Program"
180    PRINT
190    INPUT "Enter Selection (1-5): ", CHOICE
200    WHILE (CHOICE < 1) OR (CHOICE > 5)
210       BEEP
220       INPUT "Enter Selection (1-5): ",
          CHOICE
230    WEND
240    ON CHOICE GOSUB 1000, 2000, 3000, 6000
250 WEND
260 REM ** Exit Program
270 CLOSE
280 PRINT "Program complete"
999 END
1000 REM ** Create File
1010 OPEN "O", #1, "BATAVG.DAT"
1020 INPUT "Enter number of players: ",
     NUMPLAYERS
1030 GOSUB 5000 : REM ** Input and Write to Disk
1040 CLOSE #1
1050 RETURN
1990 REM
2000 REM ** Append File
2010 OPEN "A", #1, "BATAVG.DAT"
2020 INPUT "Enter number of NEW players: ",
     NUMPLAYERS
2030 GOSUB 5000 : REM ** Input and Write to Disk
2040 CLOSE #1
2050 RETURN
2990 REM
3000 REM ** Update File
3010 FOUND$ = "NO" : REM ** Flag to denote
     if player was found
3020 PRINT "Enter Name, additional At Bats,
     additional Hits: ";
3030 INPUT NAMETOFIND$, ADDATBATS, ADDHITS
3040 OPEN "O", #2, "BATAVG.TMP"
3050 OPEN "I", #1, "BATAVG.DAT"
```

```
3060 WHILE NOT EOF(1)
3070    INPUT #1, PNAME$, ATBATS, HITS, AVG
3080    IF PNAME$ <> NAMETOFIND$ THEN WRITE
           #2, PNAME$, ATBATS, HITS, AVG ELSE
           FOUND$ = "YES" : GOSUB 4000 : REM
           ** Update Player
3090 WEND
3100 CLOSE
3110 IF FOUND$ = "NO" THEN KILL "BATAVG.TMP" :
        INPUT "Name not found - press Enter",
        PAUSE$ ELSE KILL "BATAVG.DAT" : NAME
        "BATAVG.TMP" AS "BATAVG.DAT"
3120 RETURN
3990 REM
4000 REM ** Update Player
4010 ATBATS = ATBATS + ADDATBATS
4020 HITS = HITS + ADDHITS
4030 AVG = HITS / ATBATS
4040 WRITE #2, PNAME$, ATBATS, HITS, AVG
4050 RETURN
4990 REM
5000 REM ** Input and Write to Disk
5010 FOR PLAYER = 1 TO NUMPLAYERS
5020    INPUT "Enter Name, At Bats, Hits: ",
           PNAME$, ATBATS, HITS
5030    AVG = HITS / ATBATS
5040    WRITE #1, PNAME$, ATBATS, HITS, AVG
5050    PRINT
5060 NEXT PLAYER
5070 RETURN
5990 REM
6000 REM ** Print File
6010 OPEN "I", #1, "BATAVG.DAT"
6020 CLS
6030 PRINT "Name", "At Bats", "Hits",
        "Average"
6040 WHILE NOT EOF(1)
6050    INPUT #1, PNAME$, ATBATS, HITS, AVG
6060    PRINT PNAME$, ATBATS, HITS,
6070 PRINT USING "#.###"; AVG
6080 WEND
6090 CLOSE #1
6100 PRINT
6110 INPUT "Press Enter for menu ", PAUSE$
6120 RETURN
```

```
RUN
1: Create File
2: Append File
3: Update File
4: Print File
5: Exit Program

Enter Selection (1-5): 1
Enter number of NEW players: 2

Enter Name, At Bats, Hits: Bill, 3, 2

Enter Name, At Bats, Hits: Chris, 5, 3

1: Create File
2: Append File
3: Update File
4: Print File
5: Exit Program

Enter Selection (1-5): 4

Name    At Bats    Hits    Average
Bill       3         2      0.667
Chris      5         3      0.600

Press Enter for menu

1: Create File
2: Append File
3: Update File
4: Print File
5: Exit Program

Enter Selection (1-5): 3
Enter Name, additional At Bats, additional
Hits: Dana, 3, 1
Name not found - press Enter

1: Create File
2: Append File
3: Update File
4: Print File
5: Exit Program

Enter Selection (1-5): 5
Program complete
Ok
```

Lines 120 through 170 print the program menu. Line 190 inputs the user's choice. Lines 200 through 230 make sure that a correct response is input. Line 240 turns control of the program over to the subroutine of the user's choice. When the user selects option 5, the loop ends and any open files are closed at line 270. Lines 1000 through 1050 are the Create File subroutine. The file is opened for sequential Output at line 1010 and the number of players entered at 1020. The program then calls the subroutine at line 5000 which inputs player information and writes it to disk. The file is closed upon return from that subroutine. The Append File subroutine is located at lines 2000 through 2050. The file is opened in Append mode so that new information is placed at the end of the file, and the number of new players input. The subroutine at line 5000 is called to get the new player data and write it to the file. Upon return the file is closed. The file is updated by the subroutine at lines 3000 through 3120. A flag (FOUND$) is used to determine if the player to be updated has been found. Lines 3020 and 3030 input the name of the player to be updated, with the additional at bats and additional hits. A temporary file is opened for Output and the file with current player information is opened for Input at lines 3050 and 3060. Line 3070 reads the player name, at bats, and hits from the current file. If the player is the one to be updated, the flag is set to indicate that the player has been found and the subroutine at line 4000, Update Player, is called. Otherwise the player information is written as is to the temporary file. This continues until the end of original file has been reached. Line 3100 closes all open files. Line 3110 erases the temporary file and prints a message if the player name was not found, otherwise it erases the current file and renames the temporary file. Lines 4000 through 4050 update a player's information. Additional bats are added to ATBATS and additional hits are added to HITS. From this information the new average is calculated. This data is then written to file #2, the temporary file.

Note the subroutine at lines 5000 through 5070 which inputs player information and writes it to disk. A FOR loop is used to repeat NUMPLAYERS number of times. Within the loop, the player's name, at bats, and hits are input, and their batting average is calculated. The player's data is then written to the file by line 5040. This subroutine is called twice, from the Create File subroutine starting at line 1000, and the Append File subroutine at line 2000. It is perfectly legal for one subroutine to call another. In this case, having the statements which input the data and write it to the file in a single subroutine means that these same statements do not have to be repeated twice — once in Create File and again in Append File.

The subroutine at line 6000 prints the contents of the file. Line 6010 opens the file for Input. The screen is cleared and a heading printed. A WHILE..WEND loop is then used to read the data from the file and print it to the screen until the end of file is reached. The user is prompted at line 6110 to press Enter when viewing is completed.

Chapter Summary

A file is a collection of related data items stored on disk. Since files are separate from programs, they can be updated without changing any part of a program. Files can also be accessed by many programs, allowing more flexible use of the data they store. Most importantly, files allow data to be saved when the computer's power is turned off.

A sequential file is best used in situations where the data will be recalled in the same order as it was originally stored. A random-access file is best used when information is to be retrieved from a random location in the file, for example, a single name or address. This chapter explains sequential files, chapter Twelve explains random-access files.

The OPEN statement establishes a line of communication between a program and a file and prepares the file for use. It takes the form: OPEN "<mode>", #<file number>, "<file name>". There are four possible modes that tell the computer how to access the data on disk: Sequential output (O), the computer outputs data to the file starting at the beginning of the file; Sequential input (I), the computer inputs data from the file starting at the beginning of the file; Append (A), data is appended to the end of a previously created file; Random Input and Output (R) is discussed in Chapter 12. It is possible to have up to three files open at a time and each must be given a <file number> by which it is referred to in later statements. The <file name> is a unique label used by the computer to identify the file. The statement

```
20 OPEN "O", #3, "STUNAMES.DAT"
```

opens a file named STUNAMES.DAT for sequential output ("O") giving it file number 3. It is a good practice to use the extension .DAT as part of each data file name.

Communication between a program and a file is terminated using the CLOSE statement:

```
90 CLOSE #3
```

closes the file opened as file number 3.

The WRITE # statement transfers data from a program into a file and takes the form WRITE #<file number>, <variable>, <variable> .... Data stored by the variables is placed in the file with the specified file number, which must already be open. Quotation marks are automatically placed around string data and commas between both numeric and string data when data is written to a file. The statement

```
50 WRITE #3, NAME1$, AGE, TUITION
```

transfers the data in the string variable NAME1$ and the numeric variables AGE and TUITION to the file open as number 3.

Data is transferred from a sequential file to a program using the INPUT # statement which takes the form INPUT #<file number>, <variable>, <variable> .... The order in which the variables are listed in the INPUT # statement must be the same as the order in the WRITE # statement that created the file. The statement

```
50 INPUT #2, NAME1$, AGE, TUITION
```

transfers data from the file opened as number 2 to the listed variables.

To alter data in a sequential file the changed data must be transferred to a new file along with the remaining original data. After the corrected data is stored in a new file, the old file can be deleted using KILL and the new file given the name of the original file using NAME.

When a file is closed an end of file (EOF) marker is placed after the last record in the file. The EOF(<file number>) function returns true when the end of the specified file has been reached, otherwise it is false.

Since commas are used to separate data items entered into a sequential file with WRITE #, this statement cannot be used when the data contains commas. Instead the PRINT # statement can be used which places a carriage return (Enter) character after each data item to separate it from the next. It takes the form PRINT #<file number>, <string variable>. To read data from a file created using PRINT # the LINE INPUT # statement must be used rather than INPUT #.

Vocabulary

Append mode (A) - Writes data to the end of a sequential file.

CLOSE - Statement that terminates communication between a program and file.

EOF() - Function that determines whether the end of file marker has been reached.

File - A collection of related data items stored on disk.

INPUT # - Statement that transfers data from a sequential file to a program.

INSTR() - Function which returns a 0 if a specified character is not found in a string, or the position of the character if it is found.

KILL - Statement that erases a previously created file from disk.

LINE INPUT # - Statement used to read sequential files created using PRINT #.

NAME - Statement that renames an existing file.

OPEN - Statement that establishes a line of communication between a program and a file and prepares the file for use.

PRINT # - Statement used to enter data containing commas into a sequential file.

Random-access file - Stores data so that it can be easily retrieved from a random location within the file, for example, a single name or address.

Record - Complete entry in a file.

Sequential file - File which stores data so that it can be easily recalled in the same order as it was originally stored.

WRITE # - Statement that transfers data from a program into a sequential file.

Exercises

1. a) Write a program which stores 50 random numbers between 0 and 20 in a sequential file.

    b) Create a second program to retrieve the numbers, add them and print their sum.

2. a) Write a program which stores in a sequential file the names and prices of five different desserts served at Madge's Diner.

    b) With a second program, add two additional desserts to the file.

    c) Have a third program retrieve and print the information about available deserts.

3. a) Write a program which stores the first names of ten different friends in a sequential file.

    b) Create a second program which prints all the names in the file which begin with letters between D and J, or a message if none are found.

4. a) Write a program which creates a file named SEQUENCE.DAT which contains the members of the following sequence: 1000, 1001, 1002, 1003, . . ., 1128.

    b) Write a program to retrieve any member of the sequence from SEQUENCE.DAT and print it when its position in the sequence (i.e., third number, eighth number, etc.) is input:

    ```
    Which number? 3
    Number is 1002
    ```

5. a) Write a program which creates a sequential payroll file called PAY.DAT that stores each of ten person's names (last name and initial), his or her hourly pay rate, the number of dependents, and amount for a savings plan deduction for each week. Supply appropriate data in the form:

    Smith, J., 8.35, 2, 25

    This example indicates that employee J. Smith earns $8.35 an hour, has 2 dependents and deducts $25.00 a week for the payroll savings plan.

b) Write a program which reads PAY.DAT and asks you to supply the number of hours each person worked during the week. Have the program then prepare a payroll data sheet which lists the name, dependants, hours worked, gross pay, deductions, and net (take home) pay for each employee. Assume a tax rate of 25%, with 2% being subtracted from this rate for each dependent. For example, if J. Smith worked 30 hours this week, the payroll sheet would be similar to:

```
. . .
Hours for Smith, J.? 30

             Payroll Sheet
Employee name: Smith, J.
Dependants: 2
Hours worked: 30

Gross pay:        $250.50
Savings plan:     $ 25.00
Taxes ( 21 %):    $ 47.36
Net pay:          $178.14
. . .
```

6. a) Write a program that creates a file named FRAT.DAT which contains the names, fraternities, and ages of thirty students. For example:

Thom Steves	Sigma Phi Epsilon	18
Elvie Machado	Phi Sigma Sigma	23
Eric Bloom	Theta Delta	20
Jane Siberry	Sigma Delta	19
Bob Doucette	Theta Chi	21

b) Write a program that accesses FRAT.DAT and creates a sequential file THETA.DAT which contains the names and ages of only those students who are members of Theta Delta.

c) Write a program which accesses THETA.DAT to create another sequential file THETA20.DAT and stores only those members of Theta Delta who are twenty or older.

7. There are twenty seats (numbered 1-20) in a room which will be used to administer an examination. The computer is to select seats randomly for each person taking the examination and store the person's name in a sequential file named SEATS.DAT.

a) Write a subroutine that creates and initializes (places a blank space for each name) the file SEATS.DAT.

b) Write a subroutine that randomly assigns a seat to each of twenty students whose names are in DATA statements. Each name should then be stored at the proper location in SEATS.DAT. For example, the fifth name in the file is assigned seat five. Make certain that once a seat is filled that it is not used again.

c) Write a subroutine that prints the contents of SEATS.DAT similar to:

```
Seat 1: Jack Whelan
Seat 2: Patricia Hahn
  . . .
Seat 20: Ruth Wagy
```

d) Write a program that allows the user to perform each of the three tasks by selecting from a menu:

```
Seating Assignments
   1. Initialize file
   2. Assign seats
   3. Print seat assignments
   4. Quit
Your choice (1-4)? . . .
```

8. a) Two researches, Kevin and Kim, measured the Fahrenheit temperature outside at various times during a ten hour period on a winter's day. Their results are recorded below. Create two sequential files, one for each person's data, naming each file after that person:

KEVIN		KIM	
Time	**Temp**	**Time**	**Temp**
0.0	18.1	1.0	20.9
2.1	24.0	1.9	23.3
3.8	27.2	3.5	26.1
6.0	29.3	6.0	28.9
8.0	26.6	8.2	26.2
9.0	16.1	10.0	16.0

b) Write a program that merges the two files into one file named TEMPMERG.DAT. The times should be in order. However, when the same time occurs in both Kevin and Kim's file, the average of the two temperature values should be stored in TEMPMERG.DAT for that time.

c) Write a program which retrieves and prints the contents of TEMPMERG.DAT.

9. Software Jungle sells only the top computer software packages, which have names like "QBase, version 1.01A", "Tulip 3.3, Windows edition", etc. Their cashiers want a program to help them ring up customer charges with options similar to:

```
Software Jungle Register
   1. Add a software package
   2. Delete a software package
   3. Sell a software package
   4. List all software packages
   5. Quit
```

The store's inventory is stored in a file in the format:

"<package name>"
<copies in stock>, <cost>

For example,

"ZapBASIC, Developer's edition"
5, 249.95

indicates that there are 5 copies of ZapBASIC, Developer's edition available at $249.95 each.

Write a program using subroutines which allows the cashier to perform the tasks listed above. Adding a package adds a new product to the file, while deleting removes a product. Each time a copy is sold, print a sales ticket showing the cost plus 7% sales tax, and decrease the number in stock by one.

10. The Drama Society has decided to use the computer to print out tickets for a play it will perform at the local auditorium. To reserve a seat, a clerk enters the name and the row and seat number desired. There are ten rows with five seats to a row. The program creates a file named SEATS.DAT which stores the seat assignments. Make sure that a seat may not be chosen more than once.

a) Write a main program which gives the user the opportunity to choose between the following options:

```
Theater Seating
   1. Initialize file
   2. Enter a seat reservation
   3. List all empty seats
   4. Print seating list
   5. Quit
Your choice (1-5)? . . .
```

b) Write a subroutine to perform each of the tasks listed above. Be certain not to allow the same seat to be reserved twice.

Advanced Exercise

The following exercise requires the development of a detailed algorithm. The program should not be written until all details of the algorithm have been worked out.

11. The school's new coin collecting club needs a program to keep track of its ten members and their five most valuable coins.

a) Establish a sequential file named COIN.DAT. It should contain each member's name followed by a brief description of five of his or her most valuable coins. If a member has fewer than five coins, then blanks should be used.

b) Write a program, UPDATE.BAS, which performs the following functions using subroutines:

1. Allows the descriptions of each member's coins to be changed as he or she trades with club members.
2. Changes the names and coin descriptions of members who are either joining or leaving the club.
3. Produces a print out of all members names and coin descriptions.

Chapter 12

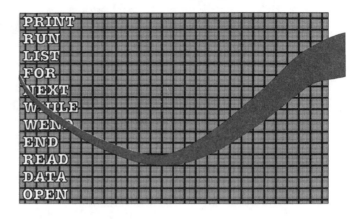

Random-Access Files

OPEN

FIELD

LSET

RSET

PUT

GET

LOF ( )

Objectives

Chapter Twelve

After completing this chapter you will be able to:

1. Open files in random-access mode using OPEN.

2. Convert numbers to strings so that they can be stored in a random-access file.

3. Use FIELD to partition a buffer in memory to fit the structure of a record.

4. Transfer data from a program to the buffer using LSET and RSET.

5. Transfer data from the buffer to disk using PUT.

6. Transfer data from a file to the buffer using GET.

7. Determine the length of a file using the LOF() function.

8. Access multiple files.

9. Convert string data containing numbers back to numeric values.

A random-access file is similar to the sequential files studied in Chapter 11, with the exception that each record in the file may be accessed individually — the previous records do not have to be read first. To read the last record in a sequential file, every record of data preceding it must be read in sequence. However, any record in a random-access file can be read without reading any of the others. Updating a random-access file is easier because the contents of one record can be updated without accessing the rest of the file, and no temporary file is needed. Unlike a sequential file, which is opened for a specific mode (Input or Output), a random-access file can be both read from and written to in the same mode.

12.1 Random-Access File Records and Buffers

Unlike sequential files, the length of the records in a random-access file is specified when the file is created, and is the same for all of the records within a given file. BASIC assumes a maximum record length of 128 characters, but this may be changed when BASIC is started. For example, typing

```
BASIC /S:256
```

starts BASIC and changes the maximum record length to 256 characters. The largest record size available is 32,767 characters.

A single record in a random-access file need not hold only one item of data but may contain many different pieces. The only restriction is that the data may not use more space than the specified size of the record.

To exploit the power offered by random-access files, it is necessary to understand how the computer stores information. For file processing, BASIC could have been designed to put each small item of information on the disk as soon as that information was made available. However, since accessing the disk is time consuming, it is more efficient to transfer information to the disk in complete records. This requires a temporary storage space in memory, called a "buffer", where information is stored until a record is complete.

The buffer is similar to an office IN/OUT basket whose purpose is to hold information prior to its filing. With sequential files the user has no control over the interaction between the buffer and the disk.

Instead, the computer automatically determines when the buffer is full and then transfers its contents to the disk. Random-access files, however, give the programmer complete control over both the structure of the buffer's contents and its transfer to and from the disk.

The increased power of random-access files also brings some increased complexity. The process of transferring data between a program and a random-access file involves the following series of steps:

1. Using the OPEN statement, the file is specified, opened, and a buffer made ready to receive data.

2. The buffer is partitioned to fit the structure of each record using the FIELD statement.

3. Data is placed in the buffer using the LSET and RSET statements.

4. The data in the buffer is written to the file using the PUT statement.

5. To retrieve data from the file, the GET statement is used.

6. Finally, the open file should be CLOSEd.

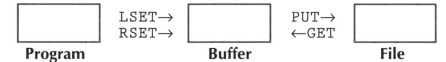

Review these steps carefully so that you understand how each step interacts with the others.

12.2 Random-Access OPEN

Like sequential files, random-access files are created using the OPEN statement. The format for opening random-access files is:

OPEN "R", #<file number>, "<file name>", <record length>

where "R" stands for a random-access mode, and the record length is the total number of characters (places) in a single record. Specifying the "R" mode automatically creates a storage area in the computer's memory called a buffer whose size is the same as the record length.

OPEN "R", #3, "EMPLOYEE.DAT", 50

opens a random-access file named EMPLOYEE.DAT as file number 3, with each record in the file containing 50 characters. A 50 character buffer is automatically created.

12.3 Converting Numbers To Strings

Unlike sequential files which can store any type of data, random-access files store all data as strings. This requires numeric data to be converted to strings before being stored. The functions MKI$(), MKS$() and MKD$() perform this operation, converting an integer, single precision or double precision number into a string:

Function	Operation
N$ = MKI$(N%)	Converts an integer (N%) into a two character string (N$).
N$ = MKS$(N!)	Converts a single precision number (N!) into a four character string (N$).
N$ = MKD$(N#)	Converts a double-precision number (N#) into an eight character string (N$).

12.4 The FIELD Statement

After the OPEN statement creates a buffer for the file, the FIELD statement is used to organize the buffer so that data can pass through it between the program and the file. The FIELD statement partitions the buffer into regions, each of which holds a string and is referenced by a specific string variable. The simplest form of the FIELD statement is:

FIELD #<file number>, <length> AS <string variable>

For example,

```
30 OPEN "R", #2, "PAYROLL.DAT", 45
40 FIELD #2, 45 AS X$
```

Line 30 opens the PAYROLL.DAT file and automatically creates a 45 character buffer. The FIELD statement at line 40 reserves the entire 45 characters in the buffer for the string variable X$. Note that both the OPEN and FIELD statement specify file number 2.

When more than one piece of data must be stored in a record, it is possible to partition the buffer to hold more than one string. The statement

```
40 FIELD #2, 20 AS A$, 25 AS B$
```

reserves the first 20 characters of the buffer for the contents of A$ and the last 25 characters for the contents of B$. To better visualize how data is stored in the buffer, it is a good practice to diagram the buffer as illustrated below:

Buffer for PAYROLL.DAT

A$	B$
20 characters	25 characters

Review

1. Create proper OPEN and FIELD statements for the each of following situations. Include a diagram of the buffer:

    a) A file named XYZ.DAT which has a record length of 10 which stores 1 piece of data.

    b) A file named PAYROLL.DAT which has a record length of 50 which stores 3 pieces of data: a name, number of hours worked, and a payrate.

c) A file named GPA.DAT which has a record length of 20 which stores 2 pieces of data: a name and a grade point average.
d) A file named INVENTRY.DAT which has a record length of 8 which stores 2 pieces of data: a part number and the number of items in stock of that part.

12.5 LSET and RSET

The FIELD statement reserves a certain number of spaces for string variables in the buffer, but it does not transfer any data to it. To do this, it is necessary to use the LSET and RSET statements. The form for both is:

LSET <buffer string variable> = <string to be placed in buffer>

or

RSET <buffer string variable> = <string to be placed in buffer>

The <buffer string variable> is the name of a variable listed in the FIELD statement. For example,

```
40 FIELD #2, 20 AS A$
50 LSET A$ = "Hello"
```

Besides transferring strings to the buffer, RSET and LSET modify the strings to make sure that they properly fit the space allotted in the FIELD statement. In the example above, A$ has reserved 20 characters in the buffer. Because "Hello" is only 5 characters long, LSET adds an additional 15 spaces to A$. If the string is longer than the space allocated in the buffer it is truncated. These operations are performed by both LSET and RSET.

The LSET statement left justifies a string by adding needed spaces to the right end of the string. In the example above, A$ would store "Hello" followed by 15 spaces. RSET justifies by adding spaces on the left end. If line 50 were changed to

```
50 RSET A$ = "Hello"
```

A$ would store 15 spaces followed by "Hello". Remember that both LSET and RSET truncate excess characters from the right end of a string which is larger than the space specified in the FIELD statement.

Most programming situations require blanks at the end of a string rather than the beginning, so the LSET statement is used more frequently than RSET.

This program demonstrates how LSET and RSET change the strings assigned by them:

```
10 REM ** Demonstrates LSET and RSET **
20 PRINT "How characters are buffered"
30 OPEN "R", #1, "SAMPLE.DAT", 20
40 FIELD #1, 5 AS A$, 15 AS B$
50 LSET A$ = "ABCDEFG"
60 LSET B$ = "ABCDEFG"
```

```
70 PRINT "Using LSET"
80 PRINT "  (" A$ ")",  "(" B$ ")"
90 RSET A$ = "ABCDEFG"
100 RSET B$ = "ABCDEFG"
110 PRINT "Using RSET"
120 PRINT "  (" A$ ")",  "(" B$ ")"
130 CLOSE #1
999 END
```

```
RUN
How characters are buffered
Using LSET
   (ABCDE)        (ABCDEFG           )
Using RSET
   (ABCDE)        (           ABCDEFG)
Ok
```

Line 30 opens a random-access file using file number 1 with the name "SAMPLE.DAT" and a record length of 20 characters. A buffer is automatically created to match the record length. Line 40 divides the buffer into 2 sections to hold the variables A$ (5 characters) and B$ (15 characters). A$ and B$ are then given values using LSET, and those values printed at line 80. The parentheses are not stored in the buffer, but are used to show how the contents of A$ and B$ are affected by LSET and RSET. Lines 90 through 120 then perform the same operations using RSET. In both cases, the "FG" is truncated because A$ may only store 5 characters. Note the differences between the value of B$ when LSET and RSET. LSET added spaces to the right of the letters, and RSET to the left. Finally, line 130 closes the SAMPLE.DAT file.

Review

2. Write a program to create a random-access file named MAILING.LST. The buffer should be divided into 5 areas as follows:

Variable	Meaning	Maximum Length
N$	Name	(20 characters left justified)
ADDRESS$	Street Address	(25 characters left justified)
CITY$	City	(20 characters left justified)
STATE$	State	(20 characters left justified)
ZIP$	Zip Code	(10 characters right justified)

12.6 PUT

LSET and RSET only transfer data from the program to the buffer, and do not transfer the contents of the buffer to the disk. The PUT statement is used to transfer the data in the buffer to a record in the file. Each record is numbered sequentially, from one to the number of records in the file.

The form of the PUT statement is

PUT #<file number>, <record number>

where <file number> is the file number specified in the OPEN statement and record number refers to the position in the file where the record is to be placed. If the record number is not specified, the data is transferred to the record immediately after the last record accessed by the program. For example,

```
50 PUT #2, 4
```

instructs the computer to transfer the current contents of the buffer into the fourth record of the file opened as number 2. If the next PUT statement executed does not specify a record number, the data in the buffer is transferred to the fifth record in the file.

12.7 Keyboard Input and Buffers

String variable names used in a program should be different from those used in the buffer. This is necessary because the computer overwrites data stored in the buffer if the same variable names are used. For example, a program using INPUT to get data from the user should have different variable names in the INPUT and FIELD statements. The data read into the INPUT variables should be assigned to the FIELD statement variables using LSET and RSET.

This program creates the file ADDRESS.DAT and allows the names and addresses for any number of people to be placed in it:

```
10 REM ** Creates ADDRESS.DAT **
20 OPEN "R", #1, "ADDRESS.DAT", 40
30 FIELD #1, 15 AS PERSON$, 25 AS ADDRESS$
40 INPUT "Enter name (DONE to stop): ", NAME1$
50 WHILE NAME1$ <> "DONE"
60    INPUT "Address"; ADDR$
70    LSET PERSON$ = NAME1$
80    LSET ADDRESS$ = ADDR$
90    PUT #1
100   PRINT
110   INPUT "Enter name (DONE to stop): ",
      NAME1$
120 WEND
130 CLOSE #1
140 PRINT "File created."
999 END
```

```
RUN
Enter name (DONE to stop): John Camper
Address? 12 Military Trail

Enter name (DONE to stop): Mary Nash
Address? 444 Swan Cove

Enter name (DONE to stop): Jane Caputti
Address? 1389 Camden Avenue

Enter name (DONE to stop): DONE
File created.
Ok
```

Line 20 opens the random-access file ADDRESS.DAT as file number 1 with a record length of 40 characters. The buffer is partitioned at line 30 into 2 sections, one which is 15 characters long and is referenced by PERSON$, and another which is 25 characters long and is referenced by ADDRESS$. The user inputs the first name at line 40. Lines 50 through 120 create a loop which executes until the user enters DONE for the name. Notice that the variable names used in the INPUT statements are not the same as those described in the FIELD statement. Lines 70 and 80 place the data input into the buffer left justified. The PUT at line 90 writes the data currently in the buffer to the file. Because no record number is specified, the record is appended to the file. The file is closed and a message printed at lines 130 and 140.

After running this program, the contents of ADDRESS.DAT are:

```
John  Camper      12 Military Trail
Mary  Nash        44 Swan Cove
Jane  Caputti     1389 Camden Avenue
```

Review

3. Modify the mailing list program from Review 2 so that it takes the record stored in the buffer and transfers it to a disk file. Write the program so that any number of names may be entered.

12.8 GET

The GET statement transfers data from a file to the buffer. Again, the data is transferred based on the buffer as described in the FIELD statement. GET has the form:

GET #<file number>, <record number>

For example,

```
90 GET #3, 12
```

transfers the contents of record number 12 to the buffer associated with file number 3. Like PUT, the GET statement transfers data from the record following the last record accessed if no record number is specified. If no record number is specified in the next GET statement after line 90 above, the data from record number 13 will be read from the file.

If the record number specified by GET is less than 1, BASIC generates a "Bad record number" error. If the record number is greater than the number of records in the file, the buffer is filled with nulls (ASCII character 0).

The program on the next page retrieves and prints the name and address of a person stored in the ADDRESS.DAT file created in Section 12.7:

```
10  REM ** Reads ADDRESS.DAT **
20  OPEN "R", #1, "ADDRESS.DAT", 40
30  FIELD #1, 15 AS PERSON$, 25 AS ADDRESS$
40  INPUT "Which record (0 to stop)"; RECORD
50  WHILE RECORD > 0
60     GET #1, RECORD
70     PRINT PERSON$
80     PRINT ADDRESS$
90     PRINT
100    INPUT "Which record (0 to stop)"; RECORD
110 WEND
120 CLOSE #1
130 PRINT "File closed."
999 END
```

```
RUN
Which record (0 to stop)? 2
Mary Nash
444 Swan Cove

Which record (0 to stop)? 3
Jane Caputti
1389 Camden Avenue

Which record (0 to stop)? 1
John Camper
12 Military Trail

Which record (0 to stop)? 0
File closed
Ok
```

Line 20 opens the random-access file ADDRESS.DAT as file number 1 with a record length of 40 characters, and line 30 partitions the buffer. The first record number is read from the user at line 40. Lines 50 through 110 form a loop which GETs that record from the file and prints the contents of the buffer. When the user enters a 0 for the record number, the loop ends and the file is closed at line 120.

12.9 Calculating File Length: LOF()

The LOF() function returns the length (number of characters) of a specified file:

LOF (<file number>)

LOF's value represents the total number of characters in the file. To determine the number of actual records, LOF() is divided by the record size. Adding line 25 to the program in Section 12.8 above

```
20  OPEN "R", #1, "ADDRESS.DAT", 40
25  PRINT "There are" LOF(1) / 40 "people in
    the file."
```

prints:

> There are 3 people in the file.

The LOF() value was divided by 40, the size of the buffer as declared in the OPEN statement.

Review

4. Write a program to access the MAILING.LST file created in Review 3. Have the user input a number to select the record the computer should GET. Print the data from this record or the message "No Data Found" if there is no data for that record number.

12.10 Accessing Multiple Files

It is possible to work with up to three random-access files simultaneously within a single program. The only requirement is that each file have a separate file number.

This program uses two files. The first, ADDRESS.DAT was created in Section 12.7 and stores names and addresses. The second file, HOBBY.DAT stores a hobby for each person in ADDRESS. Note how the file numbers are used to keep the data in each file separate within the program:

```
10 REM ** Reads ADDRESS.DAT and creates
            HOBBY.DAT **
20 OPEN "R", #1, "ADDRESS.DAT", 40
30 FIELD #1, 15 AS PERSON$, 25 AS ADDRESS$
40 NUMRECS = LOF(1) / 40 : REM ** Number of
   records
50 OPEN "R", #2, "HOBBY.DAT", 30
60 FIELD #2, 15 AS N$, 15 AS HOB$
70 FOR RECORD = 1 TO NUMRECS
80    GET #1, RECORD
90    PRINT "Hobby for " PERSON$;
100   INPUT HOBBY$
110   LSET N$ = PERSON$
120   LSET IIOB$ = HOBBY$
130   PUT #2
140 NEXT RECORD
150 CLOSE
160 PRINT
170 PRINT "Files closed."
999 END
```

```
RUN
Hobby for John Camper    ? Duck Decoys
Hobby for Mary Nash      ? Biking
Hobby for Jane Caputti   ? Rock climbing

Files closed.
Ok
```

After running this program, the contents of HOBBY.DAT are:

```
John  Camper      Duck Decoys
Mary  Nash        Biking
Jane  Caputti     Rock climbing
```

ADDRESS.DAT is opened in line 20 and the buffer partitioned in line 30. The number of records in the file is calculated by line 40. Lines 50 and 60 create and partition a file named HOBBY.DAT which has two fields, a name and a hobby, both with length 15. The loop at lines 70 through 140 reads a record from ADDRESS and uses the name to prompt the user for a hobby. Both the name and the hobby are then written to HOBBY.DAT at line 130. Because this PUT does not have a record number, each new record is appended to the file. After each record in ADDRESS has been processed, the loop ends and the files are closed at line 150. Omitting a file number from the CLOSE statement closes all open files.

12.11 Converting Strings to Numbers

When converted numeric data is retrieved from a random-access file it is stored as a string. Before it may be used, the data must be converted back to numeric format using one of the following functions:

Function	Operation
N% = CVI(N\$)	Converts a two character string (N\$) into an integer (N%).
N! = CVS(N\$)	Converts a four character string (N\$) into a single-precision number (N!).
N# = CVD(N\$)	Converts an eight character string (N\$) into a double-precision number (N#).

These are the compliments of the functions described in Section 12.3 which convert numeric values to strings. In order for the above functions to work correctly, the value in N\$ must have been converted to a string using one of those functions.

This program creates a file of 10 random numbers, then picks one from it:

```
10 REM ** Creates and reads file of numbers **
20 RANDOMIZE TIMER
30 OPEN "R", #1, "NUMBERS.DAT", 4
40 FIELD #1, 4 AS NUM$
50 FOR I = 1 TO 10
60   N = INT(RND * 100) + 1
70   PRINT N
80   LSET NUM$ = MKS$(N)
90   PUT #1
100 NEXT I
110 INPUT "Which record (1-10)"; REC
120 GET #1, REC
```

```
130 N = CVS(NUM$)
140 PRINT "The number is" N
150 CLOSE #1
160 PRINT "File closed."
999 END
```

```
RUN
 78
 44
 5
 27
 13
 89
 28
 41
 38
 50
Which record (1-10)? 4
The number is 27
File closed.
Ok
```

NUMBERS.DAT is created by lines 30 and 40. The loop at lines 50 through 100 executes 10 times, each time picking a random number, converting it to a string at line 80, and writing it to the file. Because the PUT at line 90 does not specify which record to write the data to, each new record is appended to the file. Lines 110 and 120 get a user-specified record from the file. Line 130 converts the string back into a number, and it is printed at line 140.

12.12 End of Chapter Problem

This chapter ends by solving a problem which requires a carefully thought out algorithm. Once the algorithm has been developed, we can then determine what input and output variables are needed and assign appropriate variable names. This program is a modified version of the End of Chapter program from Chapter 11. It illustrates some of the advantages of using random-access files over sequential files.

A baseball team needs a program to keep track of their players' batting averages. The players' statistics are kept in a random-access file named BATAVG2.DAT. Besides creating this file, the program should be able to add new players, update averages, and print a table of the players with their respective averages from the data in the file. Each player's uniform number corresponds to their record number in the file.

Algorithm:

1. Choose which option the user wishes to perform (create, add players, update, print or exit).
2. Perform the requested routine(s):
   a) Create File: Initialize the file. Enter the player information.
   b) Add Players: Find out number of new players. Enter the player information.

    c) Update Player: Get the number of the player to update. Check if record exists. Enter updated player information.

    d) Print File: Print player information for every record in the file that contains information.

    e) Exit: Close all files and leave the program

Since Create File and Add Players perform similar activities, they both call a subroutine to enter the player information and calculate the batting average. A conversion routine is used to convert all numeric data to strings and PUT the information on disk.

Buffer:

Player Name	PLAYER$
At Bats	AB$
Hits	H$
Average	AVERAGE$

Input:

Player Number	NUM
Player Name	PNAME$
At Bats	ATBATS
Hits	HITS
Number of Players	NUMPLAYERS
New At Bats	ADDATBATS
New Hits	ADDHITS

Output:

Player Number	NUM
Player Name	PNAME$
At Bats	ATBATS
Hits	HITS
Batting Average	AVG

```
10 REM ** Program to keep track of batting
        averages **
100 REM ** Main program
110 WHILE CHOICE <> 5
120    CLS
130    PRINT "1: Create File"
140    PRINT "2: Add Players"
150    PRINT "3: Update Player"
160    PRINT "4: Print File"
170    PRINT "5: Exit Program"
180    PRINT
190    INPUT "Enter Selection (1-5): ", CHOICE
200    WHILE (CHOICE < 1) OR (CHOICE > 5)
210       BEEP
220       INPUT "Enter Selection (1-5): ",
          CHOICE
230    WEND
240    ON CHOICE GOSUB 1000, 2000, 3000, 6000
250 WEND
260 REM ** Exit Program
270 CLOSE
280 PRINT "Program complete"
999 END
```

```
1000 REM ** Create File
1010 OPEN "R", #1, "BATAVG2.DAT", 20
1020 FIELD #1, 12 AS PLAYER$, 2 AS AB$,
     2 AS H$, 4 AS AVERAGE$
1030 GOSUB 8000 : REM ** Initialize file
1040 INPUT "Enter number of players: ",
     NUMPLAYERS
1050 GOSUB 5000 : REM ** Input Player
     Information
1060 CLOSE #1
1070 RETURN
1990 REM
2000 REM ** Add Player to File
2010 OPEN "R", #1, "BATAVG2.DAT", 20
2020 FIELD #1, 12 AS PLAYER$, 2 AS AB$,
     2 AS H$, 4 AS AVERAGE$
2030 INPUT "Enter number of NEW players: ",
     NUMPLAYERS
2040 GOSUB 5000 : REM ** Input Player
     Information
2050 CLOSE #1
2060 RETURN
2990 REM
3000 REM ** Update Player
3010 INPUT "Enter player number: ", NUM
3020 OPEN "R", #1, "BATAVG2.DAT", 20
3030 FIELD #1, 12 AS PLAYER$, 2 AS AB$,
     2 AS H$, 4 AS AVERAGE$
3040 GET #1, NUM
3050 IF PLAYER$ <> "EMPTY         " THEN PNAME$
     = PLAYER$ : INPUT "Enter additional At
     bats, Hits: ", ADDATBATS, ADDHITS :
     GOSUB 4000 ELSE INPUT "Player not found
     - press Enter", PAUSE$
3060 CLOSE #1
3070 RETURN
3990 REM
4000 REM ** Update File
4010 ATBATS = CVI(AB$) + ADDATBATS
4020 HITS = CVI(H$) + ADDHITS
4030 AVG = HITS / ATBATS
4040 GOSUB 7000
4050 RETURN
4990 REM
5000 REM ** Input Player Information
5010 FOR I = 1 TO NUMPLAYERS
5020   INPUT "Enter Number, Name, At bats,
       Hits: ", NUM, PNAME$, ATBATS, HITS
5030   AVG = HITS / ATBATS
5040   GOSUB 7000 : REM ** Conversion routine
5050 NEXT I
5060 RETURN
5990 REM
```

```
6000 REM ** Print File
6010 OPEN "R", #1, "BATAVG2.DAT", 20
6020 FIELD #1, 12 AS PLAYER$, 2 AS AB$,
     2 AS H$, 4 AS AVERAGE$
6030 CLS
6040 PRINT "Name", "At Bats", "Hits", "Average"
6050 PRINT
6060 FOR RECORD = 1 TO 99
6070    GET #1
6080    IF PLAYER$ <> "EMPTY       " THEN
        PRINT PLAYER$, CVI(AB$), CVI(H$), :
        PRINT USING "#.###"; CVS(AVERAGE$)
6090 NEXT RECORD
6100 CLOSE #1
6110 PRINT
6120 INPUT "Press Enter for menu", PAUSE$
6130 RETURN
6990 REM
7000 REM ** Conversion Routine
7010 LSET PLAYER$ = PNAME$
7020 RSET AB$ = MKI$(ATBATS)
7030 RSET H$ = MKI$(HITS)
7040 RSET AVERAGE$ = MKS$(AVG)
7050 PUT #1, NUM
7060 RETURN
7990 REM
8000 REM ** Initialize File
8010 FOR RECORD = 1 TO 99
8020    LSET PLAYER$ = "EMPTY"
8030    PUT #1, RECORD
8040 NEXT RECORD
8050 RETURN
```

```
RUN
1: Create File
2: Add Players
3: Update Player
4: Print File
5: Exit Program

Enter Selection (1-5): 1

Enter number of players: 2
Enter Number, Name, At bats, Hits: 5,
Freitas, 5, 4
Enter Number, Name, At bats, Hits: 47,
Hengy, 8, 3

1: Create File
2: Add Players
3: Update Player
4: Print File
5: Exit Program

Enter Selection (1-5): 4
```

```
Name            At Bats         Hits            Average
Freitas         5               4               0.800
Hengy           8               3               0.375

Press Enter for menu

1: Create File
2: Add Players
3: Update Player
4: Print File
5: Exit Program

Enter Selection (1-5): 2

Enter number of NEW players: 1
Enter Number, Name, At bats, Hits: 12,
Rohrman, 6, 5

1: Create File
2: Add Players
3: Update Player
4: Print File
5: Exit Program

Enter Selection (1-5): 3

Enter player number: 5
Enter additional At bats, Hits: 2, 1

1: Create File
2: Add Players
3: Update Player
4: Print File
5: Exit Program

Enter Selection (1-5): 4

Name            At Bats         Hits            Average
Freitas         7               5               0.714
Rohrman         6               5               0.833
Hengy           8               3               0.375

Press Enter for menu

1: Create File
2: Add Players
3: Update Player
4: Print File
5: Exit Program

Enter Selection (1-5): 5
Program complete
Ok
```

Lines 100 through 250 print the program menu and accept the user's input. Based on the user's choice, the desired subroutine is called. The Create File subroutine starting at line 1000 opens the file for random access. The file is then initialized using the Initialize File subroutine at line 8000. This subroutine writes "EMPTY" for the name in each record. By doing this we can check the validity of the record before printing and updating. After initialization, the number of players is input and the Input Player Information subroutine starting at line 5000 is called. This subroutine prompts the user for player information. From these statistics the player's average is calculated. The Conversion Routine is then called and the player information is transferred to the buffer and then to disk using the player number as the record number. The record is now considered active because it does not have "EMPTY" as the name. The Add Players subroutine works in much the same way. In this case, the file need not be initialized. Information is obtained in Input Player Information subroutine. Data is transferred to the buffer and then to disk in the Conversion Routine. The information is PUT into the record corresponding to the players' uniform number. Update Player GETs the player record according to the number input by the user. Update Player updates the ATBATS, HITS and the AVERAGE and information is written to disk using the Conversion Routine. Active records in the file, as indicated by a name other than "EMPTY", are printed using the Print File subroutine at line 6000.

Review

5. The End of Chapter program does not stop the user from attempting to enter a new player or update an existing player with a number greater than 99 or less than 1. Modify the program to print a message and restirct player numbers to the range 1-99 should this occur.

Chapter Summary

To read a record in a sequential file, every record preceding it must be read in sequence. In a random-access file any record can be accessed without reading any of the others. Updating a random-access file is easier because the contents of a single record can be updated without accessing the rest of the file. Also, a random-access file can be both read from and written to in the same mode.

The maximum record length in a random-access file is 128 characters, unless this is changed when BASIC is started. Entering BASIC /S:256 starts BASIC and changes the maximum record length to 256 characters.

Before data is transferred from the computer to a random-access file it is temporarily stored in an area of memory called a buffer. The structure of the buffer's contents and its transfer to disk is controlled by the programmer.

A random-access file is opened using the OPEN statement in the form OPEN "R", #<file number>, "<file name>", <record length>. The statement

```
20 OPEN "R", #2, "STUDENT.DAT", 40
```

opens a random-access file named STUDENT.DAT as file number 2, with each record in the file containing 40 characters.

Because random-access files store all data as strings, numeric data must be converted to strings before being stored. The function MKI$(N%) converts an integer to a two character string, MKS$(N!) converts single precision number into a four character string, and MKD$(N#) converts a double-precision number into an eight character string.

The FIELD statement is used to partition the buffer into regions, each of which holds a string and is referenced by a specific string variable. Its form is FIELD#<file number>, <length> AS <string variable>. The statement

```
30 FIELD #2, 15 AS NAME1$, 25 AS ADDRESS$
```

reserves 15 characters in the buffer for file number 2 for the string variable NAME1$ and 25 characters for ADDRESS$.

The LSET statement, which takes the form LSET <buffer string variable> = <string to be placed in buffer>, is used to transfer string data from a program to the buffer left-justifying it. If the string is less than the space reserved for it, blank spaces are added to the right. If the string is too large it is truncated from the right. RSET performs the same function except that it right justifies the string and adds needed spaces to the left. The statement

```
40 LSET NAME1$ = "Jonathan"
```

transfers the string Jonathan to the buffer partitioned by the FIELD statement above left-justifying the string and adding seven spaces.

The PUT statement transfers data from the buffer to disk and takes the form PUT #<file number>, <record number>. The <record number> refers to the position in the file where the record is to be placed. For example,

```
50 PUT #2, 15
```

transfers the current contents of the buffer to record 15 of the file open as number 2. If the next PUT executed does not specify a record number, the data in the buffer will be transferred to record 16.

String variable names used in a program must be different from those used in the buffer because the computer overwrites data stored in the buffer if the same variable names are used.

The GET statement transfers data from a file to the buffer and takes the form GET #<file number>, <record number>. For example,

```
80 GET #2, 12
```

transfers the contents of record 12 to the buffer from the disk file. If no record number is given data is transferred from the record following the last record accessed.

The LOF() function returns the length of (number of characters stored in) a specified file. Dividing LOF() by the number of characters in a record gives the number of records. For example,

```
90 PRINT LOF(2) / 40
```

displays the number of records for file 2 created above. The number of characters in a single record is the buffer size.

Three random-access files may be open simultaneously within a single program. Each file must have a separate file number.

Since numeric data is stored as a string in a random-access file it must be converted back to its original numeric format using one of the following function: CVI(N$) converts a two character string into an integer, CVS(N$) converts a four character string into a single-precision number, and CVD(N$) converts an eight character string into a double-precision number.

Vocabulary

Buffer - Area in memory used to temporarily store data which will be transferred to a file.

CVD(N$) - Function that converts an eight character string into an double-precision number.

CVI(N$) - Function that converts a two character string into an integer.

CVS(N$) - Function that converts a four character string into a single-precision number.

FIELD - Statement used to organize the buffer.

GET - Statement used to transfer data from a file to the buffer.

LOF() - Function that returns the length (number of characters) of a specified file.

LSET - Statement used to transfer string data from a program to the buffer, left justifying the string and adding blank spaces on the right.

MKD$(N#) - Function that converts a double-precision number into an eight character string.

MKI$(N%) - Function that converts an integer into a two character string.

MKS$(N!) - Function that converts a single precision number into a four character string.

PUT - Statement used to transfer data from the buffer to the file.

RSET - Statement used to transfer string data from a program to the buffer, right justifying the string and adding blank spaces on the left.

Exercises

1. Store the 26 letters of the alphabet in a random-access file named ALPHABET.DAT. Have a program pick five random numbers from 1 to 26 and use these numbers to create and print a five letter "word" made up from the letters stored in ALPHABET.DAT.

2. a) Write a program which stores the titles of ten books in a random-access file named BOOKS.DAT.

   b) Write a second program which reads BOOKS.DAT file and creates a new file containing all the titles beginning with letters from N to Z, inclusive.

3. a) Create a random-access file named ACCOUNTS.DAT that contains the customer name and current balance for an unknown number of savings accounts:

   ```
   RUN
   Name (or END)? Fred Ziffel
   Starting balance? 500.00
   Account number 1 assigned.

   Name (or END)? Peter Jones
   Starting balance? 400.00
   Account number 2 assigned.

   Name (or END)? Jill Montana
   Starting balance? 700.00
   Account number 3 assigned.

   Name (or END)? END
   File closed.
   Ok
   ```

   b) Write a program that allows a bank teller to update ACCOUNTS.DAT whenever an individual makes a deposit or withdrawal:

   ```
   RUN
   Entering a 0 stops the program.
   Account (or 0)? 1
   D)eposit or W)ithdrawal? W
   Amount? 600
   Transaction recorded

   Account (or 0)? 3
   Deposit (D) or withdrawal (W)? D
   Amount? 50
   Transaction recorded
   ```

```
Account (or 0)? 0
File closed.
Ok
```

c) Write a program using the file ACCOUNTS.DAT that sends letters of warning to the holders of all overdrawn accounts or letters of congratulations to those with accounts containing $500 or more informing them that they will be receiving a toaster in the mail:

```
RUN
Dear Fred Ziffel:

It has come to our attention that your
account is overdrawn by $100. Please make a
deposit for at least that amount immediately.
Thank you.

Sincerely,

The BANK

Dear Jill Montana:

You have an exceptionally large account
balance. You will be receiving a toaster in
the mail as an award.

Sincerely,

The BANK
Ok
```

4.   a) Create a random-access file named CARS.DAT to record how many full-sized, mid-sized and compact cars a dealer sells each month for a twelve month period.

b) Write a program that retrieves information from the file CARS.DAT for a specific month and then print a bar graph comparing the sales of the three sizes of cars:

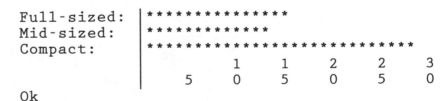

```
Which month (1-12)? 12

Full-sized: |***************
Mid-sized:  |*************
Compact:    |*******************************
            |        1    1    2    2    3
            |   5    0    5    0    5    0
Ok
```

5.   a) Write a program that creates a random-access file STUDENTS.DAT which contains the names, fraternities and ages of thirty college students.

b) Write a program that accesses STUDENTS.DAT and creates a file named SIGMA.DAT which contains the names and ages of only those students who are members of the SIGMA CHI fraternity.

c) Write a program that accesses STUDENTS.DAT and randomly selects twenty-five students for seats in a classroom with five rows, five seats in a row. Have the computer print a seating plan for the class, placing each student's name at the correct seat location.

6. a) Establish a random-access file named SAYING.DAT which contains wise sayings. Each sage remark is to consist of up to 128 characters. The number of sayings is to be determined by the user.

    b) Write the program to retrieve and print any one of the wise sayings in SAYING.DAT.

    c) Modify the program part (b) to display a random saying.

7. a) Write a program that creates a random-access file named WORDS.DAT, which contains 25 words.

    b) Write another program to pick 5 random words from the file and print a "sentence" consisting of the words. Place spaces between the five words and append a period to the end.

Advanced Exercises

Each of the following exercises requires the development of a detailed algorithm. The program should not be written until all details of the algorithm have been worked out.

8. The computer is to be used to store information on charge account customers at the Buy Low Department Store in a random-access file named CHARGE.DAT. The data on each customer is to be stored in a single record with the record number serving as the customer's charge account number.

    Write a program using subroutines that creates a file CHARGE.DAT in which the name, street address, city, state, zip code and total unpaid balance for each customer is stored. Have the program perform each of the following functions:

    a) Update the balances by adding to the unpaid balance when sales are made and subtracting when bills are paid.
    b) Send a bill to each customer at the end of the month. If the total due exceeds $800.00, the message YOUR ACCOUNT EXCEEDS YOUR CHARGE LIMIT, PAY IMMEDIATELY is printed at the bottom of the bill.
    c) Closes the account of a customer who has paid his or her balance and moved away. (Hint: Place all blanks in the record.)
    d) Opens an account for a new customer using the first empty record.

9. a) Write a program that creates a random-access file named SAVINGS.DAT that can be used by a bank to store information about ten depositors. Each depositor's name, social security number, complete address (number and street, city, state, and zip code), and account balance are to be included.

   b) Have the program allow any of the information, including the balance of the account, to be changed or updated:

   ```
   RUN
   Depositor's Account Number? 2
   Name: Mark Walter
     (1) Change Name
     (2) Change Social Security Number
     (3) Change Address
     (4) Change Balance

   Option? 4
   Old Balance: 155.63
   New Balance? 183.76
     . . .
   ```

   c) The bank gives its depositors 0.5% interest per month compounded monthly. Add a routine to the above program that can be run at the end of each month to add the interest earned to the balance of each account.

Chapter 13

Searching and Sorting

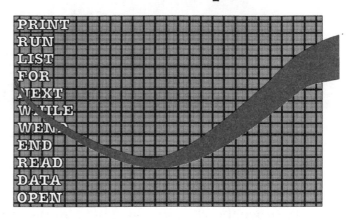

Objectives

Chapter Thirteen

After completing this chapter you will be able to:

1. Sort data using a bubble sort.

2. Improve the efficiency of a bubble sort using a WHILE...WEND loop and a flag.

3. Exchange data between variables using SWAP.

4. Search a previously sorted list to find an item using a binary search.

*A*s the title suggests, this chapter explains techniques for searching and sorting data. Since the topics covered in this chapter involve considerable use of material covered in previous chapters of this book it should not be read until that material is understood thoroughly.

13.1 Bubble Sort

When working with a large amount of data it is usually advisable to sort it first. A list of names might be sorted into alphabetical order, or a list of numbers might be sorted into ascending or descending order. One of the most fundamental and easiest sorting techniques is known as the "bubble" sort. In a bubble sort the program starts at the bottom of the list, then proceeds sequentially to the top, comparing each item in the list with the one above it. If the two elements are not in the proper order, they are interchanged. In this way the name that comes first alphabetically in the list is "bubbled" to the top of the list. For example, given the initial list

Lester   ← **Top**
Diane
Bruce
Susan
Eli   ← **Bottom**

the program starts by comparing the names Susan and Eli. Because Eli comes alphabetically before Susan, the names are switched and the list becomes:

Lester
Diane
Bruce
Eli
Susan

Next, Bruce and Eli are compared. Because Bruce comes before Eli, no change is made. Then Diane and Bruce are compared and interchanged, so the list becomes:

Lester
Bruce
Diane
Eli
Susan

Bruce and Lester are then compared and interchanged. The order of the names in the list now becomes:

> **Bruce**
> **Lester**
> Diane
> Eli
> Susan

Bruce, the name that comes first alphabetically in the list, is now at the top of the list. Now the program starts over at the bottom of the list, and the name that comes next alphabetically is "bubbled" up to its proper position. After the procedure has been repeated enough times, the order of the list becomes:

> Bruce
> Diane
> Eli
> Lester
> Susan

In general, to sort a list which contains N elements, this process must be repeated *N-1* times.

The algorithm below is for a bubble sort which takes an array of names containing N elements and sorts it so that it ends up in increasing order:

Initial Conditions:
N$ = array of names
N = number of elements in the array N$

Step 1: `FOR I = 1 to N-1`
Step 2: `  FOR J = N TO 2 STEP -1`
(Start from the bottom of the array and work to the top.)
Step 3: `    IF N$(J) < N$(J-1) THEN TEMP$ = N$(J) :`
`N$(J) = N$(J-1) : N$(J-1) = TEMP$`
(Switch names when N$(J) < N$(J-1))
Step 4: `  NEXT J`
Step 5: `NEXT I`

The loop starts at the bottom of the list and proceeds sequentially to the top, as you can see from the loop starting at N with a -1 decrement in Step 2. During the execution of this loop, each element is compared with the previous one. If they are not in the correct order, the elements are interchanged, thus putting them into the correct order. This way, elements not in proper order are moved up or down the list towards their correct positions.

Notice how data is switched in step 3 when N$(J) < N$(J-1). First, TEMP$ is assigned the value of N$(J), then N$(J) is assigned the value of N$(J-1) and finally N$(J-1) is assigned the value of TEMP$. TEMP$ is needed to hold the value of N$(J) while the switch is being made, otherwise the value would be erased. This can be demonstrated using the first switch made in the list of names between Susan and Eli:

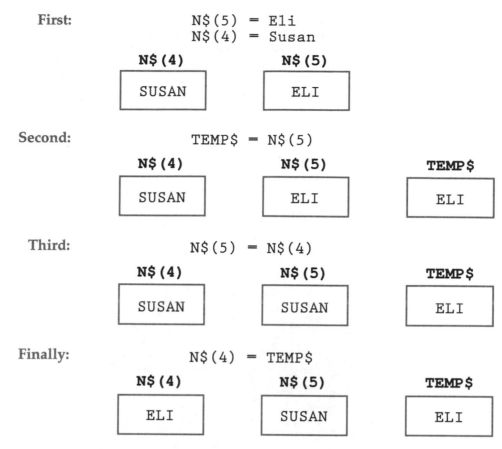

First:
$$N\$(5) = Eli$$
$$N\$(4) = Susan$$

N$ (4)   **N$ (5)**

| SUSAN | | ELI |

Second:
$$TEMP\$ = N\$(5)$$

N$ (4)   **N$ (5)**   **TEMP$**

| SUSAN | | ELI | | ELI |

Third:
$$N\$(5) = N\$(4)$$

N$ (4)   **N$ (5)**   **TEMP$**

| SUSAN | | SUSAN | | ELI |

Finally:
$$N\$(4) = TEMP\$$$

N$ (4)   **N$ (5)**   **TEMP$**

| ELI | | SUSAN | | ELI |

and the switch is complete.

This program uses a bubble sort to sort a list of 5 names stored in an array:

```
10 REM ** Sorts list of 5 names using
              Bubble Sort **
20 NAMES = 5
30 DIM N$(NAMES)
40 GOSUB 1000 : REM ** Read data into list
50 PRINT "   Unsorted Data"
60 GOSUB 2000 : REM ** Print list
70 GOSUB 3000 : REM ** Sort list
80 PRINT "   Sorted Data"
90 GOSUB 2000 : REM ** Print list
999 END
1000 REM ** Read names
1010 FOR I = 1 TO NAMES
1020  READ N$(I)
1030 NEXT I
1040 RETURN
1990 REM
2000 REM ** Print the list
2010 FOR I = 1 TO NAMES
2020   PRINT "Element #"; I; ": "; N$(I)
2030 NEXT I
2040 PRINT
2050 RETURN
```

```
2990 REM
3000 REM ** Bubble sort
3010 FOR I = 1 TO NAMES-1
3020    FOR J = NAMES TO 2 STEP -1
3030       IF N$(J) < N$(J-1) THEN TEMP$ =
              N$(J) : N$(J) = N$(J-1) : N$(J-1)
              = TEMP$
3040    NEXT J
3050 NEXT I
3060 RETURN
9000 REM ** Names to sort
9010 DATA LESTER, DIANE, BRUCE, SUSAN, ELI
```

```
RUN
   Unsorted Data
Element # 1 : LESTER
Element # 2 : DIANE
Element # 3 : BRUCE
Element # 4 : SUSAN
Element # 5 : ELI

   Sorted Data
Element # 1 : BRUCE
Element # 2 : DIANE
Element # 3 : ELI
Element # 4 : LESTER
Element # 5 : SUSAN
```

The main program calls three subroutines to perform the major tasks; reading the data, sorting the data, and writing the data (input, process, output). The subroutine at lines 1000 through 1040 uses a FOR...NEXT loop to read the unsorted values for the N$ array from DATA. Lines 2000 through 2050 print the contents of the array and their corresponding element numbers. Lines 3000 through 3060 use the bubble sort to sort the array. Notice how when the value of N$(J) is less than the value of N$(J-1) the two values are switched by employing a temporary variable TEMP$ at line 3030.

Review

1. Write a program that accepts a list of twenty numbers as input and then sorts them into descending order.

13.2 Making the Bubble Sort More Efficient

Efficiency is the cornerstone of a properly structured, well written program. For example, there are several ways to make the bubble sort in Section 13.1 more efficient. One way is to employ a WHILE...WEND loop instead of the FOR...NEXT to avoid unnecessary passes through the loop, or "iterations." It is possible that a list is sorted after only a few passes, but the FOR...NEXT continues to scan the list even though no swaps are made. If a WHILE...WEND loop and a flag are used instead, the program only scans a properly sorted list once and then terminates.

13.3 SWAP

Rather than employing the swapping routine used in line 3030 in the program in Section 13.1, it is simpler and more efficient to use the SWAP statement. For example, the swap

```
90 TEMP$ = N$(I) : N$(I) = N$(I-1) :
   N$(I-1) = TEMP$
```

can be replaced by:

```
90 SWAP N$(I), N$(I-1)
```

Employing the two techniques mentioned above, the bubble sort subroutine in Section 13.1 becomes:

```
3010 WHILE FLAG$ <> "No Swap"
3020   FLAG$ = "No Swap"
3030   FOR J = NAMES TO 2 STEP -1
3040     IF N$(J) < N$(J-1) THEN SWAP N$(J),
         N$(J-1) : FLAG$ = "Swap"
3050   NEXT J
3060 WEND
3070 RETURN
```

Notice how the flag FLAG$ is used to determine when the list is properly sorted — if no swaps are made during the execution of the FOR loop then the list is in order and the WHILE terminates.

This method has more statements than the previous version yet is still more efficient. Do not confuse efficiency with program size. It is often necessary, as in this case, to add a few more statements to get the most efficient program. At this level of your study we will use speed as the only criteria for determining program efficiency. However, advanced computer science courses take a more formal approach to this topic, including factors such as memory space required, etc.

Review

2. Rewrite your program from Review 1 to employ a WHILE...WEND loop and the SWAP statement.

13.4 Binary Search

A binary search is one of the fastest and easiest methods for searching a previously sorted list of data in order to find a specific item. A binary search can be thought of as the "divide and conquer" approach to searching. In general, a list of data is divided into two halves. It is then determined if the item to be found would occur in the first or second half of the list. The process is then repeated on that half of the list until the item is found or the list contains no more elements to be checked. Because the size of the list being searched is decreased by half each time, the binary search is very fast.

To determine which half of the list to check, the program compares the item in the middle of the list with the item being searched for. If the two match, the search is complete. If the middle element is greater than the item being searched for, the desired item must fall in the first half of the list; otherwise, it is in the second half of the list. The appropriate half is then in turn divided in half and the middle element of that sub-list is compared with the item being searched for. This process is repeated until the exact position of the desired item is determined. For example, to find the location of the letter I in the alphabet (a previously sorted list) we start by finding the middle letter of the alphabet:

A	B	C	D	E	F	G	H	I	J	K	L	M	N	O	P	Q	R	S	T	U	V	W	X	Y	Z
1	2	3	4	5	6	7	8	9	10	11	12	13	14	15	16	17	18	19	20	21	22	23	24	25	26

Strictly speaking, there is no "middle" letter in the alphabet because it contains an even number of letters so we must round up or down. The index of the middle of any list of data can be found with the formula

```
MID = INT((LOW + HIGH) / 2)
```

where LOW is the index of the lowest element of the section being examined and HIGH is the index of the highest element. In the case of the first pass through the alphabet, the index of the lowest element is 1 (A) and the index of the highest element is 26 (Z). We use INT() to round the result down to the nearest whole integer. Therefore, the index of the middle element of the alphabet is

```
INT((1 + 26) / 2) = INT(13.5) = 13
```

which corresponds to the letter M. Since M comes after I, we continue the search on the first half of the alphabet.

The index of the middle element of the first half of the alphabet is

```
INT((1 + 12) / 2) = INT(6.5) = 6
```

which corresponds to the letter F. Since F comes before I the computer continues its search in the upper half of the current list. The index of the middle element of this new section to be checked is

```
INT((7 + 12) / 2) = INT(9.5) = 9
```

which corresponds to the letter I, the desired letter, so the search is over. The algorithm for a binary search on an array of names (N$) is given below:

Initial Conditions:
        LOW = index of first element in list to search
        HIGH = index of last element in list to search
        MAX = number of elements in the array
        F$ = element to search for
        N$ = array to search

```
Step 1:    LOW = 1
Step 2:    HIGH = MAX
           WHILE <item not found> AND <still items to check>
Step 3:      MID = INT((LOW + HIGH) / 2)
Step 4:      IF F$ = N$(MID) THEN <element is found>
Step 5:      IF N$ > N$(MID) THEN LOW = MID + 1
                                ELSE HIGH = MID - 1
           WEND
```

The condition <item not found> is handled by the IF statement in step 4 which will set a flag. The condition <still items to check> may be expressed as LOW <= HIGH. When LOW > HIGH then all items in the list have been checked and the item is not found.

This program demonstrates the use of a binary search. When a person's name is entered, the program prints out that person's name and telephone number or a message if the person's name is not on the list:

```
10 REM ** Demonstrates Binary search **
20 MAX = 20 : REM ** Size of list
30 DIM N$(MAX), TELE$(MAX)
40 GOSUB 1000 : REM ** Read list
50 INPUT "Enter name to be searched "; F$
60 FLAG$ = "NOT FOUND"
70 GOSUB 2000 : REM ** Search list
80 IF FLAG$ = "FOUND" THEN PRINT N$(MID),
   TELE$(MID) ELSE PRINT "Not found"
999 END
1000 REM ** Read list
1010 FOR X = 1 TO MAX
1020    READ N$(X), TELE$(X)
1030 NEXT X
1040 RETURN
1990 REM
2000 REM ** Search list
2010 LOW = 1 : HIGH = MAX
2020 WHILE FLAG$ = "NOT FOUND" AND LOW <= HIGH
2030    MID = INT((LOW + HIGH) / 2)
2040    IF F$ = N$(MID) THEN FLAG$ = "FOUND"
2050    IF F$ > N$(MID) THEN LOW = MID + 1
        ELSE HIGH = MID - 1
2060 WEND
2070 RETURN
9000 REM ** Data: Name, Phone number
9010 DATA ABBOTT, 555-1234, BIDWELL, 555-7821
9020 DATA CARRINGTON, 555-1654, DAVIDSON, 555-9892
9030 DATA DELOREAN, 555-1243, DEMPSEY, 555-1423
9040 DATA EVERHEART, 555-1423, FAIRCHILD, 555-9999
9050 DATA FERRIS, 555-6666, GOLDBERG, 555-2634
9060 DATA HARRISON, 555-1267, JONES, 555-1256
9070 DATA KEMP, 555-2434, NOONAN, 555-2434
9080 DATA PETERS, 555-1765, PETERSON, 555-1298
9090 DATA ROBERT, 555-9821, ROBERTS, 555-8765
9100 DATA TIBBETTS, 555-0742, TRANE, 555-0000
```

```
RUN
Enter name to be searched? FAIRCHILD
FAIRCHILD        555-9999
Ok

RUN
Enter name to be searched? FRANKLIN
Not found
Ok
```

Note how this program makes use of subroutines to perform major tasks. Lines 1000 through 1040 read the names and telephone numbers from DATA. Line 50 asks the user to enter a name to be searched for. At line 60 the flag FLAG$ to be used in the search's WHILE...WEND loop is assigned the initial value "NOT FOUND". Lines 2000 through 2070 use the binary search to check the list for the input name. LOW and HIGH are initialized at line 2010. Line 2020 begins a loop which searches through the list until the name is found or all elements have been checked. The midpoint of the list to be searched is calculated at line 2030 by taking the sum of the high and low element indices and dividing by 2. If the name at the midpoint of the current list is equal to the entered name, the flag is set to "FOUND" at line 2040. If the entered name is alphabetically greater than the name at the midpoint, the lower limit is raised to one point above the current midpoint, otherwise, the upper limit is lowered to one below the current midpoint. The loop ends when either the name has been found or all elements in the list have been checked. Line 80 prints out the name and phone number if found, and if not, a message.

Review

3. Write a program that stores the letters of the alphabet, in order, in a string array. The program should accept a letter of the alphabet as input and print a number corresponding to that letter's location (index) in the array. Use the binary search to locate the letter.

Chapter Summary

In a bubble sort the program starts at the bottom of a list, then proceeds sequentially to the top, comparing each item in the list with the one above it. If two elements are not in proper order, they are interchanged. In this way the element that comes first alphabetically is "bubbled" to the top. This process is repeated enough times to order a list. To sort a list of N elements usually requires that the process be repeated N-1 times. By including a WHILE...WEND loop and a flag the bubble sort can be designed to scan a properly ordered list only once and then terminate.

The SWAP statement can be used to swap data between two variables. For example,

```
30 SWAP N$(I), N$(I-1)
```

swaps the data in N$(I) with the data in N$(I-1).

In a binary search a sorted list is divided into two halves and a determination made if the item is to be found in the first or second half. The process is then repeated on that half until the item is found or the list contains no more elements to be checked. Because the size of the list being searched is decreased by half each time, the binary search is very fast.

Vocabulary

Binary search - Technique for searching a previously sorted list in which the list is divided into halves and then a determination made as to which half the item would be found. The process is repeated on that half until the item is found or the list contains no more elements to check.

Bubble sort - Technique for sorting data that starts at the bottom of a list, then proceeds sequentially to the top, comparing each item in the list with the one above it. If the two elements are not in order, they are interchanged. The process is repeated until the list is in order.

Iteration - A complete pass through a loop.

SWAP - Statement that swaps data between two variables.

Exercises

1. a) You have been hired to help produce a new dictionary. Write a program to create the sequential file WORDS.DAT. The file is to contain twenty-five words in random order.

    b) Write a program to sort the contents of the file WORDS.DAT into alphabetical order. The program should also print the sorted list.

2. Rewrite the answer to Exercise 1 using a random-access file. Instead of storing the contents of the file in an array and sorting it in memory, the program should exchange the contents of each record in the file directly. Is this approach faster or slower than the first solution to the problem? Why?

3. a) Write a program to create the sequential file PEOPLE.DAT. The file is to contain the first names and ages of fifteen people.

    b) Write a program to sort the contents of PEOPLE.DAT alphabetically by name. For example, given the list

    ```
    Rob          20
    Don          19
    Lisa         21
    ```

    the program should change it to:

    ```
    Don          19
    Lisa         21
    Rob          20
    ```

    Note the ages have been moved also.

    c) Write a program to sort the contents of PEOPLE.DAT by age. For example, given the above initial list, the computer should change it to:

    ```
    Don          19
    Rob          20
    Lisa         21
    ```

4. Write a program that uses a binary search to find the age of a person whose name is in the sorted file PEOPLE.DAT created in Exercise 3.

5. a) Create a sequential file named PHONE.DAT that contains a list of telephone numbers. The area codes are not to be included.

    b) Write a program to sort the contents of PHONE.DAT by exchange (first three digits) only. For example, given the list

```
676-2004
609-4444
676-5112
867-5309
932-6840
867-1441
```

the program should change it to:

```
609-4444
676-2004
676-5112
867-5309
867-1441
932-6840
```

6. Write a program that sorts a list of names and telephone numbers read from DATA into alphabetical order by last name. For example, given the data

```
9000 DATA PHIL COLLINS, 555-6498
9010 DATA JOHN ADAMS, 555-1640
9020 DATA BOB ATKINS, 555-1964
```

the sorted list should be:

```
JOHN ADAMS        555-1640
BOB ATKINS        555-1964
PHIL COLLINS      555-6498
```

7. a) Create a random-access file named EMPLOYEE.DAT that contains the last names, ages, social security numbers, salaries and years of service for each of a company's twenty employees. A complete set of information for each employee should be stored in a separate record.

    b) Write a program to create a sequential file named SALARY.DAT that contains only the order (record numbers) in which the records in EMPLOYEE.DAT should be recalled to produce a list of the employees in ascending order based on salary.

8. a) Using a binary search, search the file EMPLOYEE.DAT created in Exercise 7 using SALARY.DAT as an index for the name of the employee making a particular salary. For the purposes of this problem, assume that no two persons in the file are making the same salary.

b) Rewrite your answer to part (a), allowing for the possibility that there might be two or more persons in the file making the same salary.

Advanced Exercise   The following exercise requires the development of a detailed algorithm. The program should not be written until all details of the algorithm have been worked out.

9.   A small but rapidly growing electronics company wants a computerized phone directory of its employees. The program should allow the company's phone operator to input an employee's name and output his or her phone number, or input the number and output the name. Two random-access files should be used; the first, NAME.DAT, to store the names in alphabetical order along with their corresponding phone numbers, and the second, NUMBER.DAT, to store the phone numbers in ascending order along with their corresponding names.

One program should be written that performs the following four tasks. Use subroutines where appropriate. In each case a binary search should be used to locate the needed records in the two files:

1.   Allow data to be input for a new employee by shifting records in the files to make room for the new data.
2.   Allow data to be eliminated for an employee who leaves the company by shifting records so that the employees record no longer exists.
3.   Display an employee's phone number when his or her name is entered.
4.   Display an employee's name when his or her phone number is entered.

Note that after functions 1 (add data) or 2 (delete data) are performed no empty records should exist. Each file should contain all its data in properly ordered records.

APPENDIX A –
DOS Commands and Subdirectories

*T*he following is a list of system commands used under MS-DOS and PC-DOS on an IBM-PC or compatible computer. These commands may be used whenever the DOS prompt (A>) is shown on the screen. You must exit BASIC (type SYSTEM) before using these commands.

File Names

Every program and file on a disk is identified by a unique name. For this reason you have specified a file name each time you saved a new file. The general format of a file name is:

<name> . <extension>

The <name> part may be from one to eight characters long. The <extension>, which is optional, may be up to three characters long. BASIC automatically adds the extension .BAS to the file names you enter to distinguish between BASIC programs and files produced by other applications.

Only the following characters are allowed as part of a name or extension:

Letters: A, B, ... Y, Z
Numbers: 0, 1, ... 8, 9
Special Characters: #) (@ ! } { $ % & - _ ~

While the special characters shown above may be used, it is usually best to limit file names to only letters and numbers. The following are examples of valid file names:

```
CHAP1EX5.BAS
HOMEWORK.BAS
92GRADES.DAT
SCORES.TMP
```

Using DOS Commands

When starting BASIC you have used a specially prepared disk which boots DOS and then automatically loads the BASIC system. There are times, however, when you will need to have access to certain DOS (Disk Operating System) commands. To exit BASIC, type SYSTEM. The screen clears and the DOS prompt is displayed:

A>

The DOS prompt is displayed whenever DOS is ready to execute a command. To leave DOS and return to BASIC, type BASICA and press the Enter key:

A>BASICA

Once in DOS you have access to powerful commands which can change and delete files. There are certain files on your disks which should never be changed. These have names such as BASICA.COM, CONFIG.SYS and COMMAND.COM and are required to run the BASIC program. A good rule of thumb is, if the file is not a BASIC program or data file (.BAS, .DAT, or .TMP) then it should not be altered. Network users should never delete any file which is not their own.

COPY

The COPY command is used to duplicate a file or program. Its simplest form is:

COPY <original>

For example, typing

A>COPY CHAPTER1.BAS SAFETY.BAS

at the DOS prompt causes the computer to make an exact copy of the CHAPTER1.BAS file and places it in a new file named SAFETY.BAS on the same disk. Note the space after COPY and between the two file names.

A>COPY A:GRADES.DAT B:

makes an exact copy of the GRADES.DAT file on the disk drive A: and places it on the disk in drive B:, keeping the name GRADES.DAT.

To copy an entire disk, use the DISKCOPY command described in the DOS System Disk section.

DIR

To produce a listing of all of the files on a disk, type

DIR <drive>

at the DOS prompt. (This is similar to the FILES command in BASIC.) The DIR command produces a list (or directory) of the names of the files stored on the disk in the specified drive (A:, B:, etc.). For example,

A>DIR A:

lists the directory of the disk in drive A:, and

A>DIR B:

lists the directory of the disk in drive B:. To see a list of all files produced by BASIC on drive B:, type:

A>DIR B:*.BAS

RENAME

It is possible to change the name of a file using the RENAME command:

RENAME <old name> <new name>

For example,

A>RENAME B:PAYROLL.DAT B:SALARY.DAT

gives the PAYROLL.DAT file on the disk in drive B: the new name SALARY.DAT. (This is similar to the NAME command in BASIC.)

ERASE

The ERASE command is used to remove unwanted files from a disk:

ERASE <filename>

For example, executing

A>ERASE OLDFILE.BAS

removes the file named OLDFILE.BAS from the current disk. Care should be taken when using this command, because once erased, a file may not be recovered. ERASE may be abbreviated to ERA, and is similar to BASIC's KILL command.

DEL

The DEL command (for "delete") may also be used to remove unwanted files from a disk:

DEL <filename>

Executing

A>DEL B:MYFILE.BAS

removes the file named MYFILE.BAS from the disk in drive B:. Once again, care should be taken when using DEL command, because an erased file may not be recovered. Both ERASE and DEL perform the same function, and are similar to the KILL command in BASIC.

DOS System Disk Commands

Certain DOS commands may only be executed from a copy of the DOS system disk. To use these commands, the DOS disk is booted instead of the BASIC disk. Two of the most important of these commands are described on the next page.

FORMAT

New disks must be initialized, or "formatted" before the computer can use them. As an example, it is necessary to format a newly purchased disk before it may be used to store BASIC files. The form of the FORMAT command is:

```
FORMAT <drive>
```

For example, typing

```
A>FORMAT  B:
```

at the DOS prompt causes the computer to respond with the instructions:

```
Insert new diskette for drive B:
and strike any key when ready.
```

After the new disk has been inserted and a key pressed, the computer will format the disk in drive B: and print a status report when finished. Because formatting removes all previously stored information, only new or empty disks should be formatted.

DISKCOPY

The DISKCOPY command is used to copy an entire disk at one time. Its form is:

```
DISKCOPY <original drive>  <backup drive>
```

For example,

```
A>DISKCOPY  A:  B:
```

copies the contents of the disk in drive A: onto the disk in drive B:. Any old information previously saved on the disk in drive B: is destroyed. If the disk in the backup drive has not been previously formatted, DISKCOPY will format it automatically.

The Importance of Backups

Files you saved have been stored on disks, or on a network's hard disk. These files have taken time and effort to create. Businesses and other institutions that use computers have even more time invested in the data stored on their disks, and often that data is invaluable because it cannot be replaced. Chapter 2 lists several sources of potential disk damage. The most common threat is the invisible magnetic radiation which surrounds us: computer monitors, electric motors, even the small magnet found in many paper clip holders. All generate sufficient magnetic radiation to destroy or damage the files stored on a disk. Because computer disks are susceptible to different types of damage it is important to keep copies of them called *backups*, which are used should the original files become damaged.

Creating Backups of Important Files and Programs

Although it is easy to create backups of a file or disk many people do not take the time to do so. There are businesses that have lost thousands of dollars when their only copy of an important file, such as a client list data base or accounts receivable spreadsheet, has been damaged.

The simplest way to create a backup of your BASIC files is to make a copy of your data disk. This can be accomplished using the DISKCOPY command described above. The procedure for making a backup copy of a disk is:

1. Boot a DOS system disk.
2. Type the command:

    DISKCOPY A: B: <press Enter>

    Note that you must include a space after "DISKCOPY", and another between "A:" and "B:".
3. Place the disk to be copied in drive A:.
4. Place a blank disk in drive B: and press Enter.

When Enter is pressed, a complete copy of the data stored on the disk in drive A: is made on the disk in drive B:. The entire process takes only a few minutes. Once created, the disk in drive B: is a backup copy and should be stored in a safe place, away from the original disk.

A backup copy of a single file can be made using the COPY command described above. For example, suppose you want to make a copy of a data file named CLIENTS.DAT:

1. Place the data disk containing CLIENTS.DAT in drive A:.
2. Place a formatted disk in drive B:.
3. Type the command:

    COPY A:CLIENTS.DAT B: <press Enter>

(You must type a space after "COPY", and between the file name and the "B:".)

It is also possible to create backup copies of BASIC files from within BASIC by using the Save command. If the backup copy of the current program is to be saved on the disk in drive B: type

SAVE "B:<filename>"

replacing <filename> with the name of the backup file. Do not type a space between the "B:" and the file name. When Enter is pressed, a copy of the current file will be saved on the backup disk in drive B:.

Because backups are important, BASIC automatically creates a copy of the current file when you execute the SAVE command. BASIC adds the extension .BAK to indicate that it is a BAcKup file. For example, saving a modified file named CHAP1EX9.BAS actually creates two files on the disk: one named CHAP1EX9.BAS and another named CHAP1EX9.**BAK**. Should your original .BAS program become damaged, you may wish to load the backup file:

```
LOAD "CHAP1EX9.BAK"
```

A list of all backup files stored on your disk is displayed by typing

```
FILES "*.BAK"
```

It is important to keep backup disks in a different location than the original copies. That way, the chances of both copies being destroyed are low. For example, if you keep your BASIC data diskette at school, keep your backup copy at home. Businesses often store their backup copies in special fire-proof safes, or in safe-deposit boxes at a bank. Several companies have been created just to provide safe "off-site storage" for important computer data.

Remember, the data stored on a diskette is not permanent, and may easily be erased or damaged. Following the diskette handling rules given in Chapter 2, and keeping backup copies of important files in a safe place are the best insurance against data loss.

Hard Disks and Subdirectories

Many computers now come with "hard disks" or "fixed disks" in addition to floppy diskettes. A hard disk is a permanent part of a computer system, and cannot be removed and transported like a floppy disk. However, a hard disk is faster than a floppy, and can store a great deal more data. One of the reasons for using a computer network is to allow many people to access files stored on a large, shared hard disk.

Because hard disks can store thousands of files, it became necessary to provide a way to organize the files so that they could be grouped together logically, making related programs and data files easier to find and use. The solution to this problem is to divide the disk into a number of "subdirectories", and to store related files together in their own subdirectory.

The most popular analogy use to describe subdirectories views the hard disk as a large filing cabinet, containing many files. Each subdirectory acts as a separate drawer in that filing cabinet, and related files can be placed there. For example, you may have a drawer named "BASIC" where all BASIC programs and data files are stored. Other drawers could be named "DOS", "Word Processing", "1992 Taxes" and "Personal Files." Because the cabinet is divided into drawers, each of which stores files of a specific type or purpose, it is easy to locate information in the filing cabinet.

Making Subdirectories

A hard disk may be divided by creating named subdirectories using the MD (Make Directory) command from DOS:

```
MD <subdirectory name>
```

The subdirectory name must follow the same rules for file names as given in the previous section. Many people do not include an extension with subdirectory names meaning that only 8 characters are used:

```
A>MD   BASIC
A>MD   DOS
A>MD   92TAXES
```

Subdirectories may be created on other disks by specifying the disk name:

```
A>MD   B:BASIC
```

MD may also be entered as MKDIR.

Working with Subdirectories

The contents of a subdirectory may be listed by specifying the subdirectory name:

```
FILES "BASIC"        from BASIC
DIR BASIC            from DOS
```

Files may be loaded or saved in a subdirectory by including the directory name before the file name, separated by a backslash (\):

```
LOAD "BASIC\PROG10"
SAVE "BASIC\CHAP1EX8"
```

No spaces are used. Note that in both examples given above that BASIC adds the extension .BAS to the file names. Subdirectories on other disks may also be accessed:

```
LOAD "B:BASIC\PROG15"
```

A program may work with files stored in a subdirectory by listing the subdirectory name in the OPEN statement:

```
50 OPEN "I", 1, "BASIC\CLIENTS.DAT"
```

When executed, this statement opens a file named CLIENTS.DAT stored in a subdirectory named BASIC.

Multiple Subdirectories

A subdirectory may itself have other subdirectories. For example, you may wish to divide a BASIC subdirectory in sections named "PROGRAMS", "DATA", "HOMEWORK", "TESTS", etc. If you share a hard disk or network with other people, you may wish to have a personal subdirectory to store your files named "BILL" or "MARY", etc.

When accessing files stored in multiple levels of subdirectories, each subdirectory name must be separated from the next by a backslash (\). For example,

```
FILES "BASIC\BILL"
LOAD "BASIC\PROGRAMS\PROG10"
SAVE "BASIC\HOMEWORK\CHAP1EX8"
```

This multi-level structure resembles a tree. At the top is the "root" or first level, which is specified by a backslash only. Other directories are shown below it:

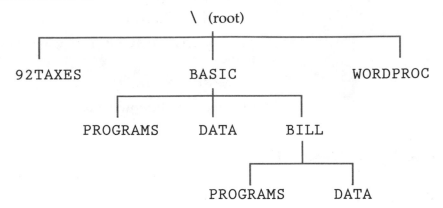

The list of subdirectory names required to access a specific file is called its "path." The complete path for a file stored in Bill's PROGRAMS subdirectory would be:

\BASIC\BILL\PROGRAMS\<file name>

The path starts with the root (\), and moves through the BASIC, BILL and PROGRAMS subdirectories. Note how each subdirectory named is separated from the next by a backslash. Paths may be used in any BASIC or DOS command that requires a filename:

```
LOAD "\BASIC\PROGRAMS\CH7EX5"
SAVE "B:\BASIC\HOMEWORK\CHAP1EX8"
50 OPEN "I", 1, "\BASIC\DATA\CLIENTS.DAT"
A>MD \BASIC\HOMEWORK
```

APPENDIX B –
PRINT USING Format Options

*T*he PRINT USING command discussed in Chapter 4 is a powerful method of formatting the output of a program. PRINT US-ING takes the form:

        PRINT USING "<format>"; <variables>

A number of different options which may appear in the <format> string are discussed below.

Numeric Formats

Symbol	Action
# (pound)	Prints a single digit. Digits to the left of the decimal point are padded on the left with blanks; to the right digits are printed as 0. The # causes numbers to be rounded:

        PRINT USING "####.##"; 5.6   prints   5.60
        PRINT USING "####.##"; 123.456   prints   123.46

A number which has more digits than specified in the format is printed in full with a leading percent sign:

        PRINT USING "###.##"; 1234.56   prints   %1234.56

, (comma)	Includes a comma in a number if it is required. Only 1 comma is required:

        PRINT USING "#,###.##"; 1234.56
                                    prints 1,234.56
        PRINT USING "#####,###.##"; 1234567.89
                                    prints 1,234,567.89

+ (plus)	Causes the sign (+/-) to be printed before or after a number:

        PRINT USING "+#####"; 123   prints   +123
        PRINT USING "#####+"; 123   prints   123+
        PRINT USING "#####+"; -123   prints   123-

** (asterisk)   Causes numbers to be printed with leading asterisks (as on some bank cheques):

```
PRINT USING "**#,###.##"; 123.45
                         prints    *****123.45
PRINT USING "**#,###.##"; 1234.56
                         prints    ***1,234.56
```

$$ (dollar)   Prints a floating dollar sign before the number:

```
PRINT USING "$$#,###.##"; 123.45
                         prints        $123.45
PRINT USING "$$#,###.##"; 1234.56
                         prints      $1,234.56
```

**$ Combines the last two options to print leading asterisks followed by a dollar sign:

```
PRINT USING "**$#,###.##"; 123.45
                         prints    ****$123.45
PRINT USING "**$#,###.##"; 1234.56
                         prints    **$1,234.56
```

^^^^ (caret)   When used with #, causes the number to be displayed in scientific notation:

```
PRINT USING "##.####^^^^"; 123.45
                         prints    1.2345E+02
PRINT USING "##.####^^^^"; 1234.56
                         prints    1.2346E+03
```

String Formats

Symbol	Action
! (exclamation)	Prints only the first character of a string:

```
PRINT USING "! !"; "Bill Freitas" prints   BF
```

\<spaces>\   Prints <spaces>+2 characters from a string. Extra characters are truncated, and smaller strings are padded on the right with spaces:

```
PRINT USING "\   \"; "Bill"        prints   Bill
PRINT USING "\   \"; "William"     prints   Willi
```

& (ampersand)   A variable length string. The entire string is printed, regardless of its size:

```
PRINT USING "&"; "Bill"            prints   Bill
PRINT USING "&"; "William"         prints   William
```

_ (underline)   A formatting character may be displayed by preceding it with an underline symbol. In the examples below, the pound (#) and exclamation point (!) are not interpreted as formatting symbols because they are preceded by underlines:

```
PRINT USING "_# ###.##"; 123.45
                  prints   # 123.45
PRINT USING "Hi \  \_!"; "Bill"
                  prints    Hi Bill!
```

Other   All non-formatting characters print as is:

```
PRINT USING "$$###.## dollars"; 123.45
                  prints    $123.45 dollars
```

Using Format Strings

The <format> of a PRINT USING statement may be stored in a string variable and used throughout the program. This allows changes to be made to only one statement in the program. For example, executing

```
10 F$ = "$$#,###.##"
20 PRINT USING F$; 123.45
30 PRINT USING F$; 1234.56
```

prints:

```
    $123.45
  $1,234.56
```

This technique makes it easy to modify the program. Changing only line 10

```
10 F$ = "**$#,###.## dollars"
```

prints:

```
  ****$123.45 dollars
  **$1,234.56 dollars
```

APPENDIX C –
The BASIC Keyboard

*T*here are a number of special keys available for use in BASIC which are described below.

The Alt Key

BASIC has a number of Alt key shortcuts for entering common commands. Using these shortcuts help speed program development, and avoids syntax errors. To use a shortcut, hold down the Alt key and press the listed key. BASIC then inserts the selected command at the current cursor location:

A	AUTO	L	LOCATE
B	BSAVE	M	MOTOR
C	COLOR	N	NEXT
D	DELETE	O	OPEN
E	ELSE	P	PRINT
F	FOR	R	RUN
G	GOTO	S	SCREEN
H	HEX$	T	THEN
I	INPUT	U	USING
K	KEY	X	XOR

The Alt key may also be used to entered characters which do not appear on the keyboard. For example, the ASCII table in Chapter 8 shows a number of characters for which there are no keys. These characters may be entered by holding down the Alt key and typing the three digit ASCII code on the numeric keypad. For example, to enter the character for the British pound, £, ASCII code number 156, hold down the Alt key and press the numbers 156 on the numeric keypad. Release the Alt key and the pound sign will appear. All three digits of the ASCII code must be entered. To enter the diamond, type Alt-003.

The Ctrl Key

The Control (Ctrl) key may be used when editing program lines. Pressing Ctrl-right arrow moves the cursor to the next word in the current line. Ctrl-left arrow moves the cursor to the beginning of the previous word. Pressing Ctrl-End erases all text from the current cursor position to the end of the statement.

Pressing the Escape key (Esc) when editing a line cancels the effects of the edit, but erases the line from the screen. The statement is still stored in the program, but LIST must again be used to display it. Ctrl-Break also cancels the effects of an edit, but leaves the line visible on the screen.

Pressing Ctrl-Enter inserts a "line feed" at the current cursor position. A line feed moves the cursor to the first position on the following line, but does not terminate the statement the way Enter does. Line feeds can be used to create special comments such as:

```
10 REM   ** Bill Freitas
            Computer Programming
            Assignment 5   **
```

In this example, a line feed was entered after "Freitas" and "Programming", and the Enter key was pressed only after the "5 **".

An important use for line feeds is in formatting IF..THEN..ELSE statements. By using a line feed after the THEN clause, we can align the THEN and ELSE, which makes programs easier to read:

```
IF HOURS > 40 THEN PRINT "Overtime"
              ELSE PRINT "Regular pay only"
```

When a program is running, pressing Ctrl-Break halts its execution. This is useful for stopping infinite loops, or when debugging. Pressing Ctrl-PrtScr (Print Screen) causes everything displayed on the screen to also be sent to the printer. This is an easy way to get a printed copy of a program's output. Ctrl-PrtScr again stops information from going to the printer.

The Function (F#) Keys

Functions keys are the keys along the top or side of your keyboard labeled F1 through F10 or F12. Each function key can perform a specific task when pressed, such as entering a command. When BASIC is first started, the function keys have the following values:

F1	LIST	F6	,"LPT1
F2	RUN←	F7	TRON←
F3	LOAD"	F8	TROFF←
F4	SAVE"	F9	KEY
F5	CONT	F10	SCREEN

These settings are listed at the bottom of the screen. The arrow after RUN, TRON and TROFF indicates that pressing that key types the command and includes an Enter. For example, pressing F2 types the command RUN and then executes it. A full listing of the function key commands may be produced by typing:

```
KEY LIST
```

The command assigned to a function key may be changed. Typing

    `KEY  <key number>,  <command string>`

assigns the <command string> to the function key with <key number>. For example,

    `KEY 10, "LIST 1-100"`

assigns function key F10 the command LIST 1-100. If KEY ON is active, the new command appears at the bottom of the screen. An Enter may be added to the command, similar to F2, by concatenating CHR$(13) which is the Enter key's ASCII value:

    `KEY 10, "LIST 1-100"+CHR$(13)`

The Enter is indicated by an arrow on the screen, ←.

APPENDIX D –
BASIC Reserved Words

*T*here are a number of reserved words in BASIC which may not be used as variable names. Attempting to use one of these as a variable results in a Syntax error:

```
10 NAME$ = "Bill"
RUN
Syntax error in 10
```

If a statement which appears correct causes a syntax error, check the list below to make certain that no reserved words have been used improperly.

Reserved Words

The following is a list of reserved words in BASIC:

ABS	CSRLIN
AND	CVD
ASC	CVI
ATN	CVS
AUTO	
	DATA
BEEP	DATE$
BLOAD	DEF
BSAVE	DEFDBL
	DEFINT
CALL	DEFSNG
CDBL	DEFSTR
CHAIN	DELETE
CHDIR	DIM
CHR$	DRAW
CINT	
CIRCLE	EDIT
CLEAR	ELSE
CLOSE	END
CLS	ENVIRON
COLOR	ENVIRON$
COM	EOF
COMMON	EQV
CONT	ERASE
COS	ERDEV
CSNG	ERDEV$

ERL	MERGE	SAVE
ERR	MID$	SCREEN
ERROR	MKDIR	SGN
EXP	MKD$	SHARED
EXTERR	MKI$	SHELL
	MKS$	SIN
FIELD	MOD	SOUND
FILES	MOTOR	SPACE$
FIX		SPC
FN<name>	NAME	SQR
FOR	NEW	STEP
FRE	NEXT	STICK
	NOT	STOP
GET		STR$
GOSUB	OCT$	STRIG
GOTO	OFF	STRING$
	ON	SWAP
HEX$	OPEN	SYSTEM
	OPTION	
IF	OR	TAB
IMP	OUT	TAN
INKEY$		THEN
INP	PAINT	TIME$
INPUT	PALETTE	TIMER
INPUT#	PALETTE USING	TO
INPUT$	PCOPY	TROFF
INSTR	PEEK	TRON
INT	PEN	
IOCTL	PLAY	UNLOCK
IOCTL$	PMAP	USING
	POINT	USR
KEY	POKE	
KEY$	POS	VAL
KILL	PRESET	VARPTR
	PRINT	VARPTR$
LEFT$	PRINT#	VIEW
LEN	PSET	
LET	PUT	WAIT
LINE		WEND
LIST	RANDOM	WHILE
LLIST	RANDOMIZE	WIDTH
LOAD	READ	WINDOW
LOC	REM	WRITE
LOCATE	RENUM	WRITE#
LOCK	RESET	
LOF	RESTORE	XOR
LOG	RESUME	
LPOS	RETURN	
LPRINT	RIGHT$	
LSET	RMDIR	
	RND	
	RSET	
	RUN	

APPENDIX E –
DOS 5 and QBasic

*A*s this text was being prepared, Microsoft released a new version of its disk operating system called DOS 5. DOS 5 no longer comes with BASICA, the BASIC interpreter described by this text. Instead, BASICA has been replaced with QBasic, a subset of Microsoft's QuickBASIC compiler.

QBasic supports most of statements found in BASICA with few modifications. QBasic also offers extensions to the BASICA language. Differences between statements in BASICA and QBasic are discussed below. Extensions in the QBasic language that are necessary for BASIC program conversion are also included in the discussion.

QBasic and BASICA

It is still possible to use DOS 5 and the BASICA interpreter. Simply copy the program named BASICA.COM (or GWBASIC.COM) from your old DOS diskette. Most versions of BASICA will run under DOS 5 without problem. Most programs written under BASICA will run under QBasic with little or no modification. Some exceptions are noted in the discussion below.

To transfer programs from BASICA to QBasic the files must be saved in ASCII format. This is accomplished by placing ", A" after the file name in the SAVE command. For example, typing

```
SAVE "CH9EOC", A
```

in BASICA saves the current program in an ASCII file named CH9EOC.BAS. This file may be read by both BASICA and QBasic.

QBasic Fundamentals

QBasic programs do not require line numbers. (However, they may be used.) Program execution is by line order and is terminated by an END statement. Since line numbers are not needed, empty (blank) lines do not require a REM statement and may by used for clarity. The BASICA program

```
10 REM ** Main Program **
20 REM
30 INPUT "Enter your name"; N$
40 PRINT "Hello "; N$
50 REM
99 END
```

becomes in QBasic:

```
REM ** Main Program **

INPUT "Enter your name"; N$
PRINT "Hello "; N$

END
```

However, the first version may be entered as shown, including line numbers, and will properly execute in QBasic.

Comments in QBasic may be in either of two forms; the REM statement or the single quote ('). Comments may be used on the same line as a statement when using the single quote — there is no need for a colon statement separator as in BASICA. The preceding program could take the form:

```
' ** Main Program **

INPUT "Enter your name"; N$
PRINT "Hello " N$

END   ' End of program
```

Variables in QBasic may be up to 40 characters long. QBasic is case-insensitive, meaning the COUNT and Count are the same variable. However, QBasic adjusts all variable references when new capitalization is used. For example, typing the statement

```
Count = 5
```

changes all references to the variable Count in the program to that capitalization. That is, every COUNT in the program automatically becomes Count.

QBasic Statements

Compound statements are not acceptable in QBasic. The BASICA format may be used for IF...THEN...ELSE statements that are short enough to fit on one line and do not require compound statements. Otherwise QBasic supports the END IF which takes the form:

```
IF <condition> THEN
     <statement>
     <statement>
       . . .
ELSE
     <statement>
     <statement>
       . . .
END IF
```

Alternatives to the ELSE (nested IFs) can be specified using the keyword ELSEIF:

```
IF <condition1> THEN
    <statements>
ELSEIF <condition2> THEN
    <statements>
ELSE
    <statements>
END IF
```

The WHILE...WEND loop in BASIC may be used in exactly the same manner in QBasic. QBasic supports variations of the WHILE...WEND, but these are not required for QBasic programs.

QBasic Commands

All commands in QBasic are selected from menus at the top of the QBasic screen using the Alt key:

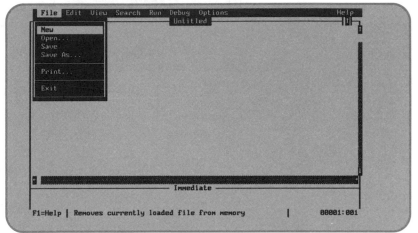

Typing a command such as RUN has no effect on the program. Instead the Start command must be selected from the Run menu (Alt-R S) to execute the program. The function key shortcut for this command is Shift-F5.

The File menu (Alt-F) contains commands to Save, Open (load) and Print programs. The Edit menu (Alt-E) allows parts of programs to be copied or moved, and new subroutines (also called "subprograms" in QBasic) and functions to be created. QBasic also has commands which aid in debugging a program, change the way the screen is presented, and other options.

Subroutines

Since line numbers are not required in QBasic programs, GOSUB and RETURN are not used for calling subroutines. (However, a program which has been entered using line numbers may use GOSUB and RETURN.) Subroutines or "subprograms" take the form:

```
SUB <Name>  (<parameter list>)
   <local variables and constants>

   <statements>
END SUB
```

SUB marks the beginning of the subroutine. Unlike subroutines in standard BASICA, QBasic subroutines are named. The name may be 40 characters long and appears after the SUB statement. The main program uses the name to call the subroutine. The parameter list is an optional list of variables and must be enclosed by parenthesis. Local variable and constant declaration is an optional list of variables and constants to be used within that subroutine only — they have no effect on the main program or any other subroutine. The statements consist of the body of the subroutine and usually perform a specific task as in BASICA. The END SUB statement acts much like the RETURN statement in BASICA. It marks the end of the subroutine and returns control back to the main program. This new format is similar to Pascal and other structured languages.

The subroutine must be declared at the beginning of a program before it may be used. The syntax is:

```
DECLARE SUB <Name>  (<parameter list>)
```

QBasic requires that all DECLARE statements precede any executable statements.

The program below demonstrates how a subroutine could be used:

```
DECLARE SUB PrintGreeting ()
' Must declare PrintGreeting before use

' ** Main Program **

CLS
PrintGreeting

END       ' End program

SUB PrintGreeting
   INPUT "Enter your name"; N$
   PRINT "Hello "; N$
END SUB
```

Subprograms/subroutines are created by selecting the New SUB command from the Edit menu (Alt-E S). QBasic creates a new "window" on the screen where the subroutine may be entered. Pressing the F2 key displays a list of subroutines. Selecting a subroutine name from this list displays it on the screen where it may be edited. Pressing F2, Home, and then Enter returns to the "main" program or "main module".

Functions

QBasic provides an alternative to the DEF FN statement which allows more complex functions to be created. (DEF FN may also be used.) Instead, creating functions is much the same as creating subprograms as described above. The syntax of a function is:

```
FUNCTION <Name> (<parameter list>)
     <local variables and constants>

     <statements>
     <Name> = <return value>
END FUNCTION
```

The keyword FUNCTION marks the beginning of a function. Unlike BASIC, QBasic functions may execute many statements in the function body before returning a value. The last statement assigns the function <Name> the value to be returned by the function. The function <Name> and <return value> must be of the same type. A function must be declared near the top of the main program using the DECLARE FUNCTION statement.

Functions are created by selecting the New FUNCTION command from the Edit menu (Alt-E F).

Should you use QBasic?

QBasic represents a dilemma for BASIC programmers. On one hand, Microsoft has given us a powerful development environment for creating BASIC programs. The integrated debugger and ability to move and copy pieces of code make it easier to create large, complex programs. However, the added complexity of local variables, parameter lists and QBasic's insistence on keeping functions and subroutines away from the main program make it harder for the beginning student. With such "overhead" QBasic's learning curve is almost equal to that of languages such as Pascal, C, or Modula-2.

There is no simple answer to this question. However, because it is possible to run older versions of BASICA under DOS 5, you can have the benefits of DOS 5 and still keep the familiar BASIC environment. Because QBasic supports the syntax of BASICA, this text may be used with QBasic to teach BASIC programming.

Index

W